Data Communication

Lynn A. DeNoia

Data Communication

Fundamentals and Applications

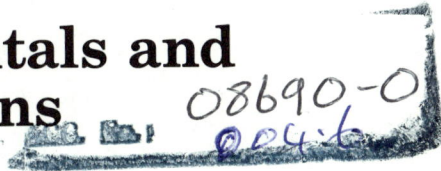

08690-0

Merrill Publishing Company
A Bell & Howell Information Company
Columbus   Toronto   London   Melbourne

Published by Merrill Publishing Company
A Bell & Howell Information Company
Columbus, Ohio 43216

This book was set in Century Schoolbook.

Administrative Editor: Vernon R. Anthony
Developmental Editor: Pam Achter
Production Coordinator and Text Designer: Jeffrey Putnam
Cover Designer: Leslie Beaber

Library of Congress Catalog Card Number: 86-62080
International Standard Book Number: 0-675-20368-6
Printed in the United States of America
1 2 3 4 5 6 7 8 9 — 92 91 90 89 88 87

The Merrill Series in Computer Information Systems

Preface

The purpose of this book is to introduce the basic concepts and technology of data communications in the broad context of computerized information systems (IS). The convergence and growing interdependence of computing and communications has made it imperative for every information systems professional to understand communications as well as computing. This is the only way systems can be made truly cost-effective. The confusion generated by AT&T's divestiture of its local telephone companies emphasizes the importance of communication systems to all our personal and professional lives. Although this text concentrates on data communication, applications of the voice technology to support data are clear. Improved understanding of one assists in understanding the other.

The material in this text does not assume any particular science or engineering background. It does depend on a basic understanding of computers, their components, and how they operate. It is aimed at an audience interested in concepts and applications rather than science and theory. It is suitable as an introduction at any level of an information systems program following introductory computing. If exercises and project work are assigned to take advantage of common additional background (such as systems analysis or design prerequisites in a particular program), a far more sophisticated course will result. Without this work, the book could also be used as a general introduction to communications technology for anyone with some computing background. In practice, however, the students seem to have more fun with hands-on projects and retain the material better than by just reading.

The information system theme is carried throughout the book, from the introduction of a system in Chapter 1 to discussions of applications in Chapter 12. The fundamentals of communication are covered in Chapter 2, followed by introductions to hardware in Chapter 3 and software in Chapter 4. Further detail on procedures and their implementation is provided in Chapter 5. These first chapters compose the core of introductory material that leads into the issues and applications.

Chapter 6 explains the regulatory context and background for communication over public facilities and introduces the characteristics of satellite communications. Specialized techniques for use of private facilities within a local area are covered in Chapter 7, and could easily be expanded as the major focus of a course. Chapter 8 looks at networks to see how much cooperation it takes to create a distributed system, while Chapter 9 considers the important management concerns for all but the very smallest networks. Putting all these pieces together for a network design is introduced in Chapter 10. Chapter 11 points out that it is no longer acceptable to wait until a communication-based information system is operational before considering privacy and security. Finally, Chapter 12 introduces some broad application areas to illustrate how system components fit together and to encourage further study or investigation.

I would like to thank my reviewers for their many helpful suggestions: Gerald D. Zarnett, Ryerson Polytechnical Institute: Darrell Z. Gobel, Catonsville Community College; John Slimick, University of Pittsburgh at Bradford; David G. Smith, University of Virginia; John K. Gotwals, Purdue University; John J. Bisbee, RCA American Communication; Reginald Yeatman, DeVry Institute of Technology-Chicago; Thomas H. Martin, Syracuse University; Paul Jacob, DeVry Institute of Technology-Columbus; Joanne Kerr, DeVry Institute of Technology-Toronto; and Marilyn Mantei, University of Michigan-Ann Arbor.

So many people have contributed to the development and production of this book that I cannot begin to thank them individually. Without my students at Bentley College, the ever-patient staff at Merrill, and the time allowed by Technology Concepts Inc. the book never would have been completed. I especially want to thank Scott Davis, John Bisbee, and Sally Callahan-Chebator for their detailed suggestions.

Contents

1 A Systems Approach

COMMUNICATION SYSTEMS

A **system** can be defined broadly as a collection of components that together accomplish a job or task. For example, a communication system comprises all the components required to provide communication. The simplest system is two people talking together. It would be difficult to separate the two people, the users of the system, from the talking, sounds, and listening that allow communication to occur. When two people talk on the telephone, however, the users are more easily distinguished from the communication system.

A simplified telephone system might incorporate a variety of components: telephone instruments, wires to connect the phones to the local office, a network of wires to connect various offices, account numbers, dialing conventions, billing procedures, switching mechanisms, and people who operate and maintain services. In this book, we will use a perspective proven useful for data processing systems to examine communication system components. We will look at hardware, software, data, procedures, and personnel. The simplified telephone system has components in each category: telephones are hardware, billing procedures are implemented in software, the items discussed during a call are data, and personnel use and maintainence of the equipment make up the specific procedures.

This book is about *data* communication systems; that is, communication systems connecting computers, peripherals, and user access devices. The major emphasis is on the hardware, the software, and how the data are packaged, but some discussion is included on operating procedures and on the personnel implications of increasingly sophisticated technology. The general context is that the communication system supports the use of computer equipment to create an information system serving a business or organization. Of course, the same components used in similar ways will support other computer equipment usage, including personal computer access to bulletin boards, for instance, but our examples will be drawn primarily from information system applications.

It is often difficult to establish the boundaries of a system; that is, deciding what is and what is not to be considered part of that system. The reasons for describing the system usually determine the boundaries as well as the level of detail in component description. A customer of our simple telephone system might be satisfied with the few details already given, but an installer would need far more information about some components and little or none about others. Our primary concern in this book is the point of view of information system designers and evaluators rather than computer scientists or communication engineers. Thus, we emphasize concepts and techniques rather than theory or mathematical foundations.

HARDWARE

Communication hardware includes all of the equipment that is employed to generate, transmit, receive, and interpret the signals that represent the data to be communicated. Terminals and computers are the sources and destinations of interest. The signals that can be generated and then interpreted on receipt are not usually in a form convenient for transmission through the communication medium. Signal conversion devices are thus required to interface sources and destinations with the medium. A telephone mouthpiece is an example of an interface. A diaphragm within the mouthpiece converts the sounds from the source into electrical impulses that can be transmitted through the telephone wires. At the other end, the receiver takes the electrical impulses from the wires and uses them to drive a diaphragm to reconstruct sounds. Internally, the telephone network may encompass various media between the calling and receiving telephones, requiring intermediate interfaces for conversions that are invisible to subscribers.

Another important aspect of communication hardware is that interface standards are necessary for individual systems or components to be compatible. Originally, all telephone instruments to be connected to a particular network had to be obtained from the company owning or selling that system. Now alternative vendors may be considered, so long as the devices conform to accepted standards and specific connection procedures are followed to ensure that no harm is done to the network by any attached device.

Many communication components that were first built as electromechanical devices were replaced later by electronic equipment for greater speed, and then by computerized equipment for greater sophistication or flexibility. This leads us to an investigation of software.

SOFTWARE

The software in typical communication systems can be divided into two categories: communication software actually assists the hardware in transferring the data between source and destination; management software coordinates or directs the use of communication resources in the system. Both types of software provide control functions to maximize system performance and flexibility. Additionally, software is often more easily changed in response to changes in technology or regulations.

Much of our communication and computing technology were developed independently of each other. After all, the telephone was invented in the 1870s and electronic computers date only from the 1940s. The old distinctions have begun to disappear, however, as more communication technology has been adapted to and incorporated into computing systems, and as more computers have been incorporated into communication systems. Although this book deals primarily with communication and management techniques in support of general-purpose computing for information system applications, it also covers a great deal about general communication systems in the process.

A particularly useful tool for structuring our investigation of data communication software is the reference model for Open Systems Interconnection (OSI), developed by the International Standards Organization (ISO). This model was designed as a vendor-independent approach to describing the communication functions required to support computing. It works both as a framework for analysis of existing networks and products and as a guide for implementing new systems. In fact, the desire to conform to OSI standards has shaped the evolution of old products and the design of new products from many computer and communication vendors.

DATA

There are two fundamental types of data to be communicated by the systems discussed in this book: *characters,* the letters, digits, and punctuation we normally think of as *text;* and *numbers,* the numerals and symbols used for *arithmetic* manipulation. Both are stored and handled internally to computers in a binary form represented by strings of ones and zeroes. Many computers use ASCII (American Standard Code for Information Interchange) to represent characters (Figure 1.1). Large IBM computers use

bit	7	0	0	0	0	1	1	1	1
positions	6	0	0	1	1	0	0	1	1
4 3 2 1	5	0	1	0	1	0	1	0	1
0000		NUL	DLE	SP	0	@	P	ˇ	p
0001		SOH	DC1	!	1	A	Q	a	q
0010		STX	DC2	"	2	B	R	b	r
0011		ETX	DC3	#	3	C	S	c	s
0100		EOT	DC4	$	4	D	T	d	t
0101		ENQ	NAK	%	5	E	U	e	u
0110		ACK	SYN	&	6	F	V	f	v
0111		BEL	ETB	'	7	G	W	g	w
1000		BS	CAN	(	8	H	X	h	x
1001		HT	EM	)	9	I	Y	i	y
1010		LF	SUB	*	:	J	Z	j	z
1011		VT	ESC	+	;	K	[	k	{
1100		FF	FS	,	<	L	\	l	|
1101		CR	GS	−	=	M	]	m	}
1110		SO	RS	.	>	N	∧	n	~
1111		SI	US	/	?	O	—	o	DEL

FIGURE 1.1 Bit Patterns of US ASCII

EBCDIC (Extended Binary Coded Decimal Interchange Code), however, and can directly handle ASCII only under special circumstances. Normally, ASCII characters must be translated into EBCDIC for processing by IBM equipment. With only two coding choices and the users of each so well known, text presents few problems as data to be communicated.

The binary coding schemes for numeric data are more complicated. Computer vendors have developed various approaches that depend specifically on the internal designs of their computers. The number of bits used for coding is first determined by the word size of the machine or by multiples of that word size. The interpretation of bits in specific positions within a code word is then determined by the type of number (e.g., integer, floating point, decimal), and the precision (within the minimum and maximum possible values that can be represented). Coding of positive and negative values also differs among computers (the UNIVAC 1108 uses one's-complement notation instead of two's-complement, for example).

At first glance, a simple agreement between source and destination on what coding scheme is used for numeric data seems to solve any compatibility problems. Unfortunately, the underlying communication systems do not easily support such an agreement.

If the data transmission is a stream of data bits, the communication components usually cannot do anything wrong with the data. If the transmission is a sequence of bytes, however, the communication system may not be able to distinguish the numeric data from communication control information that would have the same appearance in its byte packaging. This confusion occurs in the communication software, before the data passes to the application software that would recognize it as numeric data in the agreed-upon code format.

We will dicuss most of our concern for data types and codes in terms of the communication software components responsible for packaging the data into forms suitable for transmission. We will leave more complex data types and data structures as concerns for the information system applications.

PROCEDURES

Many procedures for data communication are built into the other components of a communication system. The hardware and software elements can be considered as particular ways of implementing some of the required procedures, and data formats can be considered the result of a negotiation procedure to determine the language for communication. Consequently, our discussion of procedures addresses how the hardware, software, data, and personnel interact to communicate as required by the information system application. For example, most systems have procedures for detecting service interruptions, identifying the faulty components, and isolating them for repair. These used to be accomplished manually, but many of these procedures are now being automated.

In many cases the procedural steps are so basic, so natural, so taken for granted, or so well learned, that they are seldom documented in detail. This makes it difficult to ensure that changes to a system are uniformly adopted or that new personnel are adequately trained. Even establishing an appropriate level of detail for specification of procedures can be difficult. From a communication system perspective, for example, we do not want to have to tell someone how to type, but it may be necessary to specify a detailed procedure for inserting a telephone handset (mouthpiece/receiver) into an acoustic coupler and initiating a connection. It is good practice to have written operating procedures reviewed by someone who does not usually perform them, to ensure the procedures are explicit and complete.

Our primary concern with operating procedures will be how increased automation affects system operations and what impacts new technology generates. In a telephone system, for example, consider the change from a receptionist-operated switchboard to automatic call completion in terms of any differences in interaction among subscribers and the required hardware changes.

PERSONNEL

Outside of procedures, the personnel aspects of communication systems are not treated separately or in detail. We simply assume that the purpose of the system is to be the linking mechanism between a person or computer program as the source and some other person or program as the destination. Consequently, we will concentrate on the techniques and mechanisms for communication, adding data, procedures, and personnel issues when appropriate to clarify the concepts or to give a better understanding of the application context. System designers, of course, cannot afford to maintain such a limited perspective. One measure of the success of a system is the satisfaction of its users, and a successful designer will strive to provide a system that not only meets its stated requirements, but is also pleasing to its users.

ENVIRONMENT

Data communication systems are designed to transfer the information required by an application. They may incorporate shared facilities open to public subscription, or private facilities dedicated to their own use, or both. Various components may be leased or purchased in either case. Private lines, for example, can be leased from a local telephone company to interconnect non-adjacent office buildings belonging to the same company, and the company can install private lines across its own property to interconnect adjacent buildings.

In most countries, governments or their agencies regulate communication facilities and services offered to the public. This affects both the types of offerings and the prices for service. In the United States, the Federal Communications Commission (FCC), oversees interstate communication offerings and intra-state offerings are subject to control by various state and local Public Utility Commissions (PUCs). No particular distinctions have ever been made between the public requirements and services for data communication and voice communication. The regulatory environment in Europe and much of the rest of the world is quite different. Communication services are *offered directly* (not just regulated) by government agencies for postal, telegraph, and telephone (PTT) service. In some cases, such consolidation has led to earlier improvements in communication services, such as the European international service called DATEL developed over ten years ago especially for data communication.

The regulatory situation in the United States is also complicated by the on-going merging of communication and computing technologies. The FCC has had to make distinctions between communication systems used to interconnect computers and communication systems using computers to make connections. The FCC charter provided for regulation of the second type of system, but not the first. The distinction has not been easy because the components of each look very much alike, and the FCC has been through several of its Computer Inquiry proceedings attempting to define the differences. These have so far left hazy boundaries so that disputes over categorization of particular systems have been settled on a case-by-case basis.

TYING IT ALL TOGETHER

Given the various components of data communication systems, we continue to expand on the techniques for combining pieces in specific environments to serve particular applications. This leads our discussion through the characteristics of public networks to some different approaches for small, private, or local area networks, and into distributed computing. The progression even helps to illustrate the difficulties the FCC has had with merging technologies. We see that communication has actually become a fundamental requirement of computing systems rather than an addition to them, and that communication systems also require computers to satisfy our growing demands.

From a narrow view, this might seem to complete an introduction to data communication systems. We started, however, from the perspective of communication being an important element of an information system. While the technology to transfer data is fundamental, it is not enough for most applications. To be valuable, a data communication system should be reliable and flexible enough to grow and adapt to changing conditions, and should offer or support its organization in creating strategic advantages over the competition. These concerns help to motivate our introductions to network management, design techniques, and security and privacy.

Of course, the ultimate tie required is between the technology and its application. This book offers examples and context to introduce that tie and suggest further study in the final chapter. The data communication field is developing so rapidly that some changes and improvements may even occur between the time a book on the subject is written and finally published. This book, then, is a starting point; where we go from here is our challenge.

CHAPTER REVIEW

Capsule

This book is an introduction to data communication. It starts with an explanation of basic concepts and technology, and then develops the sophistication necessary to support today's information system applications. It should provide readers with the vocabulary and context to appreciate some of the technological complexity, structure further study, and develop application requirements with appropriate communication support.

NEW TERMS

In subsequent chapters, these lists will highlight vocabulary words that are important to, or used in specific ways for, data communication concepts. We can think of this as learning to communicate about communications and technology.

QUESTIONS

In the remaining chapters, questions are provided to enhance understanding of the concepts introduced, extend the application examples, and suggest areas for further investigation. One book cannot cover every topic to the appropriate level of detail for every reader; some of the questions are intended to structure additional study and provoke more detailed thought about applications.

2 **Basic Concepts**

Much of the mystique surrounding modern communication systems is because of the specialized vocabulary which has grown up around them. In some cases, the terminology is directly carried over from the precision of the underlying science and engineering technology; in others it seems it is used as jargon to intimidate the uninitiated or unsophisticated. This chapter cuts through the mystery by relating the fundamental concepts to examples from everyday experience.

COMMUNICATION

The basic ingredients of a communication system are shown in Figure 2.1: a **source,** an originator or speaker; a **destination,** a receiver or listener; and **transmission,** a process of sending out **signals** to be propagated through a **medium.** In a classroom, for example, the instructor can be a source, the students are the destinations, and the sounds of the lecture are transmitted through the air. In a telegraph system, a sending key is used to create electrical impulses which travel through the wire to a receiving key.

Notice that just sending forth the signals is not enough to ensure **communication.** There must also be some involvement or activity on the part of the receiver(s) at the destination(s) to complete the exchange of information that communication actually implies. Communication among people goes beyond the simple sending and receiving of signals and requires that some meaning is exchanged through a common or agreed-upon system of

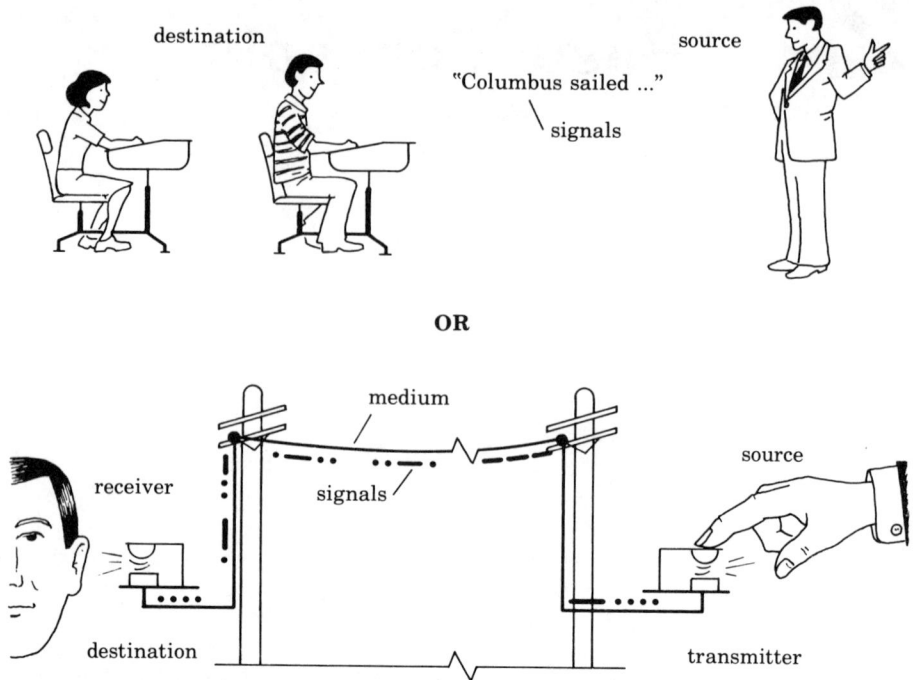

FIGURE 2.1 Elements of a communication system

symbols. Communication has not occurred unless the destination can understand or interpret the signals received. Thus if an instructor lectures in French and the students understand only German, chances are extremely slim that the lesson is communicated, even though transmission takes place.

It is useful to distinguish between **data** as a collection of symbols being transmitted and **information** as the meaningful interpretation of the symbols. The symbols of a sentence written in French can be read by a German because they come from the same alphabet, but the meaning may not be apparent. The sentence will be just data until an appropriate interpretation, in this case a translation, can be obtained to complete the communication process.

CHANNELS AND CIRCUITS

Some of the confusion that arises in communications terminology is caused by use of the same word to represent both a concept and a physical realization of that concept in a particular system. Many physical implementation techniques have been adopted from the telephone industry, whose terminology has developed over a century of historical concept, specialized technology, and convenient slang. Data processing people have picked up some of the vocabulary to use for their own needs without necessarily maintaining the underlying physical associations.

The generic interconnection between a message source and its destination, or message sink, is called a **channel.** Most of us will first think of a channel as the connection between a particular broadcasting station and our television receivers, with different channels allocated to different stations. An associated concept is that of a **circuit,** which is the complete path connecting a source with its destination(s). To be precise, this implies a channel in each direction in order to complete the circuit. A common type of electrical circuit, for example, requires two physical wires to interconnect devices. In effect, one wire carries the signal and the other wire completes the electrical ground. Both are required to create a single transmission path over the two-wire circuit. In practice, "circuit" and "channel" are sometimes used interchangeably.

Concept is sometimes distinguished from implementation by using the descriptors **logical** and **physical;** for example, the concept of a logical circuit and various physical circuits that can be used to communicate. Think of a conversation between Susan and her friend Mark as a logical circuit, and sound through the air, a telephone link, or even tin cans connected by string as various physical circuits which can connect them.

There are three modes of circuit use in communications, as illustrated in Figure 2.2. A **simplex** arrangement allows communication in one direction only. The roles of source and destination are permanently assigned. Burglar

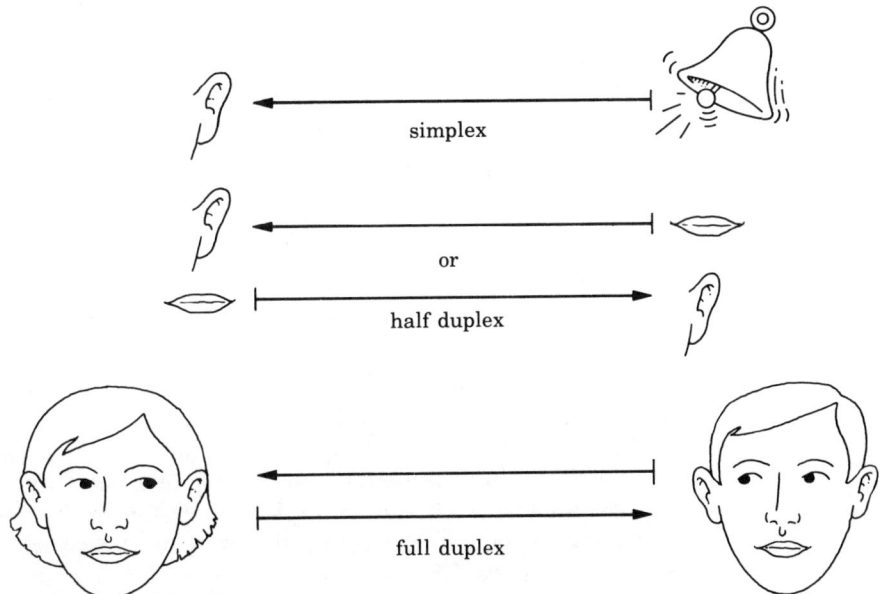

FIGURE 2.2 Modes of circuit use

alarm systems are often simplex: the protected premises are the sources and the police stations are the destinations. There is no feedback channel to ensure correct interpretation of the received signals.

In **half-duplex** (HDX) mode, transmission is allowed in only one direction at a time but the roles of source and destination are allowed to change. A Citizens' Band (CB) radio does not send and receive at the same time. People usually alternate talking with listening.

In **full-duplex** (FDX) mode, both stations are allowed to transmit simultaneously, or each station can transmit and receive simultaneously, depending on your point of view. In conversation, for example, it is quite possible for both people to talk at the same time. From one person's perspective, it is physically possible to talk and listen at the same time, but trying to do so can get confusing. There is a tendency for received words to become part of the transmission, even if they are not necessarily appropriate, or for received words to be omitted from memory. In either case, more errors result from the dual activities than from either one alone.

Notice in the examples that sometimes the physical characteristics of circuit implementations do not match their usage. A single, ordinary CB radio has both a transmitter and a receiver but is not set up to send and receive at the same time, and so could not be used for full-duplex communication. On the other hand, people are capable of transmitting in full-duplex mode, but often limit their usage to half-duplex in order to facilitate understanding. In fact, since CB radios were intended for conversations between two people, they were specifically designed to take advantage of our ordinary use limitation. The most frequent utility of full-duplex capability is to interrupt a long transmission stream. I may keep talking as long as you don't say anything. If you interrupt me, I stop to see what the problem is. In general, we will apply the terms half- and full-duplex to the usage modes of circuits. Where the distinction between usage and capability is important, we will draw specific attention to it.

SIGNALS

The techniques available to transmit the signals upon which communication is based compose an entire area of study all their own. In this text, we need only be aware of the major advantages and disadvantages of the various signaling techniques. An important consideration is the difference between analog and digital transmissions.

Analog signals are distinguished by an infinite possibility of values to represent the infinite possible variations of some transmission characteristic. An analog clock, for example, can theoretically represent an infinite number of possible time values (if the hands move smoothly and continuously around the dial).

Digital signals, on the other hand (see Figure 2.3), are characterized by a limited number of representative values. Digital clocks do not accurately

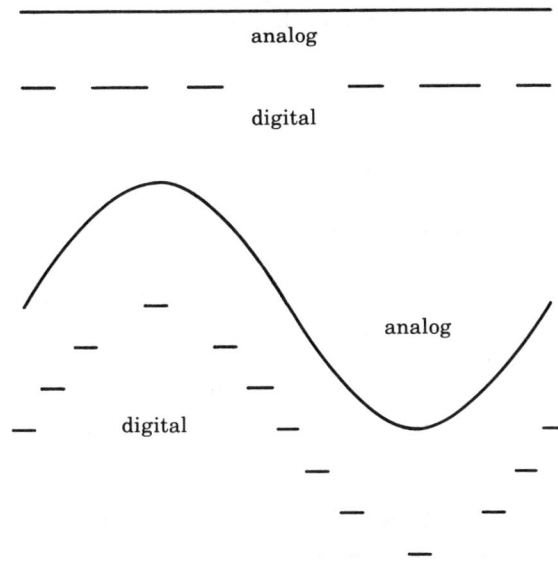

FIGURE 2.3 Analog and digital representations of signals

reflect the continually changing infinite number of time values, but choose some specific intervals or discrete steps in representation (such as minutes or seconds) which are not further subdivided in analogy to the real passage of time. Morse code is an example of digital transmission. The signal is either present or absent (turned on or off), and there are only a very limited number of discrete symbols used (dot, dash, and the different spaces between characters or words). Actually, an infinite number of different length signals are possible, but we simply choose to limit the variety we use. By comparison then, digital transmission may be simpler to accomplish (a few timers for the proper signal on, signal off durations), but it may require more effort to code or represent any richness of vocabulary. The few symbols of Morse code must be grouped into enough distinct patterns to represent all the different letters, digits, and punctuation to be transmitted.

A distinction between analog and digital which may be familiar is from computing technology. Early electronic computers used all analog techniques of adding and comparing electric current flows (continuous or smoothly measurable quantities from an infinite number of possible values), while most of our current computers use digital signals that we represent with ones and zeroes. Analog computers are still used in special situations where the extreme precision is required that can be better provided by analog techniques (industrial process control, scientific research, etc.).

Recently, data processing systems have made increasing use of communication facilities designed for transmission of analog signals (especially telephone systems) to handle digital data. We will have to be concerned with both analog and digital representations for digital data and with analog and digital transmission techniques to adequately understand the process of communication in today's environment.

TRANSMISSION

Analog Signaling

Three characteristics of analog signals which have been commonly exploited for transmission are **amplitude, frequency,** and **phase.** These may be visualized in the context of a periodic wave as in Figure 2.4. Amplitude is the distance from the central axis; frequency is the number of complete wave cycles per unit time; and phase is the relative position within one complete cycle. To be in contact, a transmitter and a receiver need a common medium and a signaling mechanism. This connection is usually provided for in electronic or electromechanical equipment by having a carrier signal sent continually from the source to the destination. The amplitude, frequency, or phase characteristics of the carrier are then varied or **modulated** in such a way that the information to be transmitted is superimposed upon and carried along with the basic signal.

Amplitude modulation (AM) is generally familiar as an entertainment radio broadcast transmission technique. The receiver is tuned to the constant carrier frequency of a particular station. The transmitter modulates or produces variations in the amplitude of the signal which can be detected and decoded by the receiver to reproduce the original information. In the case of voice, which is analog data, the amplitude values are chosen from the infinite set representing the infinite variations possible in the voice signal. Any values or variations that are introduced from other than the original voice signal are called **noise.** For digital data, we may restrict our concern to only two different amplitudes: one to represent zeroes, and another to represent ones, as in Figure 2.5.

Frequency modulation (FM) uses variations in the carrier frequency instead of amplitude. Entertainment radio again gives us a familiar example

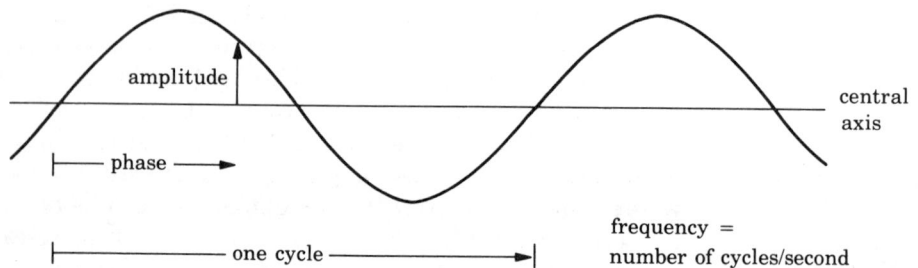

FIGURE 2.4 A periodic wave

analog carrier

digital data

transmitted signal

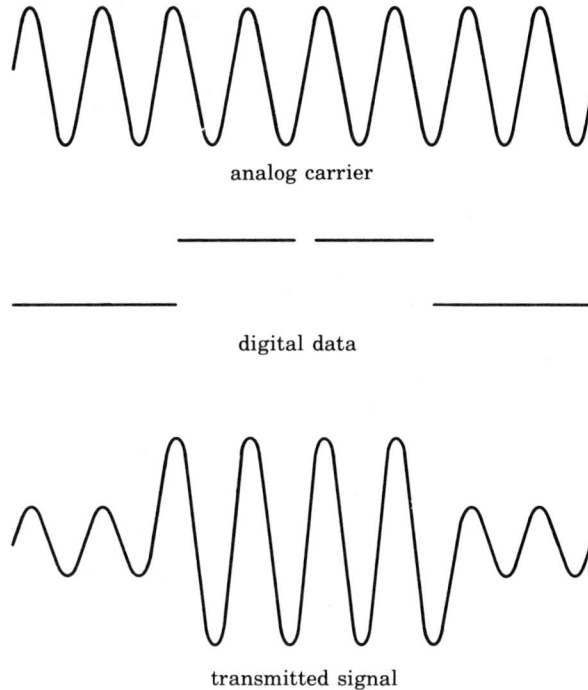

FIGURE 2.5 Amplitude modulation

for analog transmission of analog data. In this case, the basic carrier frequencies tend to be much higher so that the modulating variations are very small by comparison. The AM entertainment band is centered on about 1000 kiloHertz (kHz; one Hertz is the unit name for one cycle per second, so 1000 kHz = one million cycles per second); the FM band is in the 100 megaHertz range (MHz, one million cycles per second). For entertainment radio, this carrier frequency difference also gives much better quality sound reproduction on FM channels. For digital data, where only two variations on the basic carrier frequency are needed, either the AM band or FM band of carrier frequencies would be useful for FM transmission, Figure 2.6. Experience with entertainment radio also suggests some tradeoff considerations between the two transmission techniques: AM is more susceptible to loss of data due to external noise (like static produced by lightning), while FM can be more expensive if the higher carrier frequencies are used and because of the sensitivity required for the receiver to detect the variations properly. This latter effect is less of an issue for digital data.

Phase modulation (PM) is harder to picture than either AM or FM (Figure 2.7). Particular phase changes can be interpreted as the distinction between one and zero signals or zero and one signals. Phase modulation may

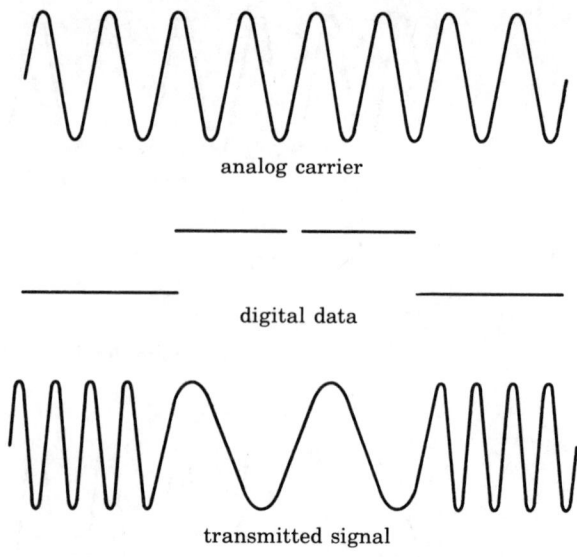

analog carrier

digital data

transmitted signal

FIGURE 2.6 Frequency modulation (frequency difference exaggerated for illustrative purposes)

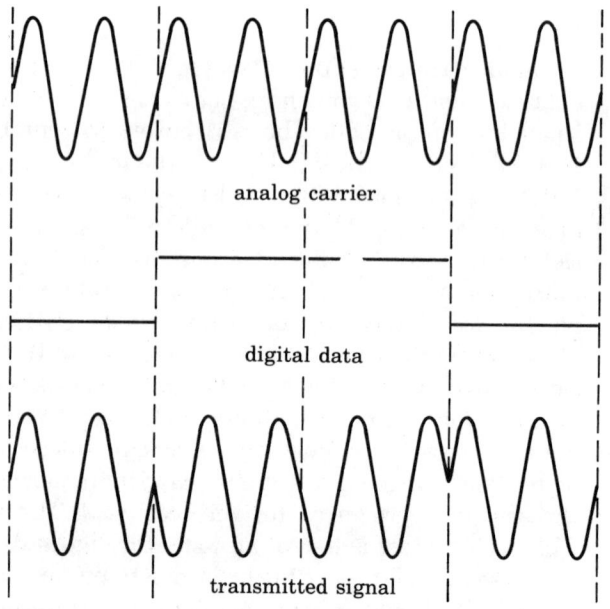

analog carrier

digital data

transmitted signal

FIGURE 2.7 Phase modulation

be less familiar, but it is the technique most commonly used for data communication. PM is much less affected by common sources of transmission noise than either AM or FM, but is susceptible to its own problem called phase jitter. This occurs when the phase is incomplete when the receiver begins to sample the incoming signal, causing confusion over what value the sample should have.

Digital Signaling

One method of transmitting signals digitally is called pulse code modulation (PCM). This is especially convenient for binary data when each pulse represents a single bit and the height of the pulse corresponds to either a one or a zero, as in Figure 2.8. Telegraph is a common example of digital transmission: the transmitter key is held down to complete an electrical circuit for the right pulse length. The pulses are transmitted by variations in the amount of electric current flowing through the wire. Another digital technique uses discrete voltage levels to represent different symbols in a pulse code.

Data may also be transmitted digitally by sampling the analog signal periodically and choosing a finite number of discrete values to represent a certain range of actual measured analog values, as in Figure 2.9. The sampling rate and the size of each range determine how well the analog signal can be reproduced at the receiver. A useful rule is that the sampling rate should be at least twice the bandwidth of the frequency range being sampled. This is often simplified to be twice the highest frequency in the range.

Choosing a transmission technique for a particular communication path is largely determined by the available medium, cost restrictions, and the tolerance for errors. Telephone transmission used to be entirely analog. Many new facilities (especially long-distance) are digital, but access to them

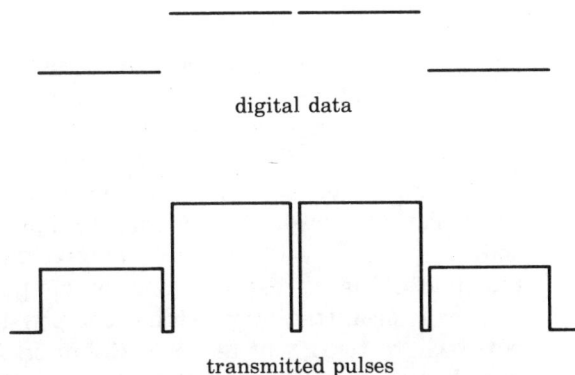

digital data

transmitted pulses

FIGURE 2.8 Pulse modulation for digital data

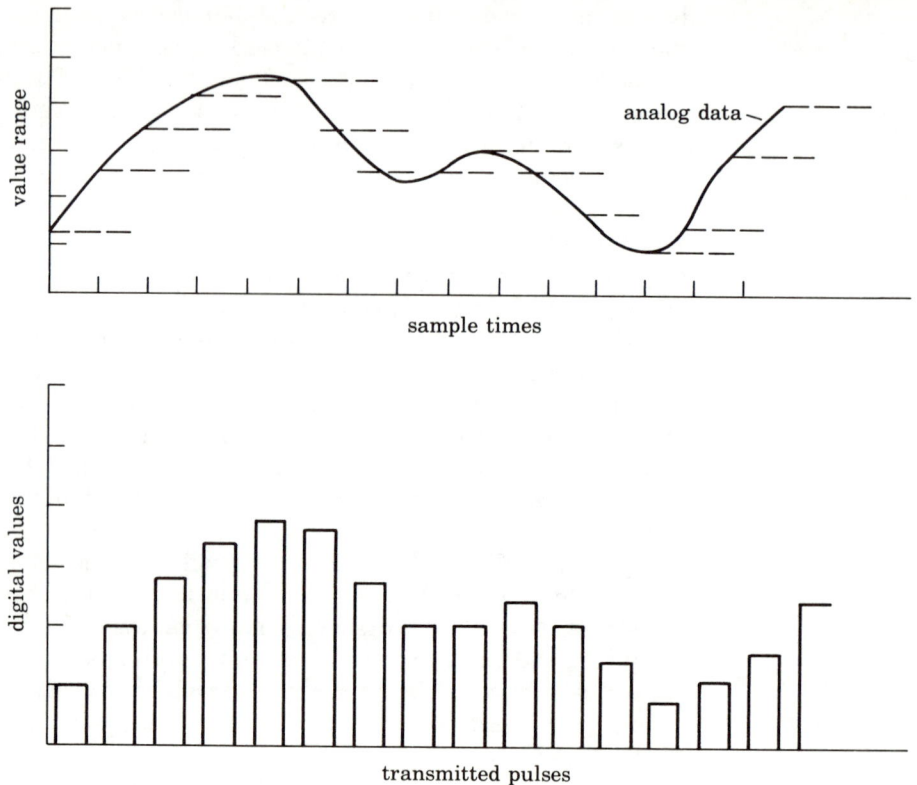

FIGURE 2.9 A digital PCM representation of analog data

is either limited or still analog, and the cost tends to be higher. Digital transmission is prevalent, however, across short-distance, private facilities.

Speed

Another important aspect of transmission is how much data can be sent in any one signal time. We commonly represent computer data in binary digits, or bits, which are usually grouped together in bytes for convenience. The two most popular character coding schemes use eight-bit bytes: EBCDIC (IBM's Extended Binary Coded Decimal Interchange Code) and ASCII (American Standard Code for Information Interchange, actually a seven-bit code plus a parity bit per byte). In both codes, each character (letters, digits, punctuation) is represented by a unique pattern of bits in the byte. Bytes may be transmitted by providing one physical path for each bit so that an entire character is sent at once, all bits in **parallel,** or they may be transferred as a sequence of bits on a single, **serial** connection, as in Figure 2.10.

data	code
"G"	01000111
"O"	01001111
bell	00000111

serial

```
0 1 0 0 0 1 1 1   0 1 0 0 1 1 1 1  0    0 0 0 0 0 1 1 1
       "G"               "O"                   bell
```

direction of transmission ←

```
0    0    0
1    1    0
0    0    0
0    0    0
0    1    0
1    1    1
1    1    1
1    1    1
```

parallel

"G" "O" bell   ⟶ time

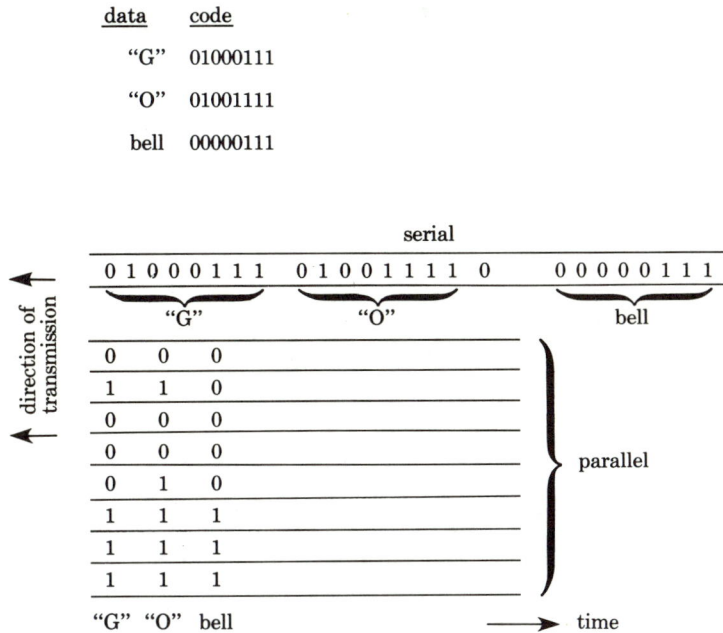

FIGURE 2.10 Serial and parallel transmission

Within and between central processing units and some peripheral devices, data transfers are made in units of one or more characters across 8-bit, 16-bit, or 32-bit parallel links. The more bits that can be sent at once, the faster the data can be transferred. When it gets too cumbersome or expensive to provide multiple physical paths, the data is again sent one bit after another over a serial link. The transmission speed is characterized in two different ways. The **baud rate** is the speed, or number of **signals per second,** successive, independent signals can be sent so that they still remain distinguishable. The **bit rate,** or the number of **bits** being transferred **per second (bps),** concerns the detail of the data being sent.

In serial transmission, bits are usually sent sequentially, one bit carried in each signal time. Thus the bit rate and baud rate are equivalent for most serial connections. Multiple bits per baud are also possible. In parallel transmission, multiple bits are sent at each signal time, so the bit rate is equal to the baud rate multiplied by the number of bits sent in parallel. Parallel transmission is used primarily within and among the closely linked elements of a computer system, such as the CPU, disks, printers, and tapes. Much

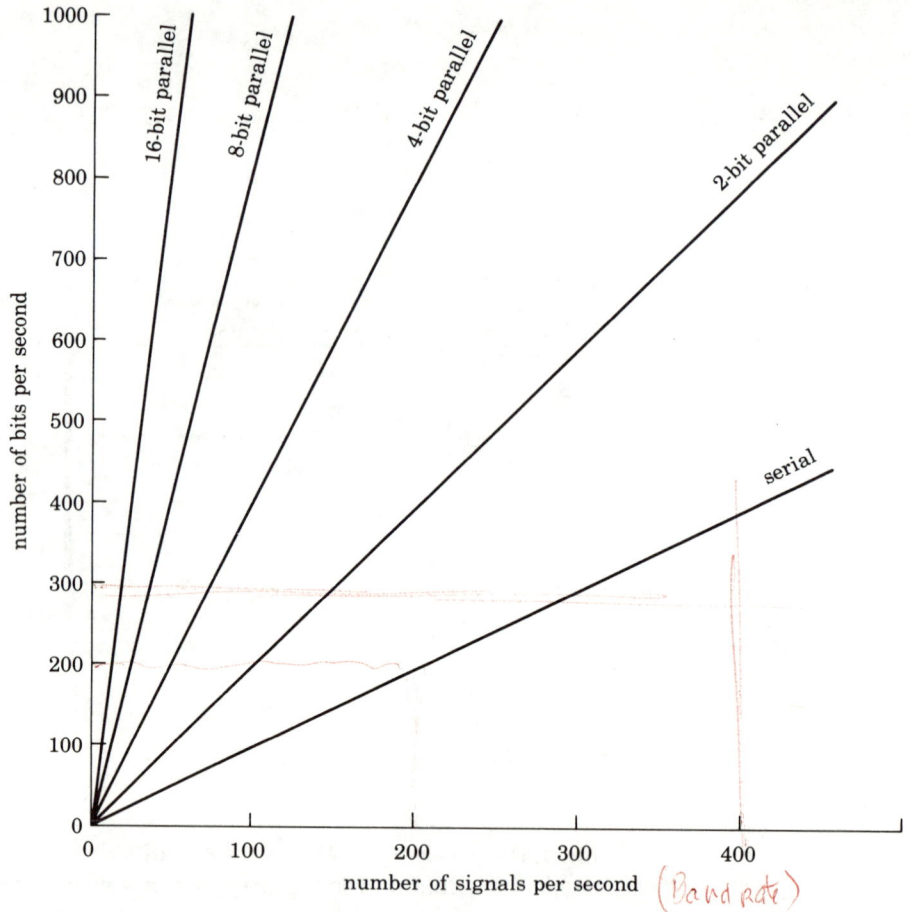

FIGURE 2.11 Relationship between bit and baud rates: bit rate = baud rate $\times$ number bits/baud

more of data communications is concerned with the serial connection of terminal devices or with connections over such long distances that parallel is not economical. It is this concentration on serial connections, where the bit and baud rates are equal, that has led to some confusion over use of the terminology. Figure 2.11 demonstrates their relationship.

Mode

The speed at which data can be sent is another important characteristic that varies among transmission techniques and devices. Low-speed transmission is especially suitable for devices which operate mechanically or intermittently. Thus the **asynchronous** mode of transmission was developed

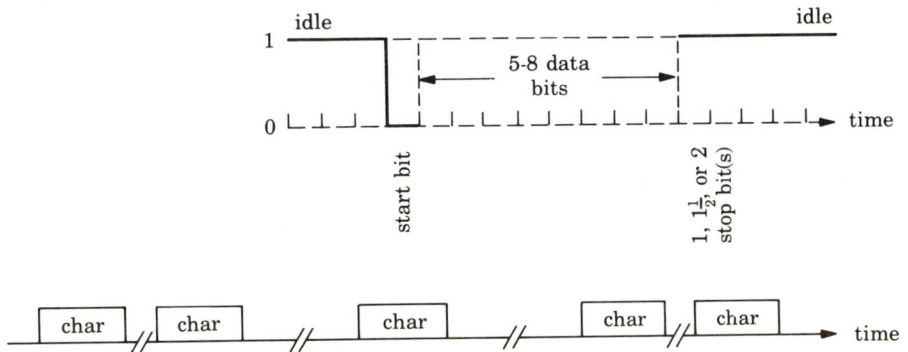

FIGURE 2.12 Asynchronous serial transmission

when teletypewriters and paper tape punches and readers were the predominant devices requiring data communication. Asynchronous devices transmit characters individually with arbitrary time intervals in between as shown in Figure 2.12. To ensure that the receiver is paying attention and ready to handle the bits in the data character, a start bit is sent first, followed by the data bits, and finally one or more stop bits (see inset in Figure 2.12). At low speeds, these ten or eleven bits are relatively easy for the receiver to handle, because slight variations in clocking between the transmitter and receiver will be small compared to the length of each bit signal, and should not add up to a problem even over the total length of the character (Figure 2.13).

When higher data rates are desirable, **synchronous** transmission is preferred to transfer a large number of characters consecutively. The beginning of a transfer becomes even more important, because the receiver must be able to ensure that its clock will stay synchronized with the transmitter over the duration of the entire group of characters. Special bit sequences called flags, which amount to the same functionality as the asynchronous start and stop bits, are placed at the beginning and end of the group rather than

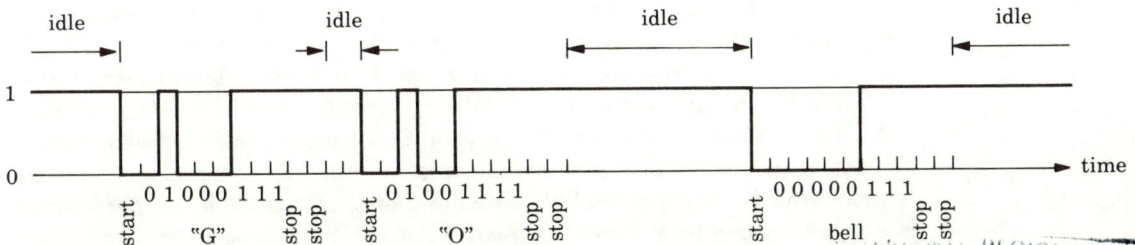

FIGURE 2.13 Sample asynchronous bit stream

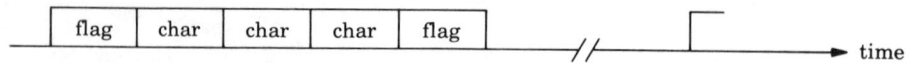

FIGURE 2.14 Synchronous serial transmission

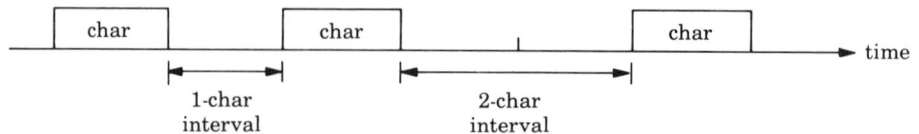

FIGURE 2.15 Isochronous serial transmission

before and after each character, as in Figure 2.14. This makes the synchronous transfer faster because no time is wasted between characters in the stream, and more efficient because the total number of non-data bits needed for synchronizing is smaller (as long as the synchronous stream is longer than a few characters). Of course, more sophisticated equipment is required to ensure the transmitting and receiving clocks stay synchronized over the entire strings of characters.

A third mode of transmission, called **isochronous** (Figure 2.15), is sometimes used for devices that have special requirements for a periodic scan or rotation rate, as in the video data required to "paint" a picture on a television screen. A start and a stop bit are placed around each character as for asynchronous transmission, but the time interval between characters must be exactly a multiple of the character length; precise clocking is required, just as for synchronous transmission. This mode can also be used to allow asynchronous terminals to transmit data at speeds faster than normally possible with simple asynchronous transmission.

CHAPTER REVIEW

Capsule

Data communication begins by sending signals from a source across a transmission medium to a destination. The circuit connecting the transmitter and receiver can be uni-directional for simplex, alternate directions for half-duplex, or bi-directional for full-duplex usage. Several different techniques are available to represent digital data as signals ready for either analog (AM, FM, PM) or digital (PCM, for example) transmission. Data bits may be sent in parallel over multiple transmission links or one bit at a time in sequence over a single serial link. The number of bits transferred per second is a common measure of communication speed. Low-speed serial transfers are usually done asynchronously, while much higher speeds can be attained with synchronous transmission. Appropriate interpretation of the signals received at the destination completes the entire process of communication.

S: source
D: destination

package:
price or item code

S

digital, optical

D

register

digital,
electronic

S

S

S

digital, electronic

D

D

digital,
printed &
hand-carried
or electronic

D

customer
display:
item, price;
subtotal, tax;
total; amount
tendered;
change due

Manager summary:
subtotals, tax, total,
amount tendered,
change due; running
total for drawer

register tape:
items, prices,
subtotals, tax
total, amount
tendered, change
due

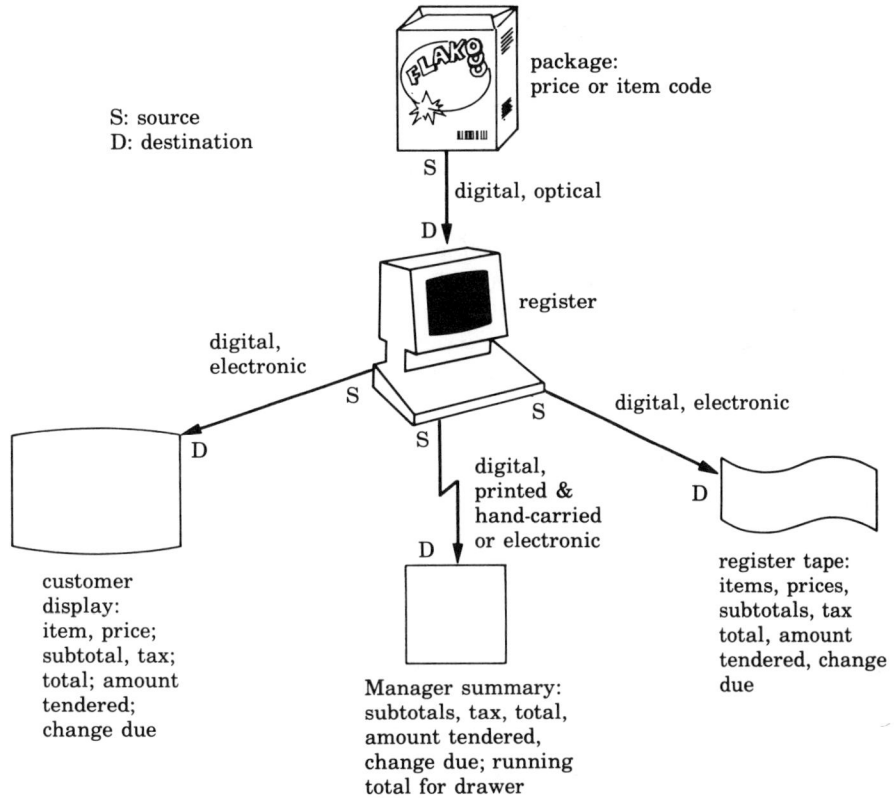

all links asynchronous, probably serial, simplex

FIGURE 2.16 Communication process for supermarket sales data

Project

From this perspective of sources, destinations, signals, and transmission, let
us begin development of a data communication system for a supermarket.
The primary sources of data are the registers and scales, the employees and
manager, the suppliers and advertisers. The major destinations for data
include the employees and manager, the customers, the suppliers and advertisers, and the government (tax reports and deposits). Signals tend to consist of sounds (oral instructions), words on paper (orders, timesheets, summaries), and money or foodstamps. Transmission is accomplished by
messenger, telephone, postal, or trucking services, and circuits are simplex,
half-duplex, or full-duplex.

  Figure 2.16 shows a communication process for sales data. Items selected
by the customer are logged by the checkstand operator at the register, ei-

ner manually by price or using an optical scanning device on the Universal Product Code. These data are processed (printed, accumulated, and taxed) and summary information, that is, the total, is produced for display (simplex) to the customer and transmission at some point to the manager. Because our system of money is essentially digital, all of the sales data are represented in or converted to (as when produce is weighed and priced) digital form.

1. Develop a list of the types of data to be communicated in the operation of the supermarket.
2. Draw flow diagrams to represent the communication process for each type of data. Identify the sources and destinations, and the signal and transmission characteristics typical in each process.

NEW TERMS

amplitude	kHz
analog	logical
asynchronous	medium
baud rate	MHz
bit rate	modulate
bps	noise
channel	parallel
circuit	PCM
communication	phase
data	physical
destination	serial
digital	signals
frequency	simplex
full-duplex	source
half-duplex	synchronous
information	transmission
isochronous	

QUESTIONS

1. What steps would ensure that communication occurred between a Canadian in Toronto and a Spaniard in Madrid? State your assumptions.
2. How could two CB radios be used to accomplish full-duplex conversation?
3. How many distinct symbols does it take to ask this question? How many would it take in Morse code? Is the written alphabet an analog or digital representation of the data to be transferred?

4. Describe how you could use your voice to illustrate any of the AM, FM, or PM techniques.

5. What kind of transmission technique do smoke signals represent? What issues would you have to consider if you were asked to come up with a code for the Indians to use?

6. In asynchronous, synchronous, and isochronous transmission, the start and stop bits used to frame individual or character groups represent non-data overhead. Compare the efficiencies of these modes by computing the ratios of data bits to total bits transferred. Consider 1000 eight-bit characters and a synchronous string length limit of 500 characters.

7. If our transmitting and receiving devices can distinguish among four different voltage levels in a given signal instead of just two, how many bits can be transmitted within a single signal element? If the voltage level can be changed 1200 times per second, what are the baud rate and bit rate?

3 Hardware

The major hardware components of a data communication system are terminals for the entry and display of data and information, conversion devices which transform signals between components, transmission media, devices for sharing those media, and computers. Many different companies manufacture communication hardware, so system designers will be concerned with compatibility among devices and with appropriate selection criteria.

TERMINALS

In an information system, terminals are major sources and frequent destinations of data communication activity. Terminal users are likely to be concerned with ease of entry and readability of the display for data characters. As hardware components of data communication systems, terminals must also have control features, such as the ability to request connection to and disconnection from the host computer system and a way to get specific attention from or interrupt the activities of the host.

A major problem in choosing terminals for communication-based computing systems is the lack of keyboard standardization for special characters and functions. Not only do key placements differ (look for characters like +, ", and :), but some terminals have "return" keys, some have "line feed," some have "newline," and others have more than one of these. In general, users have been expected to adapt to such keyboard differences through practice. The lack of standardization in the control functions, however, creates problems in connecting various terminal types to different computer systems. If the name of a control function on the terminal differs from that in the system manuals, the user is apt to get confused; if it is missing, the user may not be able to access the host services properly or at all. Incorporation of any unusual components in the terminal such as a braille printer makes it increasingly unlikely that the terminal can simply be plugged into a system and function properly, because the signals and their interpretations are even more likely to be special rather than standard.

There has been some attempt to manage hardware diversity by defining what is called a "virtual" terminal. In data communications, something **virtual** appears to exist as a physical entity although it actually may not. The purpose of the virtual terminal is to provide a standard definition for terminal functionality. Any real terminal that does not have physical characteristics conforming to the standard must have some way to emulate or generate the particular function, or be able to do without it. An Apple II personal computer, for example, does not have a "break" or "attention" key. If an Apple is used as a terminal in a system requiring the break (interrupt) function, another key combination or some software must be able to generate the appropriate signal.

A current industry trend is to include more functions in terminal hardware packages. Nearly all terminals today incorporate microprocessors, making it easy for the manufacturer or the user to continue the proliferation of terminal functions. Lack of standardization among these can have significant impact on the design choices for communication systems incorporating many terminals. Either the choice of terminals for the system will be limited, or extensive software support will be required to disguise the diversity. IBM generally uses the former approach (as with the 3270 standard terminals); independent vendors choose the latter and put the special software either in the mainframe host or in the terminals themselves.

Another important trend is the increasing use of personal computers as intelligent access points to computing facilities. Personal computers probably have more differences among keyboards than terminals do. They are also programmable in more different languages or dialects of a language (such as BASIC) than terminal manufacturers are willing to implement. These factors all suggest that standardization on a virtual terminal for data communications will become even more important than it is currently. Most personal computers can already use a variety of packages from independent software companies to emulate the functions of specific real terminals, so a standard definition would be readily championed by users but not necessarily welcomed by vendors.

A different type of communication terminal gaining in popularity for office systems is the facsimile (or **FAX**) machine to provide electronic transmission and reproduction of hard-copy documents including text, diagrams, photographs, and signatures. Here, standardized control functions are particularly important so that the FAX devices can be handled uniformly throughout the communication network.

CONNECTION

Definition of a standard electromechanical interface for connecting terminals to computer systems was originally motivated by the proliferation of non-computer manufacturing companies building terminals. In the United States, the primary standard has been **RS-232-C,** which was developed by the Electronics Industries Association (EIA) in conjunction with various manufacturers and the Bell System (Figure 3.1). Its use has become widespread for connection of computers to many kinds of peripheral equipment.

Dissatisfaction with RS-232-C as a standard is increasing, primarily because it was designed for relatively low-speed, short-distance connections, and partly because it left some connections with unspecified functions. Many vendors have taken advantage of these "free" connectors to provide

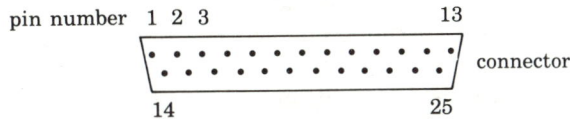

pin	name	EIA	signal
1	PG	AA	protective ground
2	TD	BA	transmitted data
3	RD	BB	received data
4	RTS	CA	request to send
5	CTS	CB	clear to send
6	DSR	CC	data set ready
7	SG	AB	signal ground
8	DCD	CF	data carrier detect
9	PDS	–	positive DC test voltage
10	NEG	–	negative DC test voltage
11	–	–	unassigned
12	SDCD	SCF	secondary DCD
13	SCTS	SCB	secondary CTS
14	STD	STD	secondary TD
15	TC	TB	transmit clock
16	SRD	SBB	secondary RD
17	RC	DD	receive clock
18	–	–	unassigned
19	SRTS	SCA	secondary RTS
20	DTR	CD	data terminal ready
21	SQ	CG	signal quality detect
22	RI	CE	ring indicator
23	–	CH/CI	data rate selector
24	SCTE	DA	serial clock transmit, external
25	BUSY	–	busy

FIGURE 3.1 RS-232-C

special functions making their products more competitive in the marketplace. Consequently, two pieces of RS-232-C-standard equipment connected do not necessarily operate in compatible ways. New EIA standards, RS-442, RS-443, and RS-449, have been developed to address these and other issues.*

SIGNAL CONVERTERS

The signals generated by data communication sources for interpretation by destinations are usually not in a form suitable for transmission. The signal converter changes source signals into a form compatible with the transmission medium and recreates the original form at the destination. The most common signal conversion devices are called **modem**s because they *modu*late and *demo*dulate a carrier signal to transfer data. For analog transmission, the source modem uses AM, FM, or PM to impress the digital data on the analog carrier. The destination modem must use the exact technique in reverse to recover the data content. For PCM digital transmission, the modems create and interpret the proper pulse relationships.

The details of signal conversion are less important in this text than the fact that numerous types of devices are available from many vendors at a large range of prices, speeds, and functionality. Source and destination modems must be compatible; that is, they must use the same modulation, timing and error detection techniques for original data to be recreated properly. Selection of modems depends upon various characteristics, such as the type of signal generated (analog or digital), the distance to be traveled, the medium (wires, radio, fiber optics) and its physical interface, the particular technique (which AM, FM, PM, PCM scheme), the speed, the type of transmission (asynchronous or synchronous), the type of data interface (RS-232-C or other), the number of devices connected together, and any special signal conditioning performed to reduce errors. Vendor reputation and equipment reliability are usually as important as cost to system designers in selection of components.

One way signal conversion devices can be categorized follows:

- *Modems* are devices that use digital signals to modulate an analog carrier for transmission, and upon receipt, demodulate to recover the original digital data. Also called long-haul modems, they are designed for use over any distance of public or private telephone facilities.
- *Modem eliminators* (null modems) are used between nearby devices to connect the appropriate data interface signals. Only one is needed to complete the link, and distances are limited according to each interface definition.

---

*An excellent introductory discussion of RS-442, RS-443, and RS-449 characteristics can be found in the second edition of *Technical Aspects of Data Communication* by J.E. McNamara (Digital Press, 1982).

■ *Line drivers* put digital signals directly onto a transmission link by giving an internal signal the power boost needed to carry it over some distance. These are typically used on private telephone-type wiring that is either customer-owned or leased from the local telephone company. Short-haul and limited-distance modems are usually of this type, as are the chips used for most RS-232-C terminal-to-computer links.

TRANSMISSION MEDIA

The media most familiar for transmission of communication signals are probably copper wires and coaxial cables. The use of such media in data communication systems has followed naturally from their progressive development for telephone and other communication systems. Short, individual device connections are often made with copper wire **twisted** in **pairs,** one wire carrying the signal and one wire completing the electrical circuit (with ground). The twisted pairs are often bundled together into multi-pair cables for convenient handling and economic packaging (Figure 3.2). Adjacent pairs must be twisted in different patterns to minimize crosstalk (signal leakage from one pair to another). Cable sizes typical from telephony include two, four, ten, twenty-five, and one hundred pairs in a single sheath. Cables usually incorporate shielding to minimize external noise entering the cable and interfering with the data signals. It is generally desirable to keep the signals confined to the cable so that they do not interfere with other equipment and are not available to unauthorized listeners.

Longer distances and connections of very many devices are usually handled by **coaxial cables,** to provide the functional equivalent of multiple pairs without the same interference problems or bulk. Originally developed for long-distance telephone links, coax is probably familiar to most people in the form of cable television installations. The cable consists of a center conductor, resembling a single fat wire, running down the middle of an outer conducting tube. The two are kept separate either by regularly spaced, non-conducting, plastic disks or by filling the space with a dielectric material similar to styrofoam (Figure 3.3). The signal quality and transmission speed for simultaneous calls over coaxial cable is a major improvement over an equivalent diameter cable of twisted pairs.

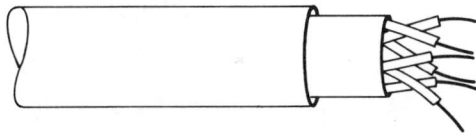

FIGURE 3.2 Twisted-pair cable

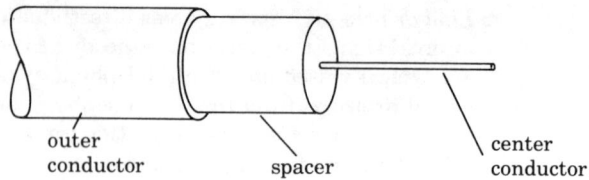

outer   center
conductor   spacer   conductor

FIGURE 3.3 Coaxial cable

Newer transmission technologies are also being transferred from telephone systems to data communications. Factors which determine appropriate uses of these media include cost tradeoffs, traffic volume, special environmental requirements, and access to supporting technical expertise. The
following lists these technologies:

- *Microwave* transmission has the potential for carrying very high traffic
  volumes, but needs fairly expensive transmitter and receiver installations and
  requires line-of-sight geography.
- *Satellite* transmission is similar to microwave, but also involves long
  transmission delays and periodic outages (as when the satellite transits the
  sun).

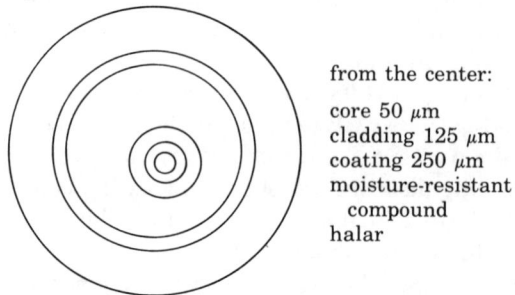

from the center:

core 50 μm
cladding 125 μm
coating 250 μm
moisture-resistant
    compound
halar

a) a tightly buffered fiber

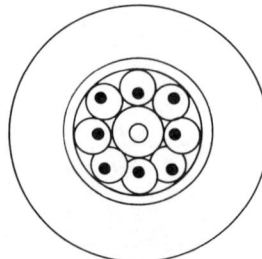

from the center:

central member (steel
    wire with overcoat)
tightly buffered fibers in
    overlength tubes
kevlar
polyethylene jacket

b) an 8-fiber cable

FIGURE 3.4 Fiber optic cable

■ *Fiber optics,* shown in Figure 3.4, provide significant weight and volume savings over equivalent capacity wire cable, but require special handling techniques for the fiber and are expensive to interface with standard computer system equipment. More types of signal conversion devices are rapidly becoming available for transmission over fiber optic cables, as are new ways to splice and terminate the cable. These developments will drive the costs for installing, using, and maintaining fiber optics down to a level that is competitive with traditional cabling. In addition, new laboratory experiments are pushing fiber transmission speeds into the billions of bits per second range, so that capacities can be expected to increase even further.

LINK SHARING

The physical circuits which are connected to computer system devices for communication are often called **line**s. This may sound strange to us in an age when microwave, satellite, and optical transmission are commonplace; the terminology is a relic of the days when all connections were made with wires. **Link**s might be a more generally appropriate term. When links connect only pairs of devices, the connections are said to be **point-to-point** (Figure 3.5). When a single link allows for connection of several devices, the connection is called **multipoint,** or the line is a multidrop line (Figure 3.6).

Link sharing can be motivated by a wide variety of factors, but the underlying concern for all of them is usually cost, especially when long-distance telephone connections are required as communication links. Data calls often last for many minutes during peak business hours when rates are most expensive. The transmission capacity of a phone link may exceed what can be used by a single device, or the one device may be active only during small intervals throughout a connected period. In either case, the cost of dedi-

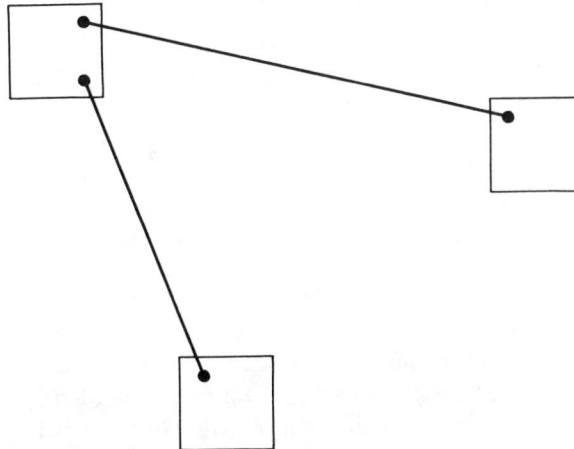

FIGURE 3.5 Point-to-point links

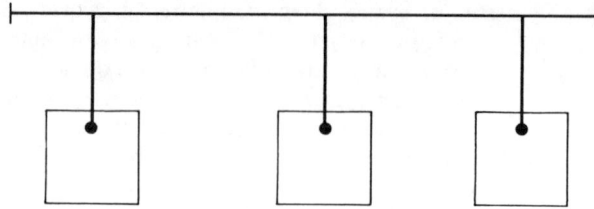

FIGURE 3.6 Multipoint link

cated links might not be warranted for individual devices, but sharing among several could change the balance of cost-effectiveness.

Another advantage of link sharing is reduced interconnection cabling, especially when large numbers of devices are connected to a central facility. This can be within a single building or across a campus. Capacity is always limited within given intrabuilding conduits, raceways, or access ducts and in aerial or underground interbuilding connections. When the space runs out, either new space must be created, or use of existing space must be re-examined. In some installations, reduced volumes of wiring lead to substantial decreases in the difficulty and costs of network maintenance. This improvement alone may be enough to justify purchase of link-sharing equipment.

Sharing by Turns

In the example of the classroom, the air is a common link among all students and the teacher. If several people speak at the same time, the sounds mix together, making it very difficult to sort out what came from each speaker. We usually agree to some sort of discipline, such as taking turns, to prevent conflict and keep things intelligible. **Polling** is a link-sharing discipline based on giving *explicit* permission to transmit.

In **roll-call** polling, a central authority lists all devices connected to the link and goes down the list, one device at a time, offering each one in turn permission to transmit. Each device holds its traffic until it receives permission, and only then transmits. This technique is common when many terminals or other low-speed devices share a fast link to a very fast device, such as a central computer. The central list may be arranged in various ways so that each device gets an equal number of turns (round-robin) or so that some devices get permission more frequently (priority schemes). Roll-call polling is especially effective when there are many devices with a reasonably steady traffic demand. If there is only intermittent traffic from a few devices, simple roll-call wastes a great deal of time checking for traffic from all the silent devices; multiple lists polled with different frequencies are more common.

Hub-go-ahead polling is a centralized scheme that reduces some of the wasted roll-call time by allowing the permission to be passed on by silent devices to the next device in line without the central authority generating a new "here is permission—do you have anything to transmit?" request. When a polled device does have traffic, it transmits after receiving permission, and then the central authority issues a new request beginning with the next device in line. Some poll message time is saved this way, but now every device must know which one is next in line after it.

Distributed polling eliminates the need for a central authority by making each device responsible for passing on the permission regardless of whether it transmits. This is usually coordinated by use of a special message called a **token.** The token is passed from device to device as the permission to transmit in much the same way relay team members pass a baton giving each in turn permission to run. As in hub-go-ahead, each device needs to know which one comes next, but token-passing is more complicated. To prevent loss or duplication of the token, each device needs a list of its successors and rules to follow should something happen to the token. Particular schemes depend on the shape, size, and transmission characteristics of the device network.

Effective polling prevents simultaneous use of the communication link by two or more devices. A less stringent approach to sharing imposes discipline only when some conflict over use of the link actually arises; this is called **contention.** Rather than preventing simultaneous transmissions, contention schemes depend on the ability of devices to detect and discard the results of them. When there are no conflicts, no restrictions are necessary and there is no overhead cost for the discipline. The cost is incurred only when it is required. If the probability of conflict is small enough, overall performance of the system is better than for polling, because no time will be wasted by devices with no traffic to send. This gives each device *implicit* permission to transmit unless something goes wrong; that is, contention occurs. These types of schemes are explained in more detail in Chapters 6 and 7.

Simultaneous Sharing

Some kinds of links offer much more transmission capacity than a single device can use effectively. In this case, we use **multiplexers** (or muxes), hardware that divides the total transmission capacity of a link into smaller portions that can be used by the individual devices wishing to share the link. The subdivisions, called **subchannels,** must be able to operate independently if speed or traffic results better than for polling are to be realized. Capacity can be divided for sharing by transmission frequency and by time.

In frequency division multiplexing (FDM), the total **bandwidth,** that is, the spectrum of frequencies which can be handled by the transmission medium, is divided into subchannels in much the same way conventional entertainment radio stations have assigned frequencies (Figure 3.7). Each device wishing to share the link is attached to the multiplexer and assigned a

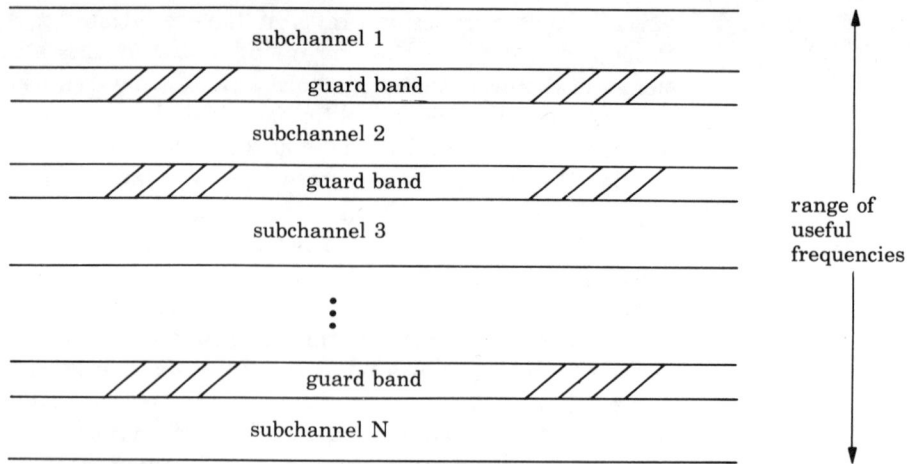

FIGURE 3.7 Frequency division multiplexing

different carrier frequency so it can transmit whenever it has traffic. All devices on sufficiently different frequencies may operate simultaneously without interfering. The multiplexer takes the simultaneous traffic from all the subchannels and transmits the appropriate frequency signals across the medium all at once. At the receiving end, the signal must be re-divided, or demultiplexed, into its subchannel frequency components. Guard bands of unassigned frequencies are required to ensure that transmissions in adjacent bands do not overlap or interfere with each other.

Time division multiplexing (TDM) leaves the frequency spectrum intact but divides the transmission time into pieces, or **slots**, that are assigned periodically to the different devices sharing the link (Figure 3.8). The multiplexer takes incoming traffic and delays it into its assigned time slot; this is commonly done one character or one bit at a time. The receiving demultiplexer must carefully clock incoming data to separate it into slots corresponding to the originals (Figure 3.9). The effective transmission rate made available to each device through its subchannel is the total speed of the link divided by the number of subchannels; that is, by the number of devices

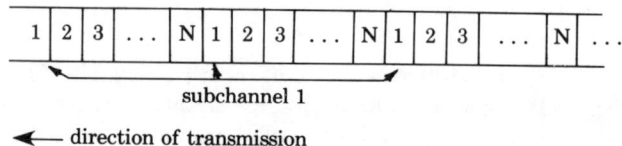

FIGURE 3.8 Slots used for time division multiplexing

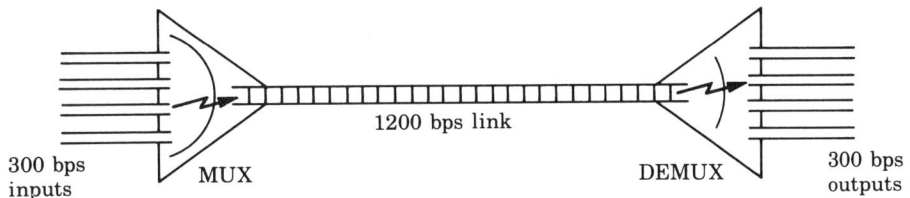

FIGURE 3.9 Time division multiplexing

that could share the link. When the allocation of slots to create subchannels is a fixed assignment, the sharing scheme is called synchronous TDM, commonly abbreviated **STDM.**

In both FDM and synchronous TDM, the assignment of devices to subchannels is static. This means when there is no traffic on a particular subchannel, that portion of the transmission capacity is wasted (Figure 3.10). Busy devices with heavy traffic cannot take advantage of the unused subchannels. Since the primary purpose of introducing multiplexing was to share the use of the link, this waste seems inappropriate. On the other hand, the sum of the transmissions of all connected devices cannot exceed the capacity of the link, or the multiplexer buffers will overflow and data will get lost (Figure 3.11).

An outgrowth of synchronous TDM called statistical TDM **(STATDM)** uses dynamic reassignment of idle subchannels to accommodate devices with data waiting to be sent. Only those devices with traffic share the entire capacity of the link, eliminating waste as in Figure 3.12. If only one device makes a request, all the slots can be assigned to it and the transmission proceeds at the maximum rate the link provides. A static assignment could provide only the one low rate determined from how often the assigned slot occurs. However, the static assignment also guarantees that one rate.

Statistical TDM is an improvement only in situations where the connected devices can take advantage of the extra link capacity available when some devices are idle. A single terminal operating at 300 bps cannot benefit from assignment of all the slots on a 1200 bps link because it can only provide data to the link at the lower rate. However, more than four 300 bps terminals might share a single 1200 bps link if their patterns of usage were such that on the average, four or fewer have traffic to transmit simulta-

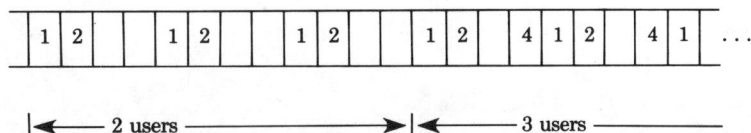

FIGURE 3.10 Idle subchannels (wasted capacity) for synchronous TDM

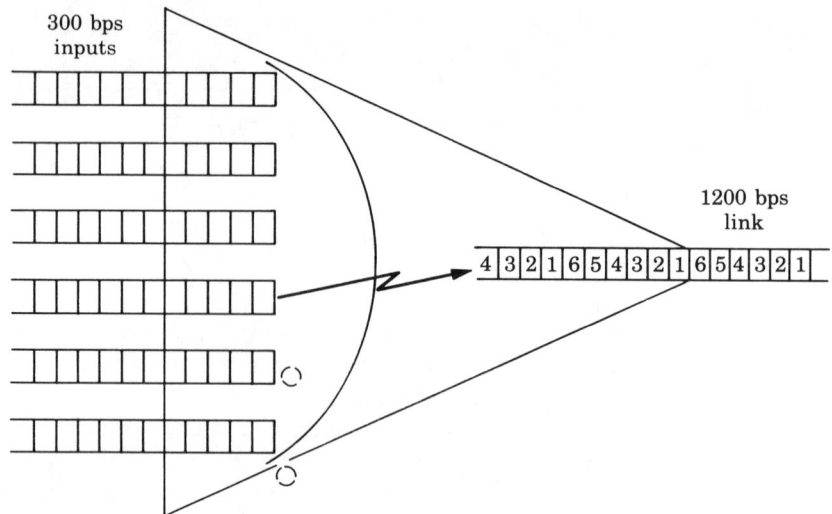

FIGURE 3.11 Buffer overflow when aggregate input rate exceeds link rate for synchronous TDM

neously. This ability to serve more devices than fixed assignment of the transmission capacity would allow is called **concentration** (Figure 3.13). Note that dynamic reassignment of slots based on the number of demands for service could potentially reduce the effective transmission rate for a single device across the link to a minimum level determined by the total number of devices active on the link. In fact, the effective link rate could go lower than the actual device rate (Figure 3.14). Statistical multiplexers must have buffer space to handle such situations. If some minimum effective link rate per device is to be guaranteed, either the number of devices will have to be limited or requests exceeding some maximum number of devices will have to be rejected. In practice, the intermittent nature of most communications traffic makes statistical multiplexing effective on the average without imposing too many restrictions or requiring enormous buffers.

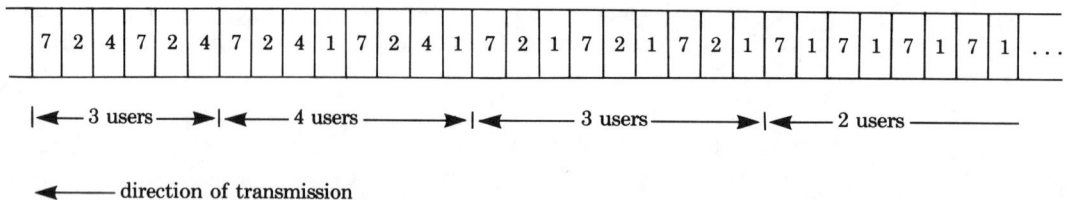

FIGURE 3.12 Statistical TDM

a) synchronous TDM: fixed assignment

b) concentration

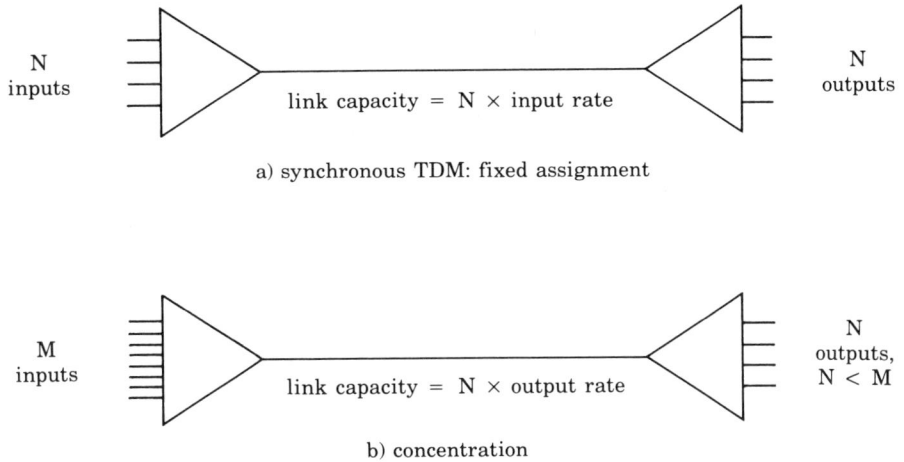

FIGURE 3.13 Concentration serves more devices

Now that we have seen some benefits of statistical TDM, we should look at some costs. If slots and devices are going to be associated dynamically, the sending and receiving multiplexers will have to keep track of the assignments. This means tagging every piece of data with source and destination addresses, or keeping tables of slot assignments and notifying the receiving multiplexer of changes. These requirements impose some management overhead and imply a level of sophistication that will make the statistical multiplexer more expensive than its synchronous counterpart. In addition, isolation of errors or malfunctions in the equipment will probably be more difficult. Inclusion of test circuitry would add even more to the purchase price. The tradeoff between cost and effectiveness would have to be weighed in each system where statistical multiplexing is being considered.

COMPUTERS

Computers are widely used to facilitate the operation of our everyday communication systems (such as the telephone); we will consider them here specifically as sources and destinations or supporters of data communication systems. Nearly all electronic digital computers are fundamentally alike as hardware; they use high-speed digital electrical signals transmitted in parallel for internal communication. They often differ, however, in their interpretations of those signals: the number of bits per word, the order in which bits are numbered or transferred if not in parallel, the internal code used to represent numbers and characters, and the kinds of instructions that can be performed. Incorporation of diverse computers into communication systems is not simply a matter of plugging the electronics together if they do not speak the same underlying languages.

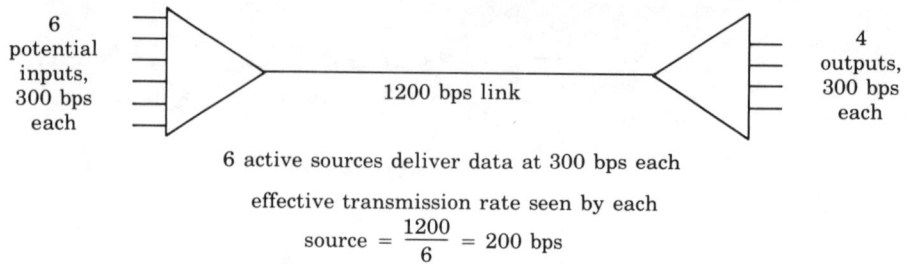

6 potential inputs, 300 bps each

1200 bps link

4 outputs, 300 bps each

6 active sources deliver data at 300 bps each

effective transmission rate seen by each

$$\text{source} = \frac{1200}{6} = 200 \text{ bps}$$

FIGURE 3.14 An overloaded concentrator

The variety of computers being used in data communication systems is increasing. Mainframe processors have traditionally served as large hosts for many terminals. As more terminals were placed in locations remote from the processor, data communications began to take on its own identity. The differences in speed between terminals and other devices and the possibilities for transmission errors were aggravated by the long-distance connections. The attendant shift from batch to interactive processing increased desires for remote access to computer facilities. The entire collection of local and remote computers, peripheral devices, terminals, and their interconnecting links has come to be known as a **network.** Simple teleprocessing networks may consist of a single host computer and many remote terminals (Figure 3.15). Distributed systems are based first on a network of computers (Figure 3.16), each of which may have its own complement of peripherals and terminals. In any case, effective allocation of network resources and management of the costs are still the major concerns of data communications.

Increasingly capable minicomputers have been taking on host computer roles in less expensive information systems, and occasionally networks of minicomputers have been used to enhance the functions of, or even to replace, single mainframes (Figure 3.17). The popularity of microprocessors for special-purpose control and as personal computers has motivated their incorporation into data communication systems as well. Such variety of processor power and roles and the diversity of manufacturers have made networks of communicating heterogeneous processors particularly interesting as solutions to information system problems.

An important special use of computers in communication systems is to free a large host from handling all its own communications traffic. A dedicated processor containing much of the communications software can be interposed to handle activity such as code conversion, buffering, line sharing, and error control (Figure 3.18). These special-purpose computers are called front-end processors (**FEPs**). They usually manage all communications traffic to and from the host CPU. The FEP may handle polling on

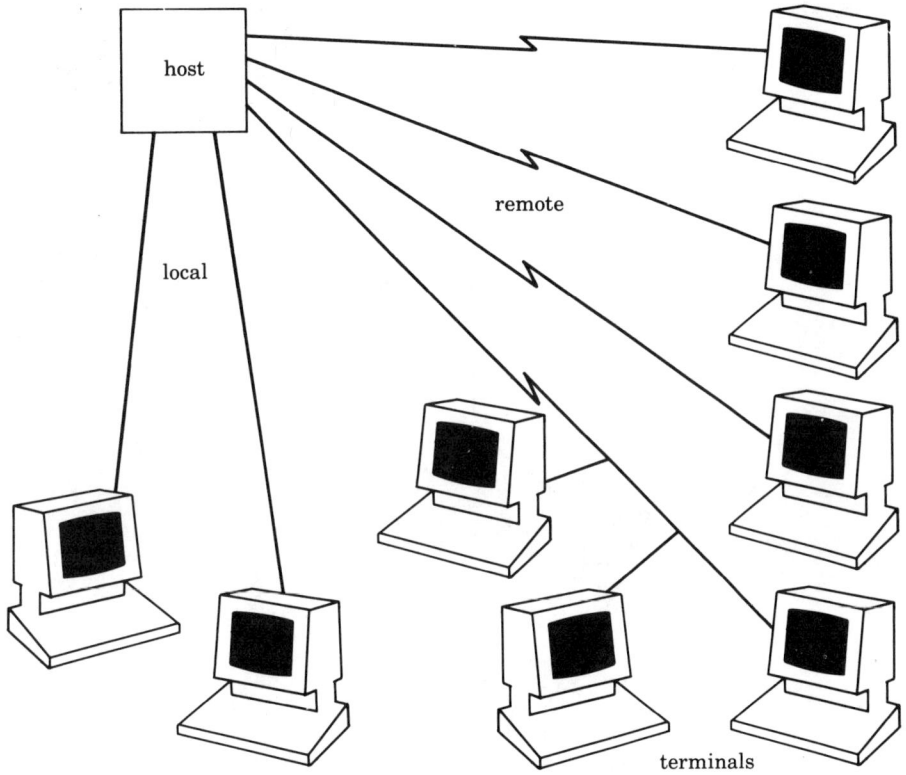

FIGURE 3.15 Simple, single-host teleprocessing network

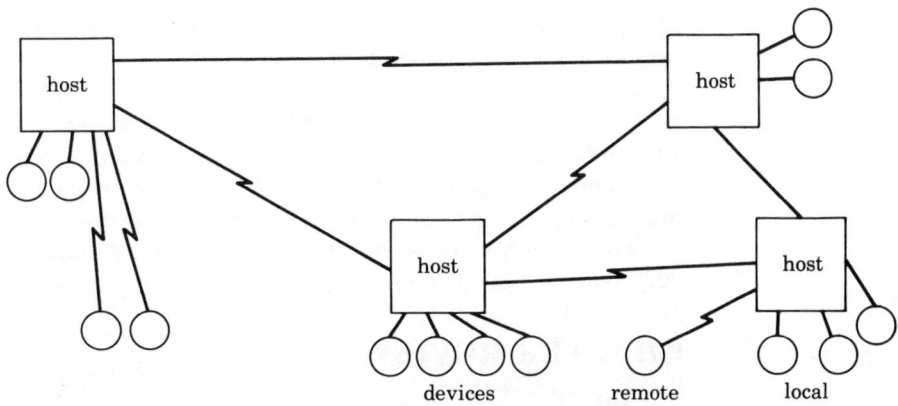

FIGURE 3.16 Multi-computer network, as in a distributed system

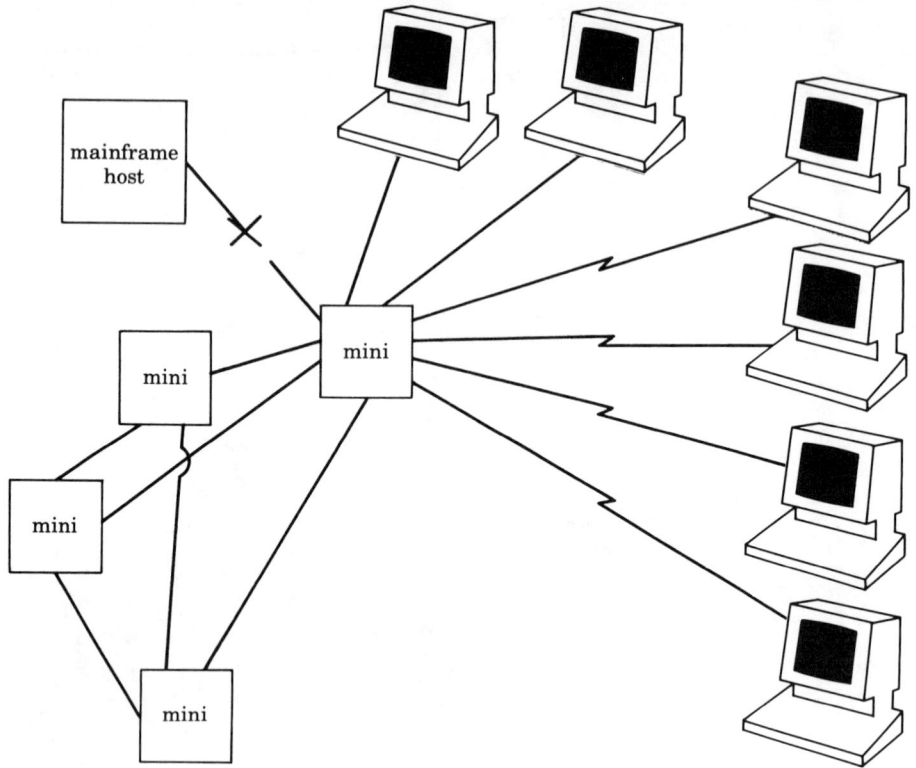

FIGURE 3.17 Network of minicomputers replaces single mainframe host

multipoint links, provide line control procedures that format outgoing messages and check incoming ones for errors, and use its own mass storage devices to log the communications activity for billing or audit trails. It is also possible to use the FEP log to save up some communications traffic when a host computer fails.

A more specialized or limited approach to front-end processing is handled by smaller computers as **protocol converters.** These are specifically designed for networks of heterogeneous components that do not speak the same underlying languages. Protocol converters typically translate between different code sets (ASCII and EBCDIC, for example) and between different communication control expectations (such as ASCII and IBM's standard 3270 terminal protocols).

CHAPTER REVIEW

Capsule

Terminals and computers are the major sources and destinations in a communications-based computer system. Modems are the devices responsible

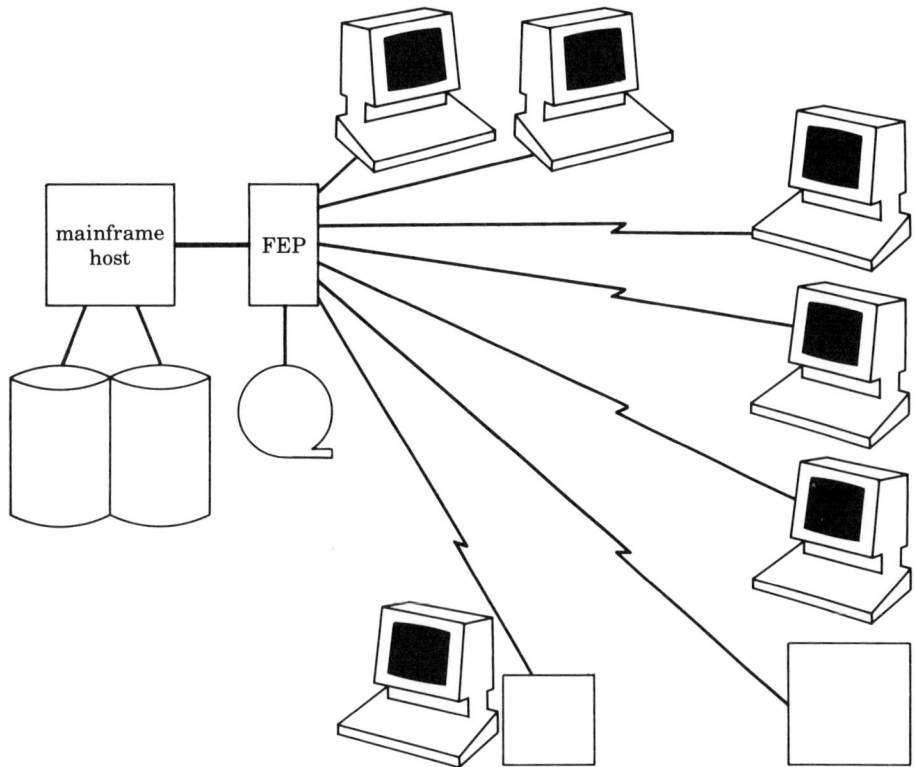

FIGURE 3.18 An FEP configuration to off-load communications processing from a busy host

for signal conversions between devices and the transmission medium. Multi-point links are commonly shared by imposing a discipline such as polling or contention on the connected devices. Point-to-point links may be shared by placing a multiplexer at each end of the link and attaching all of the devices to the muxes instead of to the shared link. The muxes subdivide the total transmission capacity of the link and enforce the sharing discipline by allocating only a portion to each device. A designer must pay careful attention to compatibility requirements if the communication system is to be built of hardware components from different vendors.

Project

Up to this point, we have not really considered a computer as part of the supermarket system, even though we have been using computer system terminology to describe the components. Let us introduce it here as an important data destination which handles application processing such as sales summarization, payroll, and inventory management. Source and destination

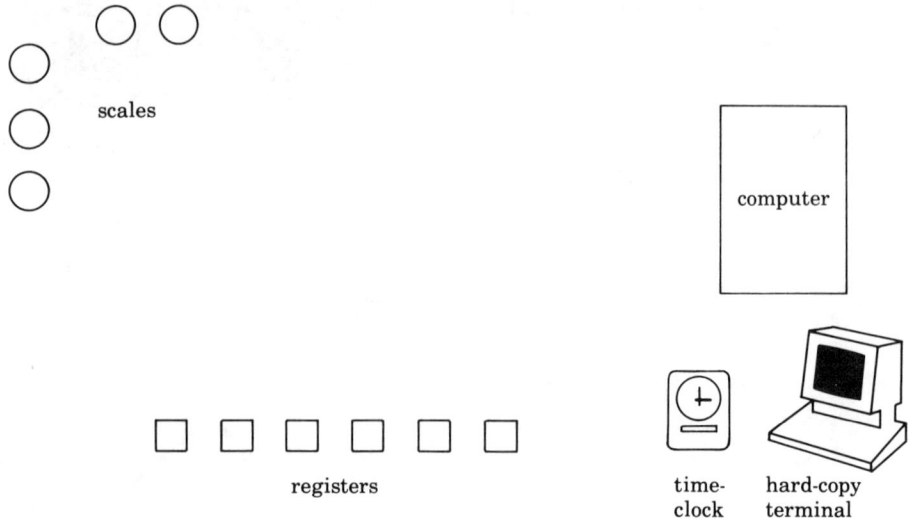

FIGURE 3.19 Supermarket floor plan

terminals will include cash registers, scales for deli meats and for fruits or vegetables, office equipment such as a calculator or typewriter, and perhaps the pricing guns.

If we assume that everything is to be eventually connected to the computer, what characteristics or options would the other elements of this data communication system need? First, the device interfaces would have to be

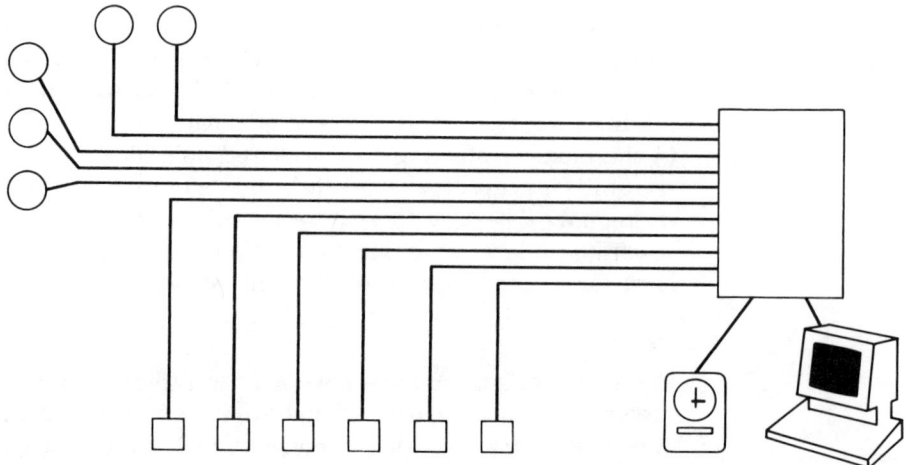

FIGURE 3.20 A twisted-pair cable plant

electronic, and standard RS-232-C connections would be preferred, if available. The most likely candidates for transmission medium would be twisted-pair, coaxial, or fiber optic cable, and suitable signal conversion devices such as line drivers or modems would be necessary. Links could be made point-to-point singly or shared, or in a multipoint arrangement with some sharing discipline.

Figure 3.19 is a sample floor layout for a typical supermarket. One possible twisted-pair cable plant design is shown in Figure 3.20.

1. What more would you have to know about the supermarket building in order to evaluate the proposed wiring plan in Figure 3.20 as an appropriate implementation alternative?
2. Discuss what advantages there might be in using multiplexers to reduce the amount of wiring suggested by Figure 3.20. Where would you put them? Discuss their potential cost effectiveness.
3. Design a multidrop twisted pair cable plant for this supermarket. What are the issues in selecting a particular polling discipline to use?
4. What sources could you use to gather data on the availability of products to implement each of the elements of our sample supermarket?
5. How would you determine the appropriateness of either fiber optic or coaxial cable in place of twisted pairs? Would you use different designs from the ones discussed above? Why or why not?

NEW TERMS

bandwidth
coaxial cable
concentration
contention
FAX
FDM
FEP
hub-go-ahead
line
link
modem
multiplexer
multipoint
network

point-to-point
polling
protocol converter
roll call
RS-232-C
slot
STATDM
STDM
subchannel
TDM
token
twisted pair
virtual

QUESTIONS

1. What standard functions would be important for a virtual terminal definition to include?
2. Recall that in two-wire circuits, one wire carries the signal and the other wire completes the electrical circuit by providing the ground.

Full-duplex communication requires the ability to transmit simultaneously in both directions. How could FDM and TDM be used to allow full-duplex connection over a two-wire circuit?

3. How many signals can be sent simultaneously across a medium being shared through FDM?

4. Does TDM allow simultaneous signals on multiple subchannels? Explain your answer.

5. Transmission rates can be shown to depend directly on the width of the frequency band used; that is, if the bandwidth is doubled, the transmission rate can be doubled. If four devices wish to share a point-to-point link equally, does TDM or FDM offer better transmission rates? Explain the difference.

6. Higher-priority devices can be handled on multipoint links by putting them in the polling list more frequently. How could different priorities among devices sharing a point-to-point link be handled with TDM? with FDM?

7. What would be some advantages of the FEP being programmable by the user (that is, by the system support specialists on site)?

4 Software

EXTENDING THE HARDWARE

The primary purpose of communication software is to make the resources of the system more readily and easily available to the users. This often means managing the resources to make them appear simultaneously available to a number of users. Other users would rather not be bothered by the details of the communication process. They just want the system to send the message when it gets a chance; the transmission format, error control procedures, destination location, and route selection are not of interest to them.

The first software introduced to assist in the use of hardware resources were the **device drivers.** These are special-purpose routines in the operating system that handle all the control signals and data transfer characteristics of a specific type of device so that a user need only issue higher level, generic I/O commands (Figure 4.1). For example, to get a line of input from the terminal, the user might want to simply say, "Read TTY." The terminal driver software would then be responsible for receiving characters one at a time from the keyboard, processing any control such as backspace, buffering the characters until the line is completed with a carriage return or other delimiter, and then forwarding the result to the requesting user.

When the hardware to be managed is a communication interface instead of a local device, the first level software is called a **communication access method,** (Figure 4.2). A very simple method would handle a single link to a specific type of terminal; a very sophisticated one would manage links shared by various remote devices. The set of rules used by access methods for governing individual communications links are called link control proce-

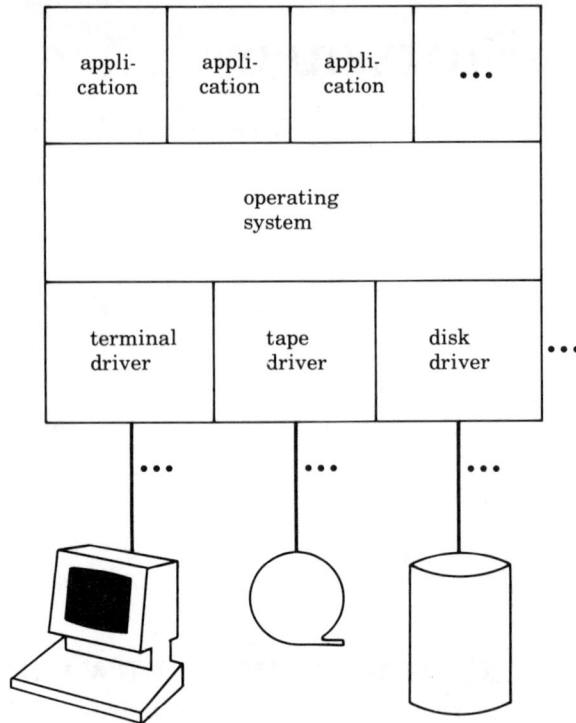

FIGURE 4.1 Device driver modules in an operating system

dures (an update of the old twisted-pair version, "line" control procedures). The best-known is IBM's Binary Synchronous Communications. Other custom procedures have been built using ASCII control characters, as in Digital Equipment Corporation's DDCMP (Digital Data Communications Message Protocol).

The most widely used and probably best-known access methods are the ones developed by IBM. **BTAM** (Basic Telecommunications Access Method) was IBM's first approach to handling communications for the S/360 processor series. It provides the basic functions to support "read" and "write" commands from users to handle asynchronous terminals and binary synchronous communications, including dialing and answering calls, polling terminals, sending and receiving messages, handling transmission errors, managing buffers, and testing the equipment. Higher levels of function, such as scheduling, controlling data flow, and data management, are left to the user. BTAM is still used by a majority of IBM installations and applications.

Several enhancements of BTAM have increased sophistication and support functions. One of current interest, **TCAM** (TeleCommunications Access Method), adds control and sharing among network resources, queues data

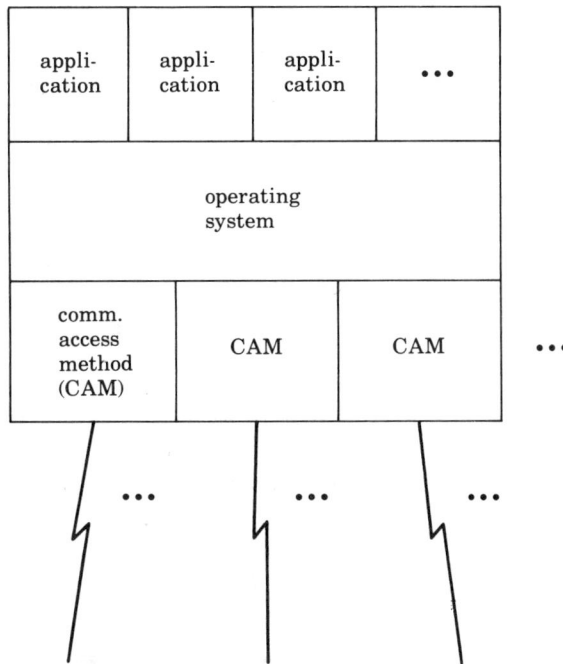

FIGURE 4.2 Communication access method modules in an operating system

for efficient use of the communication links, interfaces with various supervisory application subsystem programs, provides status monitoring and reporting, and enhances network reliability support. It is used primarily in conjunction with the time-sharing option (TSO) of IBM's advanced operating systems.

The newest access method is **VTAM** (Virtual Telecommunications Access Method), which controls communication among the logical units (the users' interfaces) of a network. In addition to all the functions of TCAM, VTAM offers the most sophisticated support for all of IBM's advanced networking products. It is designed to interact primarily with communications software in front-end processors and provides general control over all resources in a single network, including:

■ access to resources by name, without specification of network locations or physical addresses
■ sharing and allocation of network links and devices
■ status monitoring and alteration of the network configuration
■ detection and correction of network-level errors

More sophisticated function and control are built on top of the access methods in the form of communication executives or communication-based operating systems (Figure 4.3). IBM calls these "application subsystems."

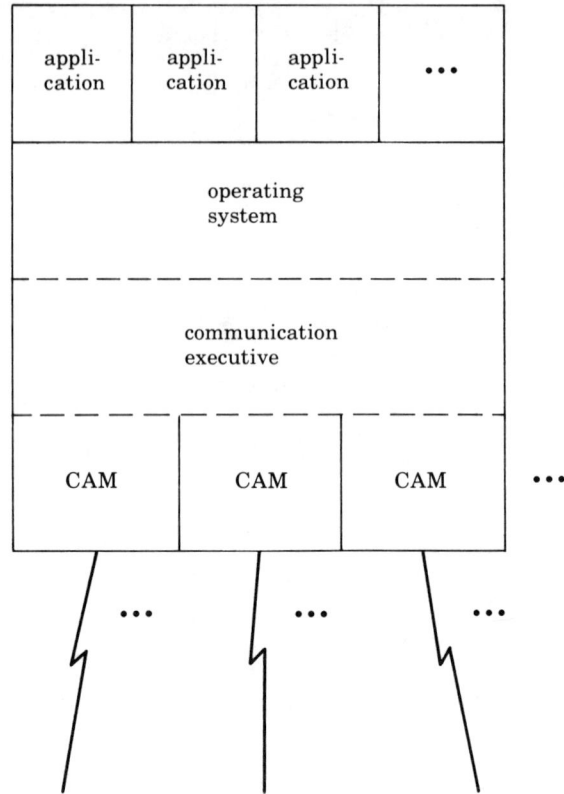

FIGURE 4.3 More sophisticated function of a communication executive managing CAM modules

Their Customer Information Control System (**CICS**) consolidates all generic support functions so that specific application programs are kept independent of the details of the underlying communication environment. A quick scan of the DATAPRO *Directory of Software* under the headings of "communication monitors and transaction processors," "terminal control programs," "CICS support," and "miscellaneous data communications" indicates the enormous number of special products available for different systems. The variety of function and capability makes it difficult to sort out and compare software from different vendors.

Applications should always be kept independent of the communication details so that detail can be changed to take advantage of the latest technological developments. Hardware changes might include new types of terminals, higher transmission speeds, particular line disciplines, amount of preprocessing by intelligent terminals, or bulk interprocessor data transfers. Software changes could be particular error handling techniques, link disciplines, addition of distributed database management, or conformity to new international standards. Applications seldom become involved with under-lying communication mechanisms.

THE LAYERED APPROACH

Communication software products translate the application input/output requirements into a form that can be handled by the communication hardware and supervises the transmission process. The simplicity of this statement belies the complexity of the tasks, as indicated by the number and sizes of the software products available to do them. We will tackle the complexity by looking in the software for levels of functions that can provide manageable chunks for understanding.

Think of communication software as concentric circles of software function surrounding the hardware (Figure 4.4). From within each ring, the view is limited to what functions are provided by the contained inner ring and what functions must be supplied to the outer containing one. These conceptual rings are called **levels** of abstraction or **layers** of software. Starting from the inside, add on one layer at a time in correspondence with extending the capabilities of the hardware by one group of functions at a time. Starting from the outside, strip away layer after layer of sophistication until reaching the core of primitive hardware functions. Communication software may also be thought of as building blocks arranged in logical layers, as in the IBM example of Figure 4.5.

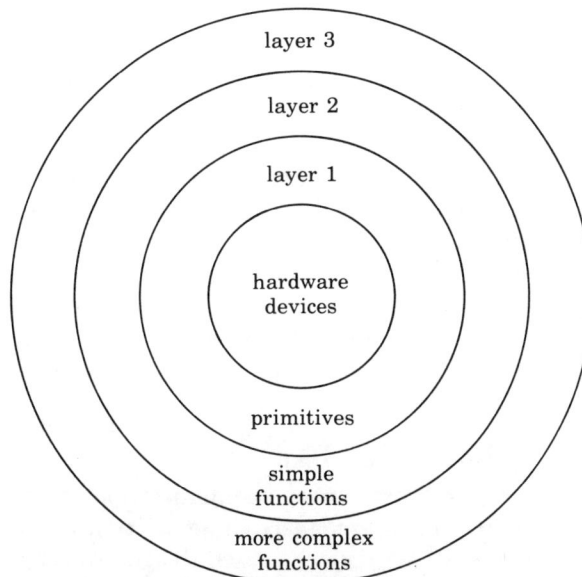

FIGURE 4.4 Circles of software function yield a layered approach to software

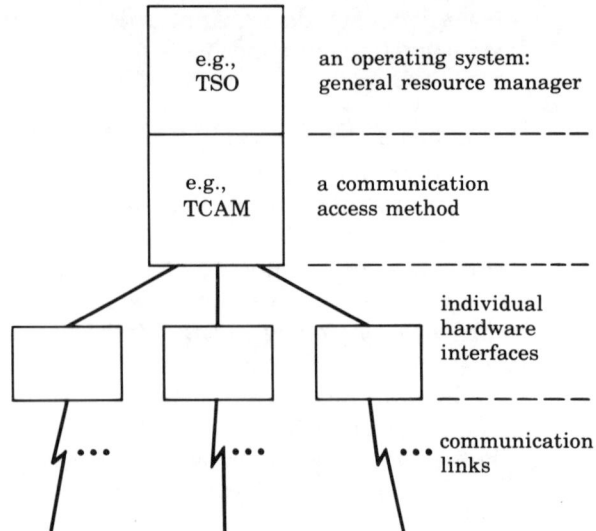

FIGURE 4.5 Example of IBM building blocks arranged in logical layers

There are many advantages in a layered approach to communication software in particular, and to other types of control software in general. The functions identified and assigned to particular layers encourage a modular approach to building the software. There functions are generally easier to understand because the jobs to be done within a single layer are more limited in scope. Application independence is fostered because the software assumes only that specific services are available, without depending on the details of their provision. Thus, hardware may be replaced as is technologically appropriate without affecting the applications, and so may lower levels of software, because internal layer mechanisms are hidden from higher layers. Maintenance of the entire system is simpler; changes do not have seemingly endless ripple effects. The layers can even serve as an implementation guide to system builders. The number of layers to be implemented on a specific processor, for example, can be chosen to fit its intended role in a network or to fit some memory size constraint. Similarly, the allocation of functions to hardware or software implementations can be made according to specific system requirements for speed or flexibility.

THE OSI MODEL
The proliferation of communication products, along with increasing user desires to interconnect different types and brands of computer equipment and systems, has motivated the International Standards Organization (ISO) to define a context for Open Systems Interconnection (OSI). It was hoped that describing the external interactions required of systems wishing to be

"open" for communication with other systems would promote the formulation and adoption of standard "rules of conversation." Such standards would not tell any vendor how to build a product, but would simply specify what functions should be provided to create an appropriate working environment for system interconnection.

The definition developed by ISO is known as the OSI **reference model.** It is a functional description, in layers, of the services required for interconnection of systems. It is based on various experiences with both experimental computer networks, such as ARPANET (a university and research net funded by the U.S. Department of Defense) and CYCLADES (a French network), and with communication products from vendors such as IBM. The model was specifically designed to have layer boundaries with well-defined interfaces that would allow for sensible implementations. The layers and boundaries were expected to indicate any standard rules needed for conversations between systems.

The reference model for Open Systems Interconnection has seven layers arranged as in Figure 4.6. The layers are briefly described here; the details are covered in the next chapter.

The **physical layer** comprises the functions and procedures for the mechanical and electromagnetic interconnection of hardware components. These include what signals should be present, when, and on what lines, and what voltages and timing are expected. The physical layer is the mechanism for transferring a stream of data bits.

The **data link layer** provides the first attempt at grouping and interpreting the bits. A frame is the basic meaningful group of bits; frames contain control information or data or both. An important function of the data link layer is to detect transmission errors and take appropriate action to correct them.

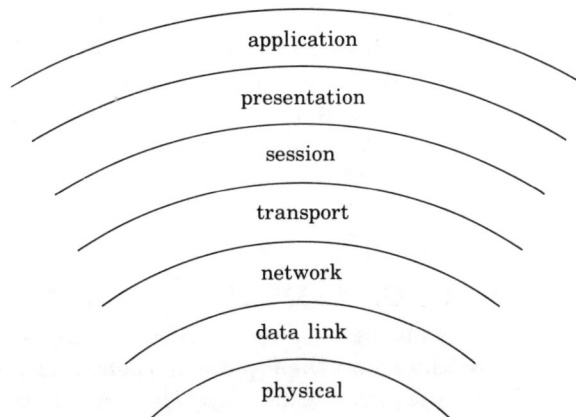

FIGURE 4.6 The OSI reference model

The **network layer** chooses a transmission path from point to point in the network and delivers the data. Opinions differ about what level of service should be provided; that is, whether deliveries should be ordered or guaranteed. These three layers, physical, data link, and network, are sometimes considered together as a *communications subnet* (or network substructure) because they were typical of the services originally offered to the public by data communication network companies. The higher levels manage functions increasingly related to applications.

The **transport layer** goes beyond the services of the network layer to ensure *end-to-end* communication. This typically means from the source to the intended destination, not in the hardware or machine sense, but from program to program or user to application in the operating context of the host systems. Most hosts support many programs and users with the appearance of simultaneity. Thus there may be multiple logical connections to be maintained between hosts, even over a single physical channel. The transport layer provides effective management of the logical paths and flow of data over those logical connections.

The **session layer** uses the connections of the transport service to provide the network user's view of the available resources. The dialogue for access and release of services, the integrity required to ensure completion of activities once begun, and the ability to recover from error situations should be handled so that users can rely on the system and know the status of their work. On a single host, users usually think of sessions as the entire login-do work-logout period. Most users appreciate periodic feedback from the system that work is in progress, and expect a notice of completion. Such status reports build confidence that the work is being accomplished.

The **presentation layer** collects non-essential, higher level functions which would be commonly useful throughout the network system. Encryption, file transfer capabilities, text compression, or definition of universal transactions (such as cash purchase, charge purchase, or refund in a retail system) typically belong in this category.

The **application layer** calls upon all of these services to handle a specified job in the information systems context of the surrounding organization: data management, inventory control, banking, and forecasting, and so forth. Agreement on the boundary between presentation and application has been very difficult to obtain; consequently, the interface has not been defined in detail.

LAYERED COMMUNICATION

How do all these layers cooperate to accomplish communication? Figure 4.7 shows that from the top down, each layer passes its requests for data transfer to the layer below. The downward-receiving layer packages the data according to its own functions and responsibilities and passes them down. When the physical layer is reached, its package is physically shipped across

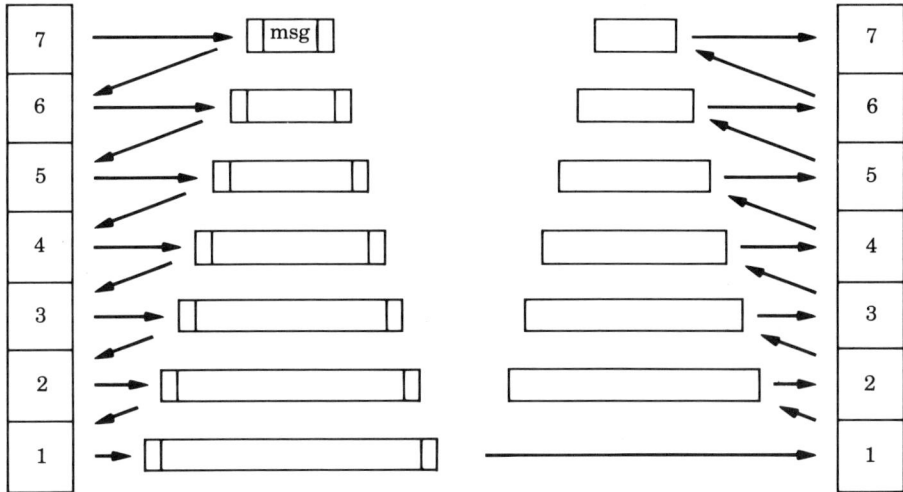

FIGURE 4.7 The layered communication process

the transmission facility to be received by the corresponding destination physical layer. Now the layer transfer process is reversed. Each upward-receiving layer interprets its own level of packaging and passes the contents untouched up to the next layer until the ultimate destination is reached. Only packaging is interpreted, created, or destroyed at each intermediate level; the contents are not disturbed in any way.

The ideas of packaging, sources, and ultimate destinations indicate the possibility that not every communication will require every level of handling. For example, a system that wishes to be treated strictly as a single terminal to another system in the network might implement only the network, data link, and physical layers (Figure 4.8). The advantages of layering will apply to these systems also, as long as they perform the proper functions and create the packaging expected by the target destination.

Blind adherence to the restricted interaction of multiple layers can sometimes be impractical for real system implementations (remember, OSI is a *model*). The overhead of many successive envelopes to be created and interpreted for a single message can impose a processing penalty and a longer delay in passing the message that is unsuitable for particular applications. In such cases, clear, functional definitions that allow higher-layer access directly to lower levels without intermediate processing are highly desirable.

NETWORK ARCHITECTURES

The ordered collection of layers, together with their function definitions, views across boundaries, and packaging rules, make up what we call a **network architecture.** It represents a plan for or a philosophy of cooperation

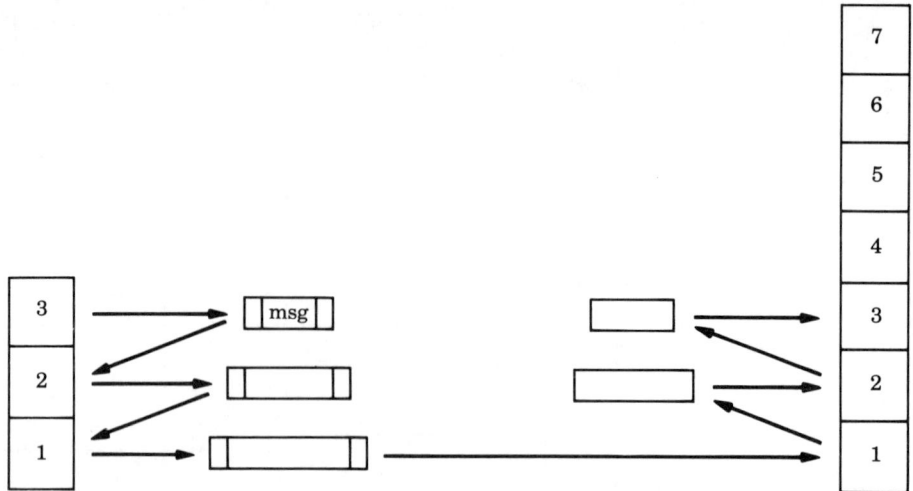

FIGURE 4.8 An example of limited layering

among the components participating in a communications-based computer network. In the same way that an architect can choose a style (baroque, Victorian, Byzantine) and a type of structure (office building, house, church, for example), system architects can choose a philosophy and a type of network structure in planning a particular system. The effort involved in creating an approach or philosophy is great enough that most architectures have been developed by large vendors of computer systems to promote sales of their own products.

Systems Network Architecture

IBM's specific plan for networking is embodied in their Systems Network Architecture (SNA). This has evolved through several versions as users have demanded more flexibility in their systems and in reaction to the OSI reference model. SNA was originally developed in response to the proliferation of IBM user applications (and products from other vendors) with special communication control procedures. The inability to share devices and procedures became a major barrier to cost-effective uses of system resources.

The logical structure of SNA is a series of layers built on top of a generally hierarchical scheme for physical interconnection of hardware devices (Figure 4.9). The major layers of SNA are shown in Figure 4.10:

- *data link control,* which frames, formats, and handles possible errors in the data stream
- *path control,* which is responsible for the physical path selections, routing table maintenance, and message segmentation and blocking

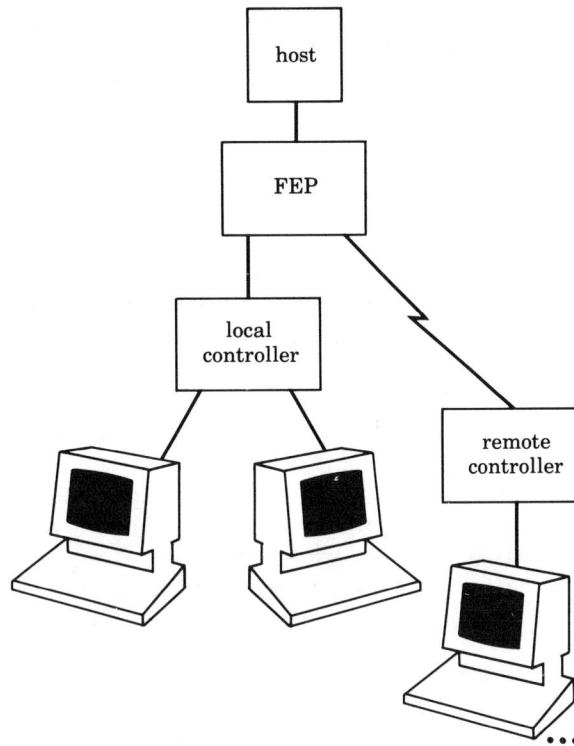

FIGURE 4.9 Hierarchical interconnection of hardware

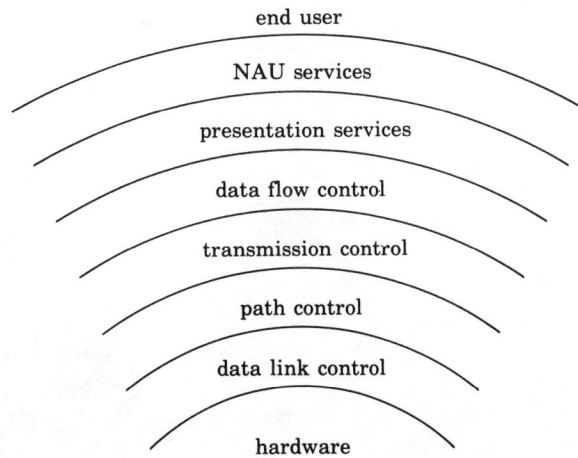

FIGURE 4.10 Systems Network Architecture: logical structure. NAU = network addressable unit

■ *transmission control,* which handles classes of service, the concept of a logical route, and traffic congestion

■ *data flow control,* which manages end-to-end flow such as the readiness of a destination to handle the potential traffic volume

■ *presentation services,* which does all format translations

■ *network addressable unit (NAU) services,* which manages the dialogue between users and applications

■ *end user,* which contains the specific application

Much more detail would be required to map accurately the functions of SNA onto the OSI reference model, but we can see that the data link layers are comparable, that path control and transmission control are roughly equivalent to the network layer, and that data flow is similar to the transport layer.

Various IBM products are available that implement the functions prescribed by SNA. Basically, an SNA network is made up of two types of **nodes;** that is, points within the network containing SNA components. These are peripheral nodes, at the lowest level of the IBM hierarchy, and subarea nodes, which link the peripheral nodes in their subarea to other subareas of the network, as in Figure 4.11. At least one subarea node will

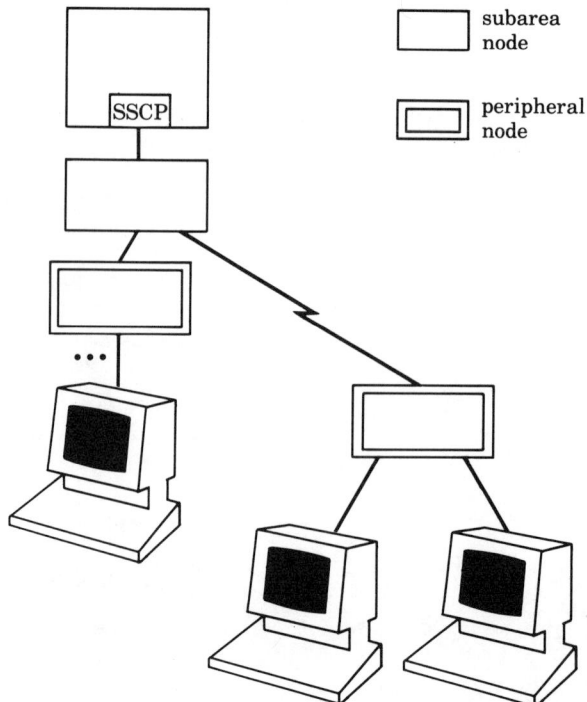

FIGURE 4.11 Nodes in an SNA network

contain a System Services Control Point (SSCP), which supervises the operation of a portion of the network, called a domain, by managing the resources, coordinating the activities, and activating hardware and software to participate in sessions.

Typically, subarea nodes with an SSCP are implemented in IBM hosts with an SNA access method. Subarea nodes without an SSCP are usually in communications control processors, such as IBM's 3705-II, running a network control program (NCP). Peripheral nodes are implemented in various cluster controllers, terminals, and systems, such as the IBM 3270 Information Display System, 6670 Information Distributor, or the System/32.

Digital Network Architecture

The plan for networking created by Digital Equipment Corporation (DEC) is called Digital Network Architecture (DNA). Like SNA, DNA has evolved beyond its original goals of providing users with a common application interface to communication facilities, sharing resources, and internally making use of standard interface definitions. It was imperative for DEC to first address the interconnection of a wide range of hardware and software components across their own dissimilar product lines (DEC-10, PDP-11, RSTS, RSX-11, and others). DNA provided the architectural model under which an entire family of **DECnet** implementations has been built as products to handle cost-effective use of resources, various topologies, availability, and extensibility by allowing for flexible protocols and functional growth.

A basic concept of DNA is the idea of a logical link, the message-oriented connection between two resource objects in the network. These objects (application programs or server programs that manage special devices or data for example) have two-part network addresses consisting of the node address within the network and an object address within the context of that particular node. The logical link provides access to a vast set of network resources in much the same way that physical links handle local resources through program calls or device interfaces. The uniform addressing of objects allows management of links to be highly distributed throughout the network. In contrast to IBM's host-dominated, hierarchical approach to systems and networks, DEC's logical link is oriented toward general interconnection of cooperating peers, much more in tune with their focus on minicomputer products.

The structure of DNA is a series of layers, as shown in Figure 4.12:

- *physical link* manages the actual hardware interconnection for transmission purposes
- *data link control* creates a communication path between adjacent nodes, using either the Digital Data Communications Message Protocol (DDCMP), or other popular standards like Ethernet or X.25
- *routing* handles paths, routing, and congestion control between source and destination nodes without making guarantees of delivery

user

network management

network application

session control

end communication

routing

data link control

physical
link

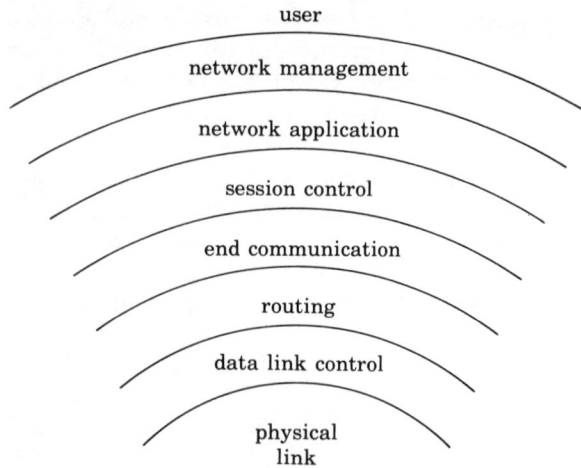

FIGURE 4.12 The layers of Digital Network Architecture

- *end communication* creates and manages logical links, provides reliable message delivery, controls flow, and manages buffers
- *session control* (relatively new), manages sessions and handles process naming and addressing
- *network application* supports user applications with generic services such as file access and transfer (Data Access Protocol), network virtual terminals, and gateways to other types of networks
- *network management* provides user access to and control of lower layer operating parameters and counters
- *user,* does specific application jobs such as remote order entry, and also handles the Network Control Program

Previous versions of DNA had no distinct session layer, and originally named the third and fourth layers opposite to the OSI reference model. DECnet implementations have been carefully structured into modules that fit within the layers of DNA and limit their interactions to well-defined interfaces. The module hierarchy shown in Figure 4.13 is somewhat more flexible than the strict layering prescribed by the OSI reference model in that functions not needed can be bypassed by direct access to the next lower layer. This ability to select modules is especially convenient in the data link layer, where access to DDCMP links, or Ethernets, or X.25 links can coexist.

ARPANET

Unlike SNA and DNA, the ARPANET is a real network implementation rather than an architecture. It is included here because it provided a large portion of the networking experience on which the OSI model and some vendor architectures were built. ARPANET is a large, geographically dis-

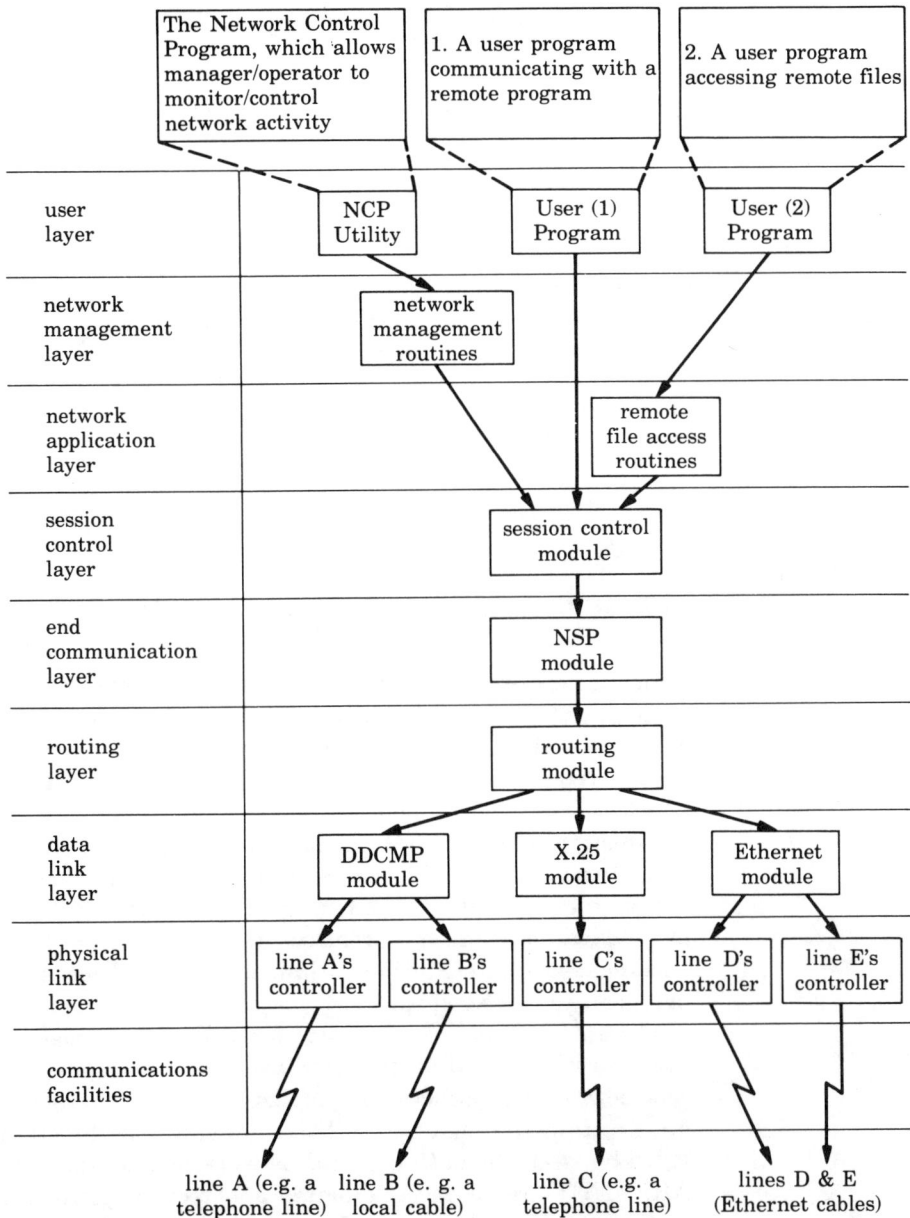

FIGURE 4.13 DNA Modules resident in a typical DECnet node. Copyright © 1982 by Digital Equipment Corporation. This information describes the Digital Network Architecture developed by Digital Equipment Corporation.

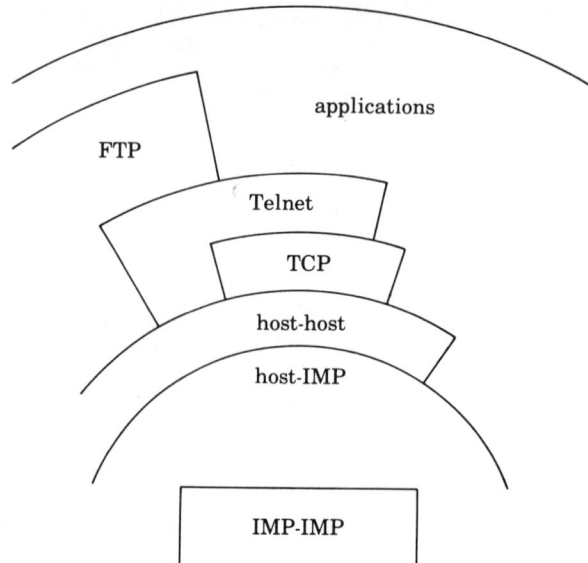

FIGURE 4.14 The logical structure of ARPANET

tributed network connecting computers at various universities and research institutions. It was originally funded by the Advanced Research Projects Agency (ARPA) of the U.S. Department of Defense to explore the technological requirements of large networks of dissimilar computer systems. Much of the development work was coordinated by Bolt, Beranek, and Newman, a Massachusetts research and consulting firm. The logical structure of the ARPANET is shown in Figure 4.14. Notice that the layers form a more hierarchical arrangement rather than falling into the concentric circles typical of the recent architectures. Advocates of the ARPANET claim this makes it more efficient in implementation because unneeded layers of overhead can be avoided.

Communication links are made between and managed by special network processors called IMPs (interface message processors), which act as the access points or interfaces for participating hosts into the network (Figure 4.15). Interaction among the IMPs provides the functionality ISO has divided between the data link and network layers. The data link functions of ARPANET are character-oriented and require positive acknowledgements to ensure correct receipt. At the network level, only a basic message delivery service is provided, and the IMPs spend extensive time keeping track of each other so that the status of paths for routing is always known.

IMP-IMP interactions, then, form the communications backbone for the attached host processors. How hosts get service from IMPs is the next level

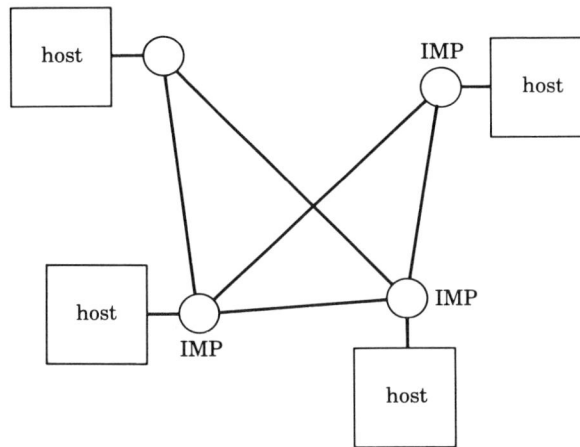

FIGURE 4.15 IMPs form and manage the ARPANET for attached host processors

of software, and then the rules for interaction among the hosts themselves are specified. These two layers do not fit the OSI model structure.

Transport level services have been offered in two different ways in AR-PANET. The original NCP (Network Control Program) assumed that the communication subnet was perfectly reliable; that nothing was ever lost or duplicated or misdirected. However, as new types of less reliable hosts were added to the network, the TCP (Transport Control Program) was introduced. TCP accepts messages of arbitrary lengths, breaks them up into packets of a maximum size, and sends each packet individually through the network. Messages must be reconstructed at the destination TCP by checking for packet losses, duplication, and correct sequencing.

ARPANET has no general session, presentation, or application layers, but some of the functions are offered as specific protocol programs. *Telnet* is a virtual terminal protocol using ASCII as the network standard code for characters and specifying certain control character meanings, such as carriage return. Options which can be negotiated through Telnet include transmission mode (HDX or FDX), remote echoing, tabulation, and page lengths. *FTP* is a file transfer protocol available on the ARPANET that allows copying of files from one node to another when certain file attributes can be made to match.

Others

Numerous other computer system vendors, such as Burroughs, Prime, Honeywell, and Data General, have also developed network architectures. Most are not so well known or widely referred to outside their user communities as those described above. One of the chief values of the OSI reference model is as a tool for comparing architectures that are quite dissimilar in appearance. We hope that eventually this will lead to easier interconnection of systems from different vendors.

CHAPTER REVIEW
Capsule

Communication software provides the interface functions needed to isolate applications from the detailed characteristics of communication hardware and procedures. A layered design approach limits the complexity of function, making the software easier to understand, build, and modify. The details of *how* each layer does its job of providing services to the next higher layer are kept hidden. In that way, internal mechanisms can be changed or updated without disturbing any other layers. The OSI reference model is a layered description of communication functions developed to promote understanding of and the potential for interconnection of communication systems from different vendors. On the basis of the model, significant international effort is taking place to standardize the services to be performed by each layer and how these will be offered to the layers above. The OSI model has also proved useful as a guide for both analysis and synthesis of communications-based computer system architectures and products.

IBM's Systems Network Architecture and DEC's Digital Network Architecture are introduced as examples of vendor approaches to networking. The OSI model can show how they are similar and different. Some of the experience on which the OSI model was based came from ARPANET, the first large packet-switching network in the U.S. Its structure is somewhat different, but the functional levels are still identifiable. Most computer vendors are now using network architectures to plan their communication within and across systems. Again, the OSI model helps to identify their similarities and differences.

Project

A major issue in the design of software for the supermarket system will be what communication software is available for the host computer system. Since we have started with a single-computer network, many of the sophisticated functions of the OSI reference model are not necessary. The underlying communications detail should be kept out of the application programs as much as possible, however. This should simplify program maintenance and improve the chances of transporting to or interconnecting with other systems.

1. Using the levels of the OSI reference model as a guide, discuss which of the major communication functions are needed in the single-computer supermarket system we have described so far.

2. What would you expect the major functions of an intelligent cash register to be? How would such devices change our ideas of the network traffic to be expected in the supermarket?

3. Would communication software be needed in the intelligent cash registers as well as in the main computer? If so, what are the functions and where are they needed?

NEW TERMS

application layer
ARPANET
BTAM
CICS
communication access method
data link layer
DECnet
device driver
DNA
ISO
layers
levels

network architecture
network layer
node
OSI reference model
physical layer
presentation layer
session layer
SNA
TCAM
transport layer
VTAM

QUESTIONS

1. What are some possible disadvantages of a layered approach to communication software?

2. Into what layers of control could the activities of a ferryboat across a river be divided using the OSI model? What is the equivalent of full-duplex service and how could it be provided?

3. Discuss what layers could be omitted if a network consisted only of two computers connected together by a single link; by several links.

4. How does TCP know when it has correctly reconstructed a message at the destination host? Think of mailing a multi-page letter by putting each page in a separate envelope.

5. Does layer similarity ensure that communication can take place? What layers are involved in a telephone call to Italy from Scotland, for example?

6. Find a description for a vendor architecture other than SNA and DNA. How does it relate to the OSI reference model?

5 Protocols and Interfaces

The most important aspect of layered communication software is that once the general functions are grouped into layers, precise definitions of how the functions should be accessed can be developed. Two definitions are of particular interest to us. A **protocol** describes how communication is carried out within a level and requires agreement among all the participants. An **interface** is at the boundary between two adjacent layers. It describes the services that are provided to the upper layer, such as how functions are requested and how results are returned.

A familiar example of a communication system is the telephone sales order depicted in Figure 5.1. The functions involved can be considered very simplistically as three layers: the telephone (a physical layer), the conversation (a session layer), and the order (an application layer). Notice that components of these layers exist at both the source and the destination.

The boundary between person and telephone could be called the instrument interface. Very simply, it specifies how a call is made and how a call is received. The basic services available at this interface include handset off-hook detection, tone generation, call connection, ring, and disconnection. The steps involved in making a call are to take the handset off-hook; listen for a dial tone; dial the number if the tone is present (further detail depends on the specific instrument); listen for the ring; connection is achieved if someone picks up in answer. To receive a call, the steps are to wait for the phone to ring, and pick up the receiver. Thus, the definition of an interface specifies how adjacent layers (in the same location) interact.

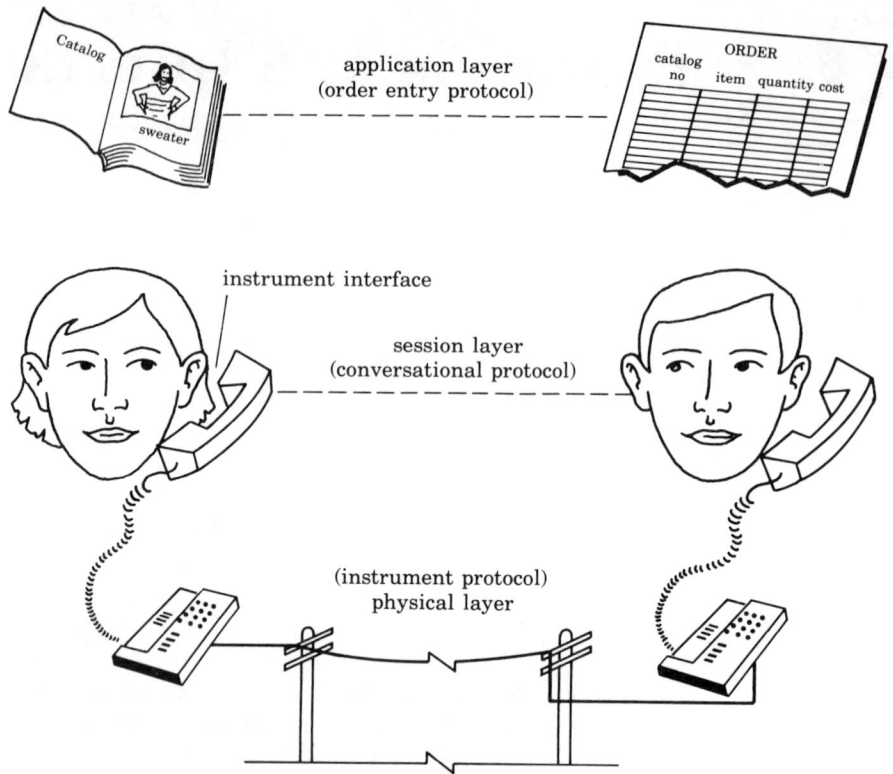

FIGURE 5.1 A layered view of a telephone sales order

Protocols, on the other hand, specify the rules for *how* the services are coordinated between the source and destination locations within a layer. Our telephone order example needs three protocols, one for instrument-to-instrument (the physical layer protocol), one for the person-to-person conversation (the session layer protocol), and one for the details of the order entry application. The instrument-to-instrument rules are enforced by the hardware, and have been defined precisely for telephone systems. In fact, the instrument protocol encompasses all of the detail about how a dialed number establishes a path from source to destination, how an instrument is notified of its calls, how calls are blocked out if a connection is already established, and so on. It is clear that for one instrument to have access to another, they must have agreed upon these details. Of course, the instruments do not "agree" to anything; it is the manufacturing and operating companies that must agree. The variety of instruments (from Western Electric, ITT, etc.) and telephone systems or services (by AT&T, MCI, etc.) available in the United States, and the fact that international calls can be made as well, indicate that extensive agreement or standardization does exist at the physical level for telephone systems.

The person-to-person or conversational protocol is much more flexible than the instrument protocol. There are some general rules such as saying hello when a call is received, saying good-bye before a call is terminated, and not talking when another person is talking. Violations of the rules at this level do not usually prevent the communication from taking place.

Some flexibility could be built into any communication layer, but it is more typical of the higher applications-oriented levels. The sales order form, for example, typically requires entry of several pieces of data for each item being ordered (for example, catalog number, item description, quantity, price). The number of fields depends on the item, and the sequence of requests and responses can be flexible as long as all relevant information is supplied.

To summarize, protocols are the rules for communication within a layer across locations; interfaces are the local rules for sending and receiving communications across layers within the context of one's own system (Figure 5.2). Internal rules may differ greatly so long as external protocol expectations are satisfied. Physical communication takes place only within the physical layer, but the protocols make it convenient to think of virtual communication occurring within each higher layer. In the telephone example, we think of the conversation as being between people, when actually the caller speaks to an instrument, the instrument transmits to the receiving instrument, which then forwards the information to the listener. If we use precise terminology, we could say that physical data transfers are made across interfaces (down the layers for transmission and up the layers for reception) while logical information is communicated through protocols (within layers across locations).

This chapter discusses some of the standards for protocols and interfaces that are widely accepted and some others still being developed.

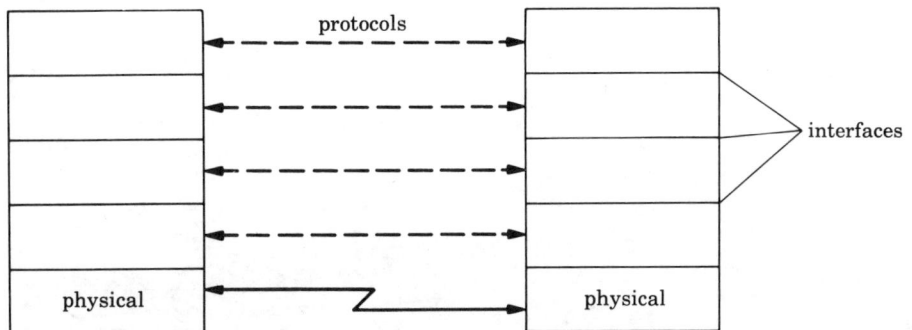

FIGURE 5.2 Protocols and interfaces

PHYSICAL LAYER

As mentioned in Chapter 3, the most common standard for interconnecting communication-based computer system devices is the EIA specification known as RS-232-C. It consists of definitions for the expected electromagnetic signal characteristics, the mechanical connection requirements, the functions of the physical interchange circuits, and some agreed-upon subsets of interchange circuits for groups of specific applications (recall Figure 3.1). These functional definitions, signal levels, wires used, and distance and voltage specifications have been adhered to faithfully by numerous manufacturers for many thousands of devices and components to create a vast breadth of hardware compatibility. The few exceptions have been known to frustrate novice users, but increasingly, the major dissatisfactions with RS-232-C are due to its speed and distance limitations.

RS-232-C cables are commonly made with connectors capable of providing up to 25 individual circuit connections (that is, 25-pin connectors) as in Figure 5.3; few devices actually use all of the circuits. In fact, it is common for certain circuits (pins) to be wired together internally, within the cable connector. Direct terminal-to-computer connections may be made, for example, with only the transmitted data, received data, data terminal ready, and signal ground circuits active. Sometimes transmit and receive alone are sufficient. More complicated devices or more sophisticated connections tend to use more of the available functions.

Users have grown increasingly intolerant of the unsuitability of RS-232-C for applications requiring higher speeds and longer-distance communications. Acceptance of newer standards for interconnection is under way. The "General Purpose 37-position and 9-position Interface for Data Terminal Equipment and Data Circuit-Terminating Equipment Employing Serial Binary Data Interchange", more commonly called **RS-449**, defines more interchange functions to extend the applicability of RS-232-C. The major barrier to acceptance of RS-449 is the sheer numbers of RS-232-C devices already installed and currently being manufactured.

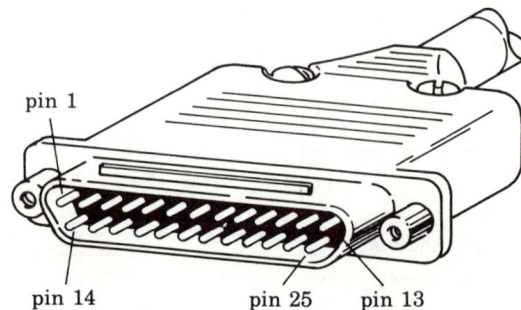

FIGURE 5.3 A 25-pin connector for RS-232-C

Internationally, many of the standards for data communications are set by the Consultative Committee on International Telephony and Telegraphy (**CCITT**), which is part of the International Telecommunications Union of the United Nations. The international physical layer standard comparable to RS-232-C is the "List of Definitions for Interchange Circuits between Data Terminal Equipment and Data Circuit Terminating Equipment," commonly called V.24. Revision efforts by the CCITT have proceeded differently from the RS-449 approach in the U.S., actually reducing the number of interchange circuits (connector pins) and compensating for the difference by adding logic to control the interface. The X.20 (Interface Between Data Terminal Equipment and Data-circuit Terminating Equipment for Start-Stop Transmission Services on Public Data Networks) and **X.21** (General Purpose Interface Between Data Terminal Equipment and Data-circuit Terminating Equipment for Synchronous Operation on Public Data Networks) recommendations have both taken this approach of fewer pins and more logic.

DATA LINK LAYER

The data link layer groups bits together to provide error-free transmission across a single link. The unit of transfer is called a **frame;** in addition to the data, it usually includes addresses (in case of multipoint links), transmission control flags, and error control information. These are arranged as preliminaries called the **header,** the main **body,** and follow-up called the **trailer.** The specific organization and interpretation of these contents are defined by the various data link protocols.

Early data link protocols were known as line control procedures. For asynchronous communication, controls were built on top of the binary character coding schemes with special characters (ASCII, for example, has characters for start of heading, start of text, end of text, and end of transmission; see Figure 1.1 for a complete listing). Synchronous communication at first extended the use of these control characters by blocking large groups of characters together for transmission but still interpreting them individually on receipt. A widely used (and current) IBM protocol of this type is Binary Synchronous Communications, commonly called bisync or **BSC**. The layout of a BSC frame is shown in Figure 5.4.

A major drawback of the character-oriented approach is encountered when data other than text are transmitted. Numeric data have entirely different internal computer formats from character data, making it possible for bit patterns that look like the special header or trailer control character codes to appear within the body of a frame. This could cause the receiver to think it had found the end of the body prematurely and try to interpret subsequent body characters as trailer information. The search for control characters can be disabled in the body of the message if even more special characters are used to identify its beginning and end. Foolproof schemes are

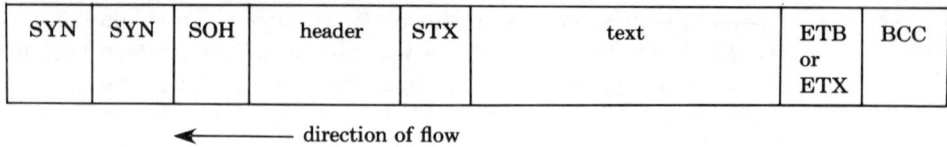

SYN	SYN	SOH	header	STX	text	ETB or ETX	BCC

←——————— direction of flow

SYN—synchronize (start bits)

SOH—start of header

STX—start of text

ETB—end of transmission block, more will follow later

ETX—end of text, no more blocks will follow

BCC—block check character, for error detection

FIGURE 5.4 BSC frame layout

difficult to concoct, and destroy the simplicity of the original protocol ideas. The approach is particularly susceptible to problems if transmission errors occur.

Character-Oriented Protocols

One way to solve the transparency problem of character-oriented techniques is used in the Digital Data Communications Message Protocol (DDCMP) of Digital Equipment Corporation. DDCMP was designed to be a very general protocol useful in many different environments, including for asynchronous or synchronous, half-duplex or full-duplex transmission. One of its most important goals was to provide compatibility with older equipment to preserve as much user investment in existing installations as possible.

The format for DDCMP data message frames is shown in Figure 5.5. The header includes a count that tells how many character-sized units (bytes)

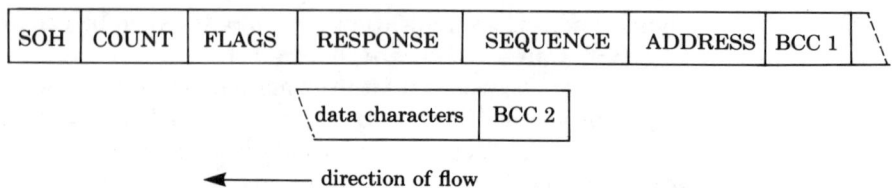

SOH	COUNT	FLAGS	RESPONSE	SEQUENCE	ADDRESS	BCC 1

data characters	BCC 2

←——————— direction of flow

SOH—start of header

BCC—block check

FIGURE 5.5 DDCMP frame format

01111110 11100010 11000001 11010011 11000101 11100010 01000000

flag   S   A   L   E   S

false flag sequence

11100011 11010110 11010111 0100000001011011111110111 1111

T   O   P $ 7

transmitter
inserts a

011111010100 ... 01111110   zero

7   M   flag

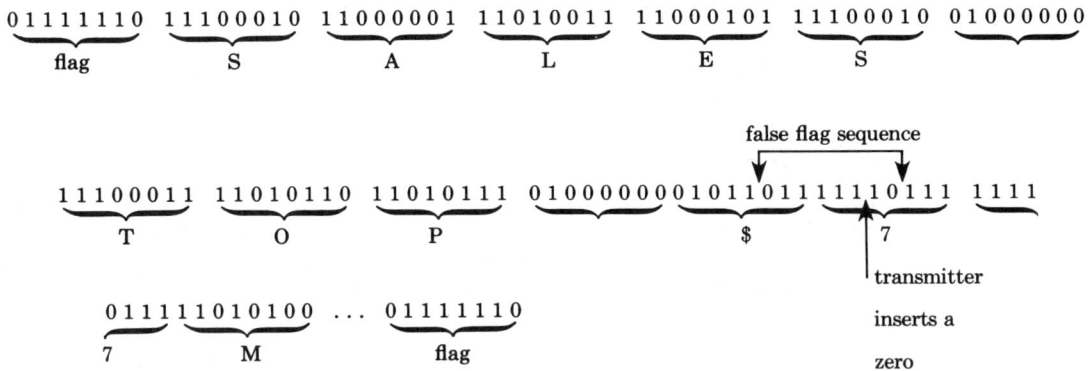

FIGURE 5.6 Bit-stuffing (zero-bit insertion)

will be in the body. Only after completing that count in the body is the trailer expected, signifying the end of the frame. To ensure correct receipt of the count, the header carries its own error check information independently of the body.

Bit-Oriented Protocols

IBM took a different tack in improving BSC. Instead of attempting to preserve compatibility with old installations, they created an entirely new approach (forcing users to invest in new equipment): a full-duplex, bit-oriented scheme called Synchronous Data Link Control, **SDLC**. It is completely bit-oriented; frames are delimited by a special sequence called a flag: six consecutive one bits between zero bits. A technique called bit-stuffing ensures that the flag sequence cannot be found anywhere inside a frame (Figure 5.6). Once a flag has been sent to begin a frame, the transmitter watches for any string of five one bits. If five consecutive ones are found, a zero bit is inserted ("stuffed") into the transmitted data stream automatically. The receiver must correspondingly discard any zero found following five ones. The protocol is thus greatly simplified at the expense of sending a few more non-informational bits in the data stream.

Figure 5.7 shows the layout of a bit-oriented frame. The header contains address information to specify the destination for the frame and a control

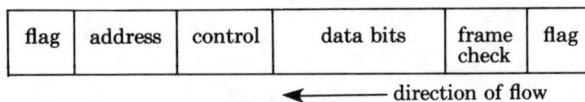

flag	address	control	data bits	frame check	flag

← direction of flow

FIGURE 5.7 Bit-oriented frame format

field to indicate the type of message (sequenced data, initialization of a connection, and so on). The body of the frame can be any length, although some practical limits have been imposed. The trailer contains a sophisticated error-checking mechanism.

Error Handling

Transmission across physical links is prone to errors from noise (spurious signal) or inaccurate interpretations due to loss of signal or quality. The data link layer is responsible for handling the results of such problems. Prevention of transmission errors is probably impossible, so detection is required. The detection process generally requires cooperation between the sender and receiver, and some agreement on what to do about the error.

A simple mechanism for error handling is called **echo checking.** All transmissions are repeated by the receiver back to the sender, who compares the echo with the original. If they are identical, the sender knows the frame was received correctly and sends the next one. If there was an error in either direction (original or echo), the two will not match and the transmission could be repeated *if* the receiver discards the previously received frame (Figure 5.8). Sequence numbers are used to keep the receiver and sender synchronized, but they are just as susceptible to damage as the data in the frame. In general, echo checking is not an adequate mechanism for computer networks.

Another way of handling errors is to shift the responsibility for detection from the sender to the receiver. This means the sender must add something to the data that would allow the receiver to determine whether or not damage had occurred. A very simple mechanism for character-oriented protocols is to add a parity bit to each character. This is especially convenient for ASCII characters where seven bits are used for the actual coding and the

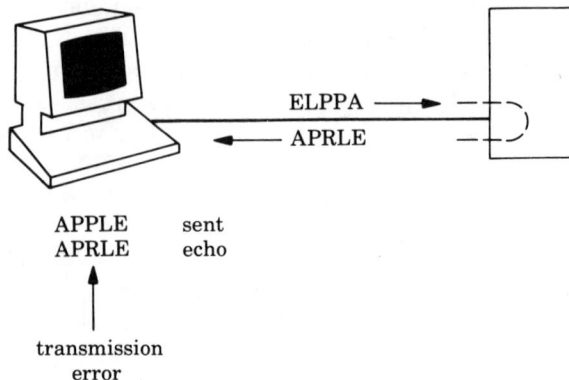

ELPPA

APRLE

APPLE sent
APRLE echo

transmission
error

FIGURE 5.8 Echo checking for error detection

```
1 0 1 0 1 0 0    T
1 0 1 0 1 0 1    U
1 0 0 1 1 1 0    N              ASCII
1 0 0 0 0 0 1    A              characters

                                ↓

   odd parity                   0 1 0 1 0 1 0 0
                                1 1 0 1 0 1 0 1
                                1 1 0 0 1 1 1 0
                                1 1 0 0 0 0 0 1

   even parity                  1 1 0 1 0 1 0 0
                                0 1 0 1 0 1 0 1
                                0 1 0 0 1 1 1 0
                                0 1 0 0 0 0 0 1
```

FIGURE 5.9 Character parity for error detection

eighth can be for parity. The value of the eighth bit is chosen according to the number of one bits in the character code, and according to agreement in the data link layer on whether to use odd or even parity (Figure 5.9). More bits are thus transmitted than actually required to represent the data, but the overhead allows simple one-bit errors to be detected. Practically, transmission errors tend to occur in bursts, so character parity alone may not be a sufficient technique.

Another parity scheme is illustrated in Figure 5.10: sending an extra "character" periodically that is made up of bits used strictly for error control. This is sometimes called a longitudinal redundancy check (LRC), because it adds another dimension of checking to the "horizontal" redundancy check of the character parity bit. Notice that for single bit errors, the combination of the character parity bits and the frame check character allows not only detection of the error, but also pinpoints the bit location in error and consequently could lead to correction of the error. With bursty errors

```
even character parity
  ↓
1 1 1 1 0 0 1 1      s
0 1 1 1 0 1 1 1      w
0 1 1 0 1 1 1 1      o
0 1 1 1 0 0 1 0      r
1 1 1 0 0 1 0 0      d
0 1 1 0 0 1 1 0      f
0 1 1 0 1 0 0 1      i
1 1 1 1 0 0 1 1      s
1 1 1 0 1 0 0 0      h


0 1 1 0 1 0 0 1  ◄── even block parity
```

FIGURE 5.10 Parity block check for error detection

for 6-bit character codes

$$CRC\text{-}12 = X^{12} + X^{11} + X^3 + X^2 + X + 1$$

for 8-bit character codes

$$CRC\text{-}16 = X^{16} + X^{15} + X^2 + 1$$

$$CRC\text{-}CCITT = X^{16} + X^{12} + X^5 + 1$$

FIGURE 5.11 Standard generator polynomials for cyclic redundancy checking to detect transmission errors

likely to cover more than a single bit, however, this correction is not usually reliable.

The cyclic redundancy check (**CRC**) is a much more sophisticated error-detection mechanism. Based on an arithmetic technique, the bits in a frame are considered to be coefficients of a polynomial. This polynomial is divided by a special standard polynomial called a generator, and the remainder from the division becomes a frame check sequence (FCS). The sender calculates the FCS for each frame (header and body) and appends it to the frame as the trailer to complete a single transmission. This is similar to the parity character technique. The receiver divides the incoming data by the same generator polynomial and checks the computed remainder against the FCS received from the sender. If they are not identical, an error is detected. Mathematical analysis has been used to select generator polynomials that give excellent protection against burst errors (Figure 5.11).

Once errors have been detected by a receiver, either they can be corrected by the receiver, or the bad data can be discarded by the receiver and the original data can be retransmitted by the sender. Error correction techniques tend to be more complex than detection, and are preferred over retransmission only under special conditions (such as on satellite links or where high security is required).

A simple retransmission scheme is called **stop-and-wait** (Figure 5.12). The sender transmits a frame, including both data and check sequence. The receiver computes a check on the data and compares it with the incoming check sequence. If they match, an **ACK** (acknowledgement frame) is returned from the receiver to the sender, and the sender transmits the next frame. If an error is detected, the bad data is discarded by the receiver, a **NAK** (negative acknowledge) is returned to the sender, and the sender retransmits the previous frame. Often the sender will set a timer after transmission, and if no acknowledgement is received before the time expires, retransmission is automatic. Frame sequence numbers are required to ensure that the receiver can detect and discard duplicate transmissions. This protects against damaged ACKs or timers that are set for too short an interval.

The stop-and-wait technique has a fairly high overhead time when few errors occur. An alternative approach is to use a continuous transmission

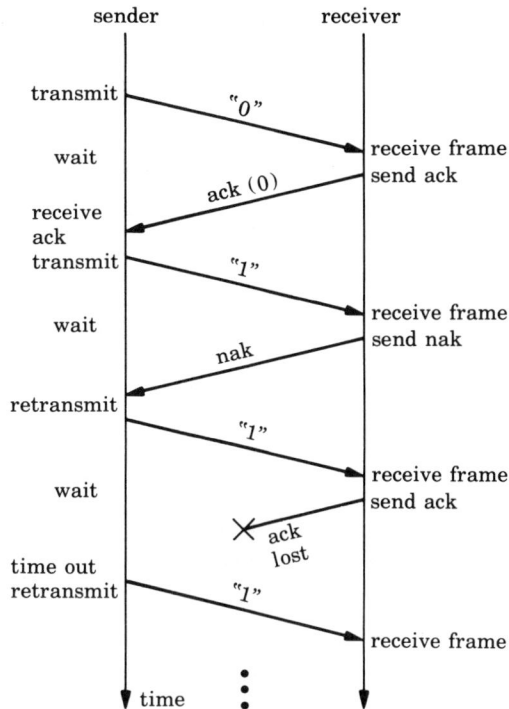

FIGURE 5.12 Stop-and-wait retransmission protocol

scheme that allows the receiver to interrupt the transmission when an error is detected. The first of these techniques is called **go-back-N** (Figure 5.13). When the receiver detects an error, it returns a NAK containing "N" plus the sequence number of the frame in error, and stops saving received frames until it gets frame "N" again. The transmitter, upon receiving the NAK, stops transmitting, goes back to frame "N", and begins transmission again with that frame. This approach obviously requires an effective interrupt channel or full-duplex connection. In practice, senders usually require positive ACKs periodically to continue transmitting. This limits the send buffer sizes on long messages.

A second continuous transmission technique is called **selective retransmission** (Figure 5.14). In this case, the receiver continues to listen after returning a NAK, and the sender restransmits only the frame specified to be in error. Again, periodic ACKs are desirable to limit buffer requirements for both the sending and receiving data link layers. Comparative analysis of the various schemes depends heavily on the characteristics of the transmission links, appropriate buffer sizes and availability, and the application requirements for accuracy.

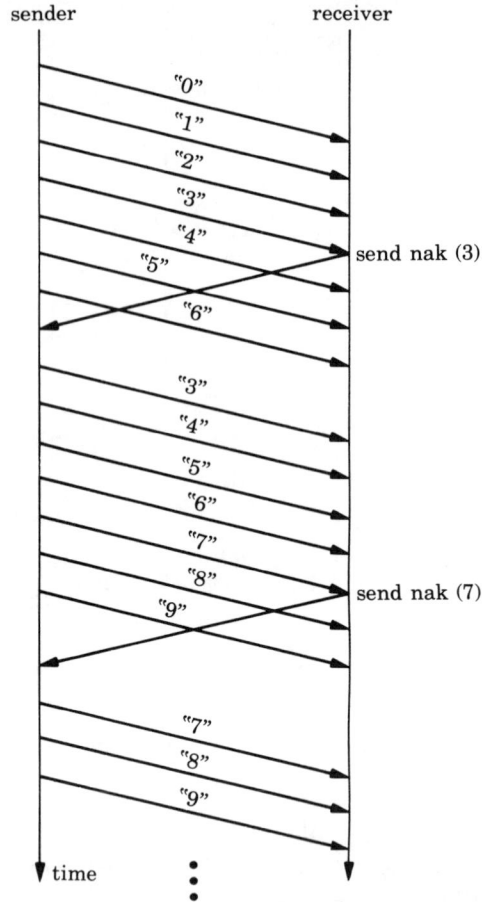

FIGURE 5.13 Go-back-N retransmission protocol

Standards

Standardization at the data link level largely follows the bit-oriented approach. The American National Standards Institute has generalized from SDLC in developing its Advanced Data Communication Control Procedures (ADCCP). ISO's High-Level Data Link Control (**HDLC**) is similar, as is the Balanced Link Access Protocol (LAPB) in CCITT's X.25 recommendation. Details of protocol operation depend on the characteristics of the particular transmission media making up the links of the network, but the frame format, sequence numbering, and the frame check sequence are now similar for most.

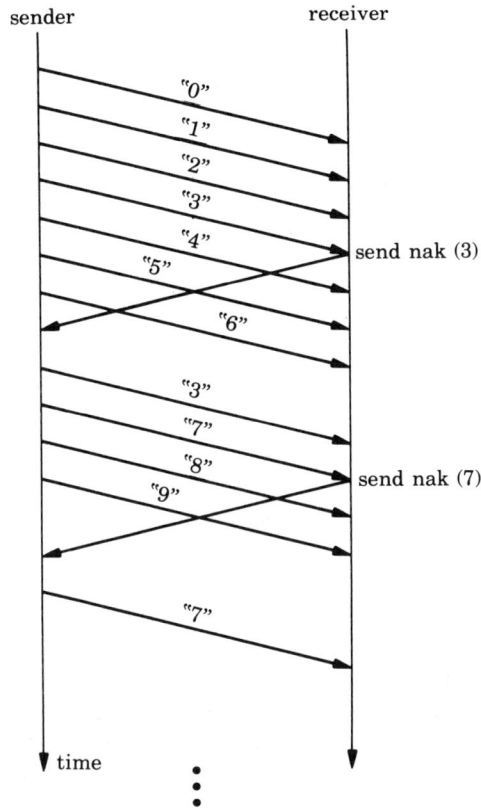

FIGURE 5.14 Selective retransmission

NETWORK LAYER

The network layer delivers messages from source to destination locations. In fact, a **network** is a set of resources connected by a set of communication links. This represents two kinds of sophistication beyond the data link level. First, there is the generalization of a link as the direct connection between just two points. At the network level, a **path** from a source to a destination might consist of a sequence of links through and including intermediate points capable of passing along the messages. This distinction is most clearly demonstrated in networks made up of point-to-point connections as in Figure 5.15, where links are labeled with lower case letters (a, b, c, etc.) and paths can be specified by concatenating the names of the locations connected (PQ, PR, QS, etc.). Non-adjacent locations are thus connected by multi-link paths between sources and destinations. When the connected locations of a network are capable of temporarily holding a message in case

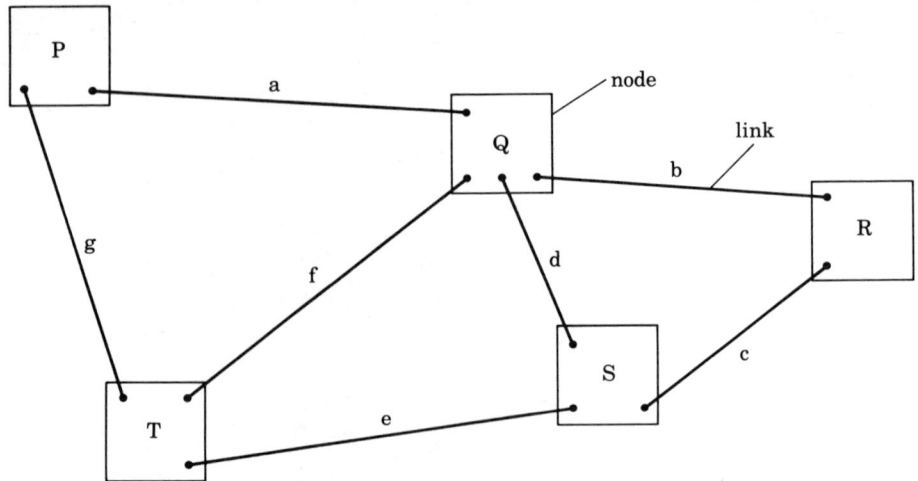

FIGURE 5.15 Point-to-point network

the next stop is busy or out of touch, the system is a **store and forward** network.

For networks having multipoint connections, Figure 5.16 shows that the distinction between the data link and network levels is only one point of view. The simple network (a) of one host with all devices on a multipoint link has three possible source-to-destination paths, each consisting of a single, direct link. Traffic from P to R travels directly; it is not sent from P to Q and then forwarded by Q to R. The more complex network (b) consists of devices which are all capable of interacting with each other. This gives six source-to-destination pairs and thus six single-link paths. The fact that links and paths correspond directly in multipoint networks will require network layer protocols (for multi-access) that are quite different from point-to-point protocols. These will be discussed in Chapters 6 and 7.

The second sophistication at the network level is the concept of a message rather than the frame of the data link layer. Think of frames as convenient units for transmission, and messages as the basic units of communication. Most messages among people are in written or spoken forms, so postal and telephone systems are convenient models for network delivery. In fact, two general approaches to the network layer have been advocated: a **virtual circuit** service roughly analogous to telephone systems, and a **datagram** service somewhat similar to postal systems.

One requirement for sending any message is to specify the location of the intended receiver, as with a telephone number or street address. In a computer network, any addressable location with intelligence is called a **node** (dumb terminals must be attached to nodes; personal computers may actu-

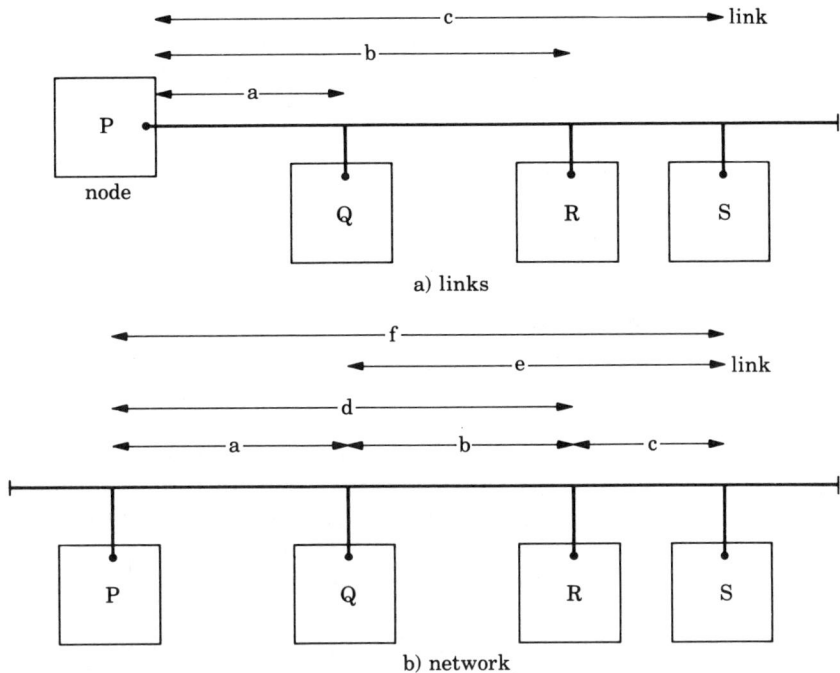

FIGURE 5.16 Multipoint

ally be nodes). Point-to-point networks may have a series of intermediate (store-and-forward) nodes on the path between source and destination. These may not be explicitly addressed at the network level, but they are required to participate in forwarding the traffic. In fact, each node must choose the next link according to local knowledge about the direction of the destination. On multi-point links, nodes physically between a source and destination do not participate in the data transfer. Thus, we are sometimes distinctly aware of the intermediate nodes along a message path, as when we ask an operator or receptionist for a particular telephone extension; other times we are not, as from which post office station a letter carrier will pick up the mail to be delivered to a particular house.

Virtual Circuit Service

A virtual circuit is a logical network connection from a source to its destination, and is maintained for the duration of a conversation. In analogy to a telephone circuit, the virtual circuit must be established or "set up" on request, maintained during data transfer, and disconnected or released on request. Advocates of the virtual circuit approach in the network layer want reliable delivery where the results of the service are always known: the message either gets through or it is refused (if it cannot be delivered). We do not begin a telephone conversation, for example, until the circuit is established *and* the right person says hello. If the connection is broken somehow, we (usually) know how much of the message got through. Otherwise, a connection is maintained for the duration of the message, and a specific action, hanging up the telephone, is required to terminate the call. Independent messages must each follow the entire connect, transfer, disconnect sequence and there is no possible confusion about the order in which those messages were sent or received.

Datagram Service

Datagram service, on the other hand, provides only a simple delivery mechanism. There are no guarantees for the quality of service (only "best effort" to deliver can be expected), and there are no relationships provided or implied among messages from the same source to a particular destination. Every message must carry complete addressing information because there are no pathways (virtual circuits) established between source and destination pairs.

Datagram users must handle all of their own assurance that messages are received and provide their own ordering schemes. Two letters mailed on the same or on different days might be received on the same or different days, in the same or opposite order, or not at all. Duplicate messages must also be detected and discarded. Datagram service pushes most of the reliability considerations upward, to be handled explicitly by the next higher level of software.

Packet Switching

Many data communication networks are built using a technique called **packet switching,** an extension or outgrowth of statistical multiplexing (Chapter 3). In large networks, we not only want to make efficient use of the available connections, we want to avoid the extra costs of installing or maintaining seldom-used or redundant paths (Figure 5.17). Too few connections, however, could mean time wasted waiting for circuits tied up with long messages. Similarly to time slots in statistical TDM, we can subdivide message transmissions at the network level to some well-defined maximum size **packet** and share the transmission capacity among those messages waiting to be sent (Figure 5.18). At each node, every packet is examined and sent off on the next link according to its destination and the status of the links (out of service, link cost, for example). Some networks even try to adapt to the perceived traffic load by choosing links according to how busy they are. Two packets of the same message could actually travel different physical routes as network conditions change over time. All packets thus contain addressing and sequencing information as well as data so that messages can be reconstructed at the correct final destination.

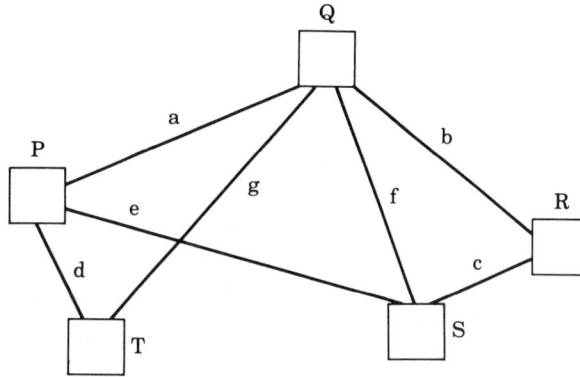

If P has very little traffic for S, link e could be
eliminated because the traffic could be routed as:

P af S, P abc S, or P dgf S.

FIGURE 5.17 Minimizing network costs

From a virtual circuit point of view, packets are analogous to the message
units of a telephone call. A phone call can be charged on the basis of how
many message units it covers, but the telephone system does not send the
units out of order or over different routes. Virtual circuit service maintains
a logical concept of the message as a whole, but allows physical transmission

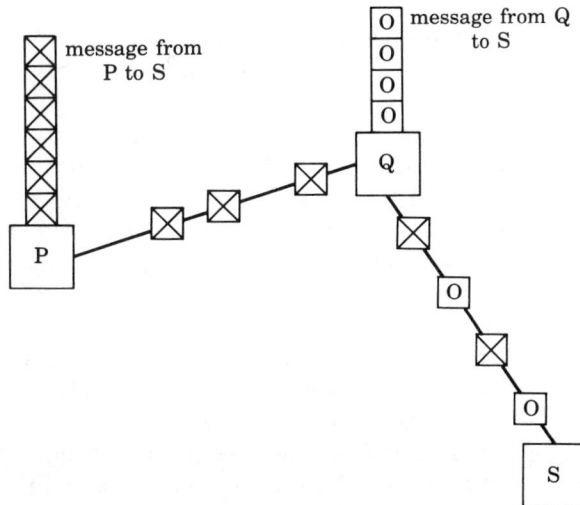

FIGURE 5.18 Packet switching to share network links

of multiple, distinct, independent packets. Once the virtual circuit is established, the network layer is totally responsible for the illusion of connection by dividing the message into packets, switching them, and controlling them to guarantee the delivery of all packets in the proper order to reconstruct the original message. Incidentally, packet networks do usually charge for message transmission service according to the number of packets sent.

A datagram service built on packet switching is similar to mailing the individual pages of a letter in separate envelopes. The network layer would accept all the envelopes and the receiver would have to collect them, put the pages back in order, and check for completeness. The pages could be sent totally independently, along different routes, at different times, however it happened to be convenient in the overall traffic picture of the network. Responsibility for numbering the pages and checking for losses or duplicates is pushed up to the next higher level.

Routing

The primary motivation behind packet switching is to make *efficient* use of the communications connections in a network. As a network management goal, this may conflict with user desires for the most cost-effective service. Consequently, **routing** decisions are usually made by choosing the "least costly" path, where the assignment of cost depends specifically on the individual network. Three steps are involved in routing decisions from a global network viewpoint: 1) determination of the path options, 2) creation of routing tables at each node to tell which is the preferred next link on the path to each destination, and 3) conversion of the tables into a form useful for dispatching each incoming packet onto an output link. In general, routing choices are provided either centrally by some type of network control center, or distributed by cooperation among the individual switching nodes.

Numerous routing techniques have been developed to satisfy the goals of different networks. They are usually characterized as *deterministic* if selecting a particular destination requires use of a specific path, as *static* or *fixed* if the routing tables do not change once established, as *stochastic* if a particular path is chosen only with some probability, or as *adaptive* if the choice depends on the observed performance characteristics in the network. SNA, for example, requires a system manager (person) to enumerate all the potential paths during network configuration prior to putting the network into operation. Thus, path options are pre-determined and fixed. Explicit routes for individual packets can be chosen from a set of available alternatives during network operation. In DNA, however, links are assigned fixed cost values and each node maintains a list of costs for the various paths to each destination. The lists can be updated dynamically during network operation by special routing messages, and paths are chosen according to the least cost available to a particular packet's destination.

Congestion Control

Another important function of the network layer is to monitor and control the data traffic to prevent overloading the network and to protect against speed mismatches, either of which could degrade the service available. This means user demands must be balanced against network capacity so that resources are allocated fairly, used efficiently, and remain available. **Flow** is determined both by the number of packets in transit and their ability to move through the network according to the buffer openings at each store-and-forward location. If capacity is exceeded or movement restricted, the traffic gets bogged down.

At the network level, the primary concern is to prevent buffer congestion in the network as a whole. Three common approaches are: (1) limiting the total number of packets circulating (first come, first served), (2) limiting the size of input buffers (restricted entry everywhere, regardless of total traffic), and (3) introducing choke packets (to shut off garrulous sources). Routing decisions also have an effect on flow, but in general they only hasten or delay potential congestion.

Standardization

Each network architecture has traditionally defined its own network layer protocol according to that vendor's view of what a network is supposed to be: SNA's path control, DNA's routing control, and so forth. The variety of approaches available for each function of the network layer has made compatibility among different products or networks difficult, if not impossible. ISO has agreed on a standard service (functional) definition for the network layer, but has not yet completed a protocol standard because implementations differ so widely and efficiency is defined so differently in actual networks.

A recommendation that is being accepted by many vendors, however, is CCITT's X.25. **X.25** defines the interface between data terminal equipment (**DTE**) that belongs to a user installation and data communication equipment (**DCE**) typical of publicly accessible data networks or subscription information networks. X.25 has three parts: a physical level recommendation, X.21 (essentially RS-232-C); a framing recommendation corresponding to the OSI data link layer called Link Access Protocol, Balanced version (LAPB); and a Packet Level Protocol (PLP), which corresponds to the OSI network layer. The Packet Level Protocol specifies how control and user data are structured into packets for network delivery, either over virtual circuits or by datagrams. The context and terminology of virtual circuits has tended to predominate; compatibility with datagram services was added after the original recommendation and could be dropped again. Communication is divided into three phases: call establishment, data transfer (including data packets, interrupt packets, and flow control), and call clearing to release a connection. Error recovery mechanisms include "reset" to re-initialize flow control, "restart" to recover from major failures, and diagnostic packets for special cases.

TRANSPORT LAYER

The transport layer is the highest of the communication-oriented levels in a network system. It is responsible for the reliable, efficient transportation of data from one end to the other, adding any functions necessary to improve the quality of service provided by the network level. The transport layer is no longer concerned with relay points or routing of the data, but concentrates on enhancing the quality of network service to support the requirements of the session layer. The transport layer is independent of communications media and technology, except for bridging the gap between network-provided services and session quality expectations (as for throughput, priority, or cost).

In our familiar telephone example, a transport connection is established when our friend Anne comes to the phone and says hello. The network layer handled the connection between our instruments; but only when we are convinced it is Anne on the other end do we transport the data of the conversation.

The complexity or sophistication of a transport layer depends largely on the level of service provided by the network layer underneath. If the network layer offers virtual circuit service, then delivery of all messages in order, without duplication, is guaranteed. There is then little work for the transport layer to do in providing the reliable, efficient connection between two end-users, and it is certainly less work than if the network provided only datagram service. In both cases, however, the transport layer must be concerned with delayed messages, with how to recover from network errors (such as "broken" network connections), with flow control, and with general network connection management (set up, keep track, release).

Just as quality of network service can be negotiated at the time a network connection is being established, the transport layer contains several classes of functions from which service and options must be chosen. The basic services provided include connection and disconnection requests and confirmations, data transmission and acknowledgement, and expedited data and acknowledgement. The five classes (or sets) of function proposed by ISO for the transport protocol are:

- 0—simple (assumes reliable, quality network service),
- 1—basic error recovery (in case the network is less reliable),
- 2—multiplexing (allows sharing of network connections by multiple sessions),
- 3—error recovery and multiplexing (extends the error handling capabilities), and
- 4—error detection and recovery (in case the network does not always find all of the errors)

Not all network nodes will support all classes of transport service, so prior agreement between source and destination is necessary to support each conversation established.

Error Handling

The basic error mechanism at the transport level is designed to provide recovery from network-signalled disconnections or resets. The sender keeps a copy of all messages transmitted, so that when a failure is indicated, the resynchronization mechanism can be invoked to retransmit appropriately. A more sophisticated approach is to provide such recovery transparently to the user of the transport service, which means transport layer data copies are kept until positive acknowledgements are received following transmission.

Error detection is available for use with networks which do not even recognize all possible error conditions. In this case, the transport layer detects lost or duplicate message blocks and maintains the proper sequence of the blocks composing a message. Timeouts, sequence numbers, and other protocol mechanisms are required for this level of service; transport layer checksums are also available through negotiation.

Flow Control

Explicit flow control is available at the transport level to minimize the potential for *end-point* buffer overflow and for network connection congestion. It is typically used when the network traffic or multiplexing load is heavy. Receivers use a credit mechanism to tell senders how much data they are willing to accept, and a "window definition" keeps track of expected sequence-numbered message blocks. Expedited data transfer is also available for special data (control signals for example) which need to be sent outside the normal data flow control. Expedited message size is limited and only one unacknowledged block can be outstanding at any time.

Sharing Connections

The multiplexing option allows several transport connections to share a single network connection. Every message block must carry a destination address so that appropriate demultiplexing can be done. ISO class 2 service provides multiplexing functions for inherently reliable networks. ISO class 3 service does the same for less reliable networks which might signal disconnect or reset failures. The particular advantage of multiplexing at this level is to minimize the (often considerable) overhead which may be associated with opening, maintaining, and closing network connections.

The opposite of multiplexing is to use more than one network connection for a single transport connection. Called splitting/recombination, it is offered to provide throughput enhancement or improved error protection for special applications.

Standardization

Agreement on transport level services and protocol has been proceeding in two different directions. The U.S. Department of Defense first selected an ARPANET approach for the transport layer, called TCP/IP (transmission control protocol and internetworking protocol). This was largely incompatible with the ISO approach, however, and subsequent consideration led to eventual adoption of the ISO standard instead.

In contrast with these differences, agreement was obtained far earlier on the transport layer as the appropriate level for provision of network interconnection services. This is usually accomplished in the form of a **gateway.** For example, CCITT Recommendation X.75 specifies how interconnection is to be made between networks that adhere to Recommendation X.25. Figure 5.19 shows that gateways may be considered as translators between a universal standard protocol and various local standard protocols. This means all traffic between networks must flow through the gateway for translation and forwarding. Other internetwork approaches have become more popular recently. There is growing interest in including internetworking functions in each node, as supported by the Department of Defense selection of IP as their internetwork protocol. Discussion continues on whether or not this should become a standard separate layer between the OSI network and transport layers.

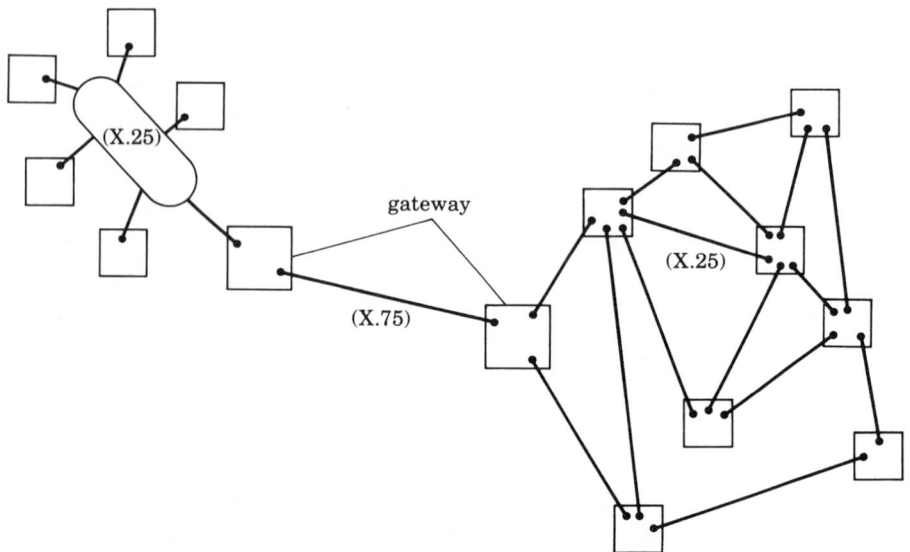

FIGURE 5.19 Gateway connecting independent networks

SESSION LAYER

The concept of a **session** encompasses the unit of interaction between an end-user and a resource in the network. We commonly think of a session as the period between logging in and logging out, terminology typical for users sitting at computer system CRT terminals. Across a sophisticated network of various computer resources, this idea generally covers the period between allocation and release of various network resources. In any case, the CRT-user's view does expose the issues that the session layer should address more generally. User identification, for example, is often handled by an account number supplemented with a password for authentication. We are just beginning to explore whether this is adequate in the larger network context.

The major responsibility of the session layer is to manage the dialogue and integrity of a session. It should be possible to guarantee that activities begun are properly completed, or, at the very least, to provide periodic checkpoints that say everything is okay so far. If a session is then interrupted or "broken", the last mutually recognized checkpoint can be used to resynchronize activities without returning all the way to the beginning of the original session activities.

Agreement is just now being reached on the services and protocols of the session layer. It is likely that some services will not be supported by all nodes, and that a negotiation process will be required at this level also.

PRESENTATION LAYER

Above the session layer, it is convenient to group together some functions that, although not necessarily essential to all, would be commonly useful to many applications. These typically include encryption for privacy, data compression for efficient transfers, virtual terminal definitions for encompassing hardware flexibility and variety, and compatible definitions of files to be transferred. Each of these services has usually been defined as a specialized protocol, independent of the others. Most have been implemented only on individual networks (ARPANET's File Transport Protocol, for example) or for particular architectures (such as DNA's Data Access Protocol).

Encryption

Encryption means disguising data so that their meaning is not readily apparent to an arbitrary receiver. More effort has been put into developing standards for encryption than for most of the other presentation layer services. Cryptography itself is a sophisticated mathematical discipline whose treatment is far beyond the scope of this book. The best-known approach to encryption is probably the Data Encryption Standard (**DES**), promulgated in the United States by the National Bureau of Standards. DES is a complex algorithm that uses a 56-bit key to encode the data. An authorized receiver reverses the algorithm and uses the same key to decode the data. As long as the key is unknown to others, the meaning of the data is kept private. Speed is achieved by implementing the algorithm in hardware. There has been some controversy over whether the 56-bit key is long enough to protect against the use of computers for breaking the ciphers, and there is a general question of how keys can be distributed without compromise.

A different approach to encryption that has been gaining recognition and popularity is called **public key** cryptography. The key distribution problem is eliminated because completely different keys are used during the encoding and decoding processes. Encode keys for each destination in a network could be put in a directory; decode keys would be kept privately. Messages would be encoded with the public keys but could only be deciphered by the destination with the correct decode key. So long as the private decode key could not be deduced from the public encode key, secure communication should be achieved.

For more discussion of encryption methods, see Chapter 11.

File Transfer

The general problem of translating files among different internal storage formats is very difficult, perhaps impossible, to solve. Early protocols had simple negotiation options, such as choice of ASCII or EBCDIC character codes, size of fixed-length records, or finding and interpreting the length field for variable records. This was often adequate to transfer simple sequential text, but seldom useful for programs, numeric data, structured records, or word processing files.

Within the restricted environment defined by SNA however, IBM has taken a much broader approach than just file transfer. An entire family of "architectures" has been developed to support creation, revision, distribution, storage, and retrieval of information in networked office systems. Included are Document Interchange Architecture (DIA), consisting of Document Distribution Services (file transfer), Document Library Services (file storage), and Application Process Services; various Document Content Architectures (DCA), providing definitions of internal file structure; and Graphic Codepoint Definitions (GCD), to deal with the limited ability of byte-oriented codes to handle the large character sets typically needed for international correspondence or for graphic displays.

Application-Specific Presentations

Presentation layer services can also be considered as a mapping between a particular application's interpretation of data and the way that data must be structured for communication. For example, graphic information is usually structured in "screens", which are rectangular arrays of "pixels", whose values represent the color and intensity of light at particular positions on the screen or image. The presentation layer establishs agreement on the order of pixel transmission, coding of pixel values, and any compression techniques used for data transmission efficiency. General agreement on such fine detail across a heterogeneous network is usually limited to the context of single applications. Parameter specification and negotiation techniques are now being developed that may eventually lead to generic standards.

APPLICATION LAYER

Protocols and standards at the application level are defined according to the particular requirements of specific applications. Even the boundary between the presentation and application layers will depend to some extent on individual points of view about what constitutes an application. To some (vendors, perhaps), a distributed database management system will be an application; to others it is a necessary tool (supporting inventory control, for example). More and more networks today are being built to satisfy numerous aspects of very large, generic applications such as banking, travel reservations, and medical information systems. The details of any one could easily fill an entire book above and beyond the underlying principles we are discussing here.

CHAPTER REVIEW

Capsule

Standardization of network protocols and interfaces is still in active negotiation today. The communication-oriented layers (physical, data link, network, and transport) seem well enough understood for point-to-point networks so that there is general agreement on the proposed standards. Multipoint network standards are still under wide discussion, as are local networks. Many of the standards groups, such as the U.S. National Bureau of Standards, ANSI, ISO, CCITT, and ECMA, are working on standardization of protocols at the higher levels of the OSI reference model. Agreement has proceeded slowly on these more application-oriented layers to ensure the diverse requirements of different applications can be adequately served.

Project

To fully appreciate the impact of protocol standards, we must expand our supermarket system to encompass a group of stores with a network interconnecting the main computer in each store. If all of the stores run the same hardware and use the same communication software, an application program can be written and installed at each site to support interaction and file transfers across the network. If different software environments occur in various locations, the process is not quite so straightforward.

1. Select a particular vendor's hardware and software system for the store computers (for example, IBM System 36, Altos 586 with Xenix). Collect the appropriate product literature to determine what support exists for a five-store network. List the protocols provided at each OSI level and describe the functions provided.
2. Select a second vendor's hardware and software system for the store computers (for example, DEC VAX 11/730 with VMS and DECnet). Discuss the requirements of matching functions between the two systems to support a network-wide pricing and inventory database.

NEW TERMS

ACK	network
body	node
BSC	packet
CCITT	packet switching
CRC	path
datagram	protocol
DCE	public key
DES	routing
DTE	RS-449
echo checking	SDLC
encryption	selective retransmission
flow	session
frame	stop-and-wait
gateway	store and forward
go-back-N	trailer
HDLC	virtual circuit
header	X.21
interface	X.25
NAK	

QUESTIONS

1. **Concentration** is often defined as a method of accepting data from more incoming links than there are outgoing links. How does this apply to statistical multiplexing? Would you say that statistical multiplexing is a concentration technique? What then is an appropriate distinction between concentration and multiplexing?
2. What advantages and disadvantages do you see to using fewer circuits and more logic to achieve physical layer standardization?
3. How do the minor differences in the frame formats and operations of bit-oriented protocols inhibit the interconnection of networks at the data link level? What makes the transport level more appropriate for network interconnection?

4. In Figure 5.15, what paths are available for traffic from node P to node S? A convenient way to name these may be to specify the link sequence between the nodes, as in "PabR".

5. Draw a diagram which represents a typical progression in packaging that maps a message into packets into frames for transmission.

6. A packet assembly/disassembly facility (PAD) has been defined to allow start-stop character mode terminals and non-X.25 nodes to exchange data with X.25 networks. Draw a diagram of where PADs might be placed in a public data network to provide connections between SNA hosts with and without X.25 interfaces.

7. What are some possible uses of expedited data at the transport level?

8. It can be said that concentration techniques provide a measure of privacy by dynamically interleaving data flows from different users. Explain.

6 Communication Environments

PUBLIC COMMUNICATION

A variety of communication service is available to individual and business subscribers in the United States. The companies offering basic services to the public are called **common carriers,** after the historical terminology of the transportation industry. Just as stagecoaches and trains "carried" passengers, the pony express and telegraph systems "carried" the mail, and various telephone systems "carry" voice and data. Much of the communication industry is also controlled by governmental agencies, as is transportation, to ensure quality service and fair rates. Detailed descriptions of the services and rates, called **tariffs,** must be approved before the services are offered to the public. Three categories of primary interest for data communication are switched, leased, and hybrid services.

Switched Services

The most familiar switched service is provided by voice telephone networks. Subscribers are directly connected to a switching facility, usually by a dedicated pair of copper wires called a **local loop.** The loop must be capable of carrying voice (or data) signals in both directions (to and from the subscriber), as well as the control signals needed to handle supervisory services such as dialing and ringing. The two major loop techniques are distinguished by the method of signaling an off-hook condition: loop-start, where off-hook completes a looped path through which current can flow; and

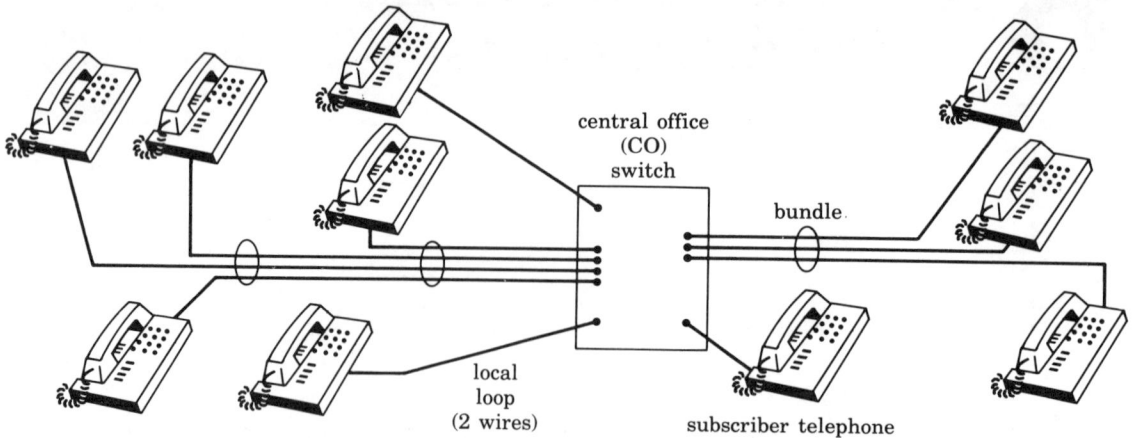

FIGURE 6.1 Local loop connections to a central office (where bundles group wire pairs from proximate locations for space and handling convenience)

ground-start where off-hook is signaled by connecting one side of the loop line to ground.

The switching center is set up to provide access to any or all of the rest of the network facilities. Individual subscribers are connected directly to a large switching complex in the **central office** (CO) of a telephone company, as in Figure 6.1. When a call is dialed, the switching center determines which two lines should be linked together to complete the connection. The selected path through the switch is then dedicated to that pair of lines for the duration of the conversation.

Business subscribers often have switching equipment on their own premises connected to the central office by a large capacity link called a shared **trunk.** Central offices are then connected by shared trunks to other central offices in their areas, as well as to a hierarchical arrangement of different types of facilities for long-distance services, as in Figure 6.2. Various new options for distribution of local service are developing along with new switching and cabling technology. These include multi-tenant office parks or buildings with their own COs and advanced fiber optic drops to individual subscribers, microwave replacement of business to CO cable trunks, and greatly expanded private network installations in place of common carrier facilities.

The data communication usage of switched subscriber networks is primarily for occasional, dial-up interconnection of devices, often at slower speeds. Low-speed services are offered by the teletypewriter exchanges: the older TELEX, and the newer TWX. Both support transmission up to 150 bits per second (bps), and are commonly used for message exchange between terminal teletypewriter devices. Telephone networks provide faster service,

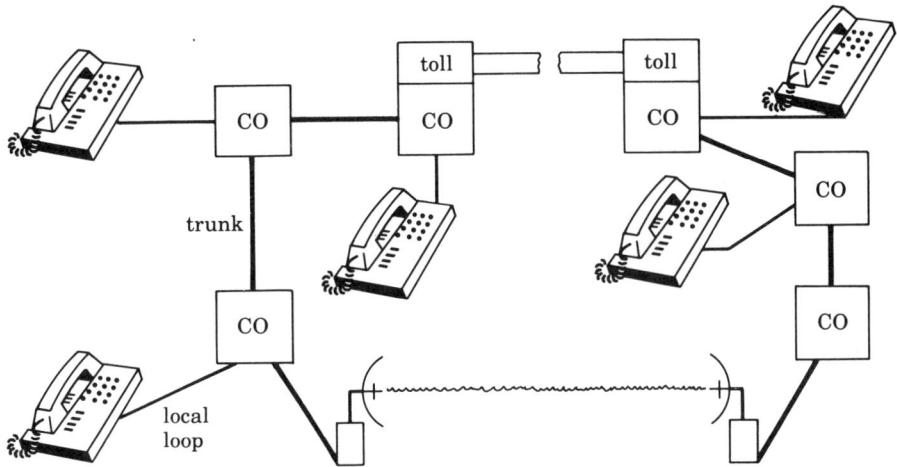

FIGURE 6.2 A telephone switching hierarchy

for example, through Direct Distance Dialing (DDD) and its less expensive version, Wide Area Telephone Service (WATS). The most common modems for access to switched facilities operate at speeds of 110 (now considered old technology), 300, and 1200 bps. Newer modem techniques and hardware offer 2400, 4800, and even 9600 bps. Use of the higher speeds is limited both by the cost of the modems and the varying quality of the phone lines and switching stations in different geographic areas.

The majority of switched service has always been provided by the various segments of the American Telephone and Telegraph Company (AT&T), which used to be known as the Bell System. Other carriers include Western Union for TELEX and TWX, the specialized (and original long-distance) carriers such as MCI and SPRINT, and a variety of new companies spawned during the deregulation of the telecommunications industry.

Several characteristics of the ordinary switched services are of special interest to data communication users. First, telephone systems were designed to handle voice traffic, which is transmitted in analog form. Computer data must be transformed from its native digital into the analog suitable for transmission, so a modem is required even for the shortest distances (see Chapter 3). Second, it can take 15 to 30 seconds or more to establish a connection when making voice telephone calls, including both access to the facilities and selection of the path to be dedicated for the duration of the call. The actual time depends on such factors as day of the week, time of day, location called, and amounts of other traffic. The automatic dialing equipment used in computer systems may have difficulty handling such variability. It must be sophisticated enough to allow both for a hierarchy of connection facilities when services from different vendors are combined (especially long-distance), and for different delays in reaching individual carrier facilities.

Once a switched connection is established, the quality of transmission can also vary from call to call, depending upon the physical equipment, interference or noise generated by the weather conditions, and the traffic conditions along the selected path. Mechanical switches make more noise than electronic ones; for example, meteorologic phenomena such as lightning can cause a great deal of static noise and cross-talk from other traffic can be very distracting. The higher the transmission speed, the more data will get damaged by such noise. Switched services offer little protection against these. High-volume users are thus restricted by the available speeds and quality of service, as well as by the costs.

Leased Services

To obtain better quality transmission for faster data communication over public facilities, it is necessary to move up to leased services. Dedicated links are provided between subscriber locations, either through direct connection or by reserving the appropriate transmission capacity through telephone company facilities. In addition, special equipment may be requested on leased lines to guarantee a particular grade or minimum quality of transmission service. This includes, for example:

- electronic instead of mechanical switching to reduce extraneous noise
- equalizers to even out or compensate for signal losses that are linear functions of transmission frequency
- echo cancelers

These links with special equipment are called **conditioned** lines.

Because leased facilities are set aside for the exclusive use of a specific customer, accessibility is assured and transmission quality is consistent. Several classes of leased service are available for use as data transmission links:

- *sub-voice grade* is for low-speed traffic up to 150 bps, and commonly handles messaging or alarm signals
- *voice-grade* covers 300-9600 bps, depending on the modem selected (higher speed usage generally requires the higher quality provided by conditioning)
- *wide-band* handles the higher speeds often desirable to interconnect computers or to use line-sharing equipment such as multiplexers

Dataphone Digital Service (DDS) from AT&T is probably the most familiar leased service. It is usually offered in specific line speed capacities: 2400, 4800 and 9600 bps links are available, primarily using special switching techniques on analog facilities. Where newer digital equipment has been installed by the carriers, more varieties of dependable service are becoming available, including a limited 56 **kbps** (kilo- or one thousand bits per second) capacity within and among certain cities.

Wide-band services are also offered at specific speeds, such as 19.2 kbps, 56 kbps, or 1.544 **Mbps**, (mega- or one million bits per second), commonly called T1, depending on the equipment owned by the carrier. Especially over long distances, various transmission techniques may be used, including microwave and satellite links. Customers determine for themselves the best uses of the total capacity being leased. As with voice services, leased data links are offered by such companies as MCI, ITT, GTE, Western Union, Satellite Business Systems, and RCA, to name a few in addition to AT&T and the Bell Operating Companies. Deregulation will theoretically result in increased competition in the telecommunications industry; interest is high in what other companies enter the data communication field.

Hybrid Services

The services we have discussed up to this point have been basically *transmission* services; the form of the signal may be changed (as between analog and digital), but the content of the data may not be modified. Another entire category of services, built as enhancements to the basic transmission capabilities, is provided by value-added networks (**VAN**s). For data transmission, the kinds of enhancements which might be most useful include code conversion (such as between ASCII and EBCDIC), protocol conversion (such as BSC or ASCII to SNA), speed matching (such as between different types of devices), cost-effective sharing of large transmission capacities (especially among low-volume users), end-to-end error control mechanisms, reliable service, and adaptability to changing customer and network demands or patterns.

Value-added services for data communication are typically offered through a network consisting of a series of packet-switching nodes located in major cities and interconnected by wide-band communication links. VAN companies may own just the nodes and lease the links from other common carriers, so that the packet-switching nodes actually add the value over the basic transmission service, or a common carrier may add packet-switching nodes to its own links to form a VAN. This combination of facilities is the reason VANs are generally considered to be a 'hybrid" service.

Most VAN subscribers access the facilities with a telephone connection to the nearest packet-switching node, and their traffic is routed and manipulated so that it reaches the destination in appropriate form. Higher volume customers may have a switching node installed on-site with their own leased link into the rest of the network. Benefits to be gained from VAN subscription include paying only for the transmission capacity actually used; avoidance of complete network design, installation, operation, and maintenance costs and headaches; access to the latest equipment and developments in communication technology; and flexibility in selection of rates and services as needs change.

REGULATION
History

The history of regulation in the communications industry is largely the history of AT&T itself. From the time it was created after Alexander Graham Bell patented the telephone in 1876, American Telephone and Telegraph grew into a multi-billion dollar company. Determining how to split such a giant corporation into smaller parts, while ensuring maintenance of the communication services so vital to industry and commerce in the United States, took the better part of ten years. It will take several more years to evaluate the results.

The first attempt to regulate telephone service occurred in 1885 within the state of Indiana, but it was not until 1910 that any federal control was imposed, when the Interstate Commerce Commission was granted power over interstate communications. By 1913, the U.S. Department of Justice had already decided that AT&T was in violation of the anti-trust laws. In response, Bell promised not to enter any new territories and agreed to interconnect all existing telephone companies to provide as nearly universal a long-distance capability as was then possible. When the Federal Communications Commission (FCC) was created in 1934 to oversee all interstate communication services, AT&T entered an age of privilege; its major restriction was a total annual corporate profit limit of 10-12 percent.

By the 1940s, AT&T consisted of Western Electric Company, the manufacturing subsidiary with exclusive rights to supply equipment to all of the Bell companies; Bell Telephone Laboratories, the research facility responsible for development and application of new technologies; Long Lines, the division providing all long-distance service; and an amalgamation of some 4700 semi-independent telephone companies. The Department of Justice made its first real attempt to break up the AT&T monopoly on provision of telephone service in 1949 by trying to split off Western Electric. The primary intent was to promote competition in the development, manufacture, and sale of telephone and switching equipment. The case was not settled until 1956, when the lawyers agreed to a consent decree allowing AT&T to keep Western Electric but forcing it to provide patents and technology to the competition through licensing agreements. AT&T was also *restricted* to the common carrier, regulated telephone communication business, so that it could not really participate in the emerging computer age.

By the 1960s, increasing difficulties over hardware competition culminated in a suit by Carterfone against AT&T. The Carterfone decision by the FCC in 1968 finally broke AT&T's stranglehold by allowing attachment to

Bell System lines of non-Bell devices that met certain technical compatibility requirements. This decision eventually led to the variety of telephone equipment and vendors available today.

But it was increasing technological changes that became the real downfall of the AT&T monopoly. Beginning in 1969 with MCI's microwave network, the FCC gave permission for several privately owned long-distance systems to become "specialized" common carriers. By 1978, court battles over anti-competitive practices had forced AT&T to allow these companies access to AT&T local loop distribution facilities at both ends of a call. In the meantime, advances in computing technology had prompted investigations by the FCC in 1966 and 1976 to distinguish between the uses of computers to support regulated communications services and the use of communications to access unregulated computer services. The regulation of data processing was certainly outside the scope of the FCC charter, but the distinction was still important because the 1956 decree prohibited AT&T from entering the computer services market.

Of course, AT&T had foreseen some of their competitive difficulties developing and had been trying to move from the old paternalistic monopoly attitudes into a posture more responsive to the service needs and requests of its customers. A proposal to provide a nationwide network allowing for terminal access to any computer finally precipitated the FCC distinctions in 1980 and 1981 between "basic" and "enhanced" services. Plain old telephone service (affectionately known as POTS) would be considered "basic," and would continue to be regulated as before. Anything more would be "enhanced," and disputes over categorization of specific offerings would be settled on a case-by-case basis. AT&T would be allowed to offer enhanced services, but only through a totally separate subsidiary.

While the FCC struggled with the long-distance and computer issues, the Department of Justice watched the MCI anti-trust suit and finally decided to tackle the competition issue more generally. Their suit was first filed in 1974. After years of haggling and tremendous expense, AT&T management decided in 1981 that breaking up the company was probably the best of the available alternatives. Negotiations between AT&T and the Department of Justice to establish the operational details began with a consent decree in 1982 under the supervision of Judge Harold Greene. The target date for divestiture was January 1, 1984; some of the procedures are still under discussion now.

Divestiture

In the early 1980s, AT&T employed over one million people, held assets worth over $300 billion, and generated revenues in excess of $50 billion annually. It was generally structured as in Figure 6.3, with all local distribution of subscriber services handled by the 24 Bell operating companies (**BOCs**): 20 of these BOCs were wholly owned and two more were primarily

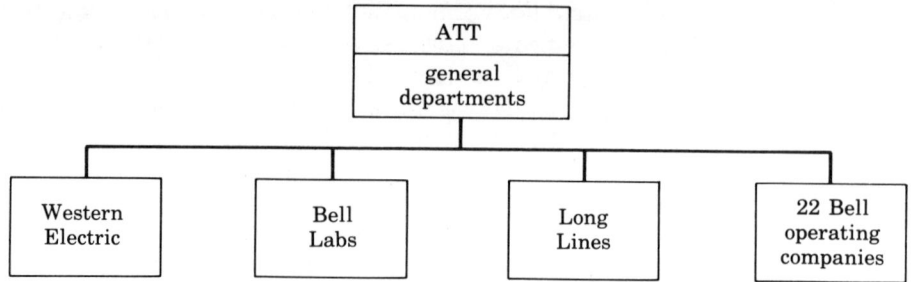

FIGURE 6.3 Structure of AT&T prior to divestiture

held by AT&T. Only two (Southern New England Telephone of Connecticut and Cincinnati Bell of Ohio) were independently owned and consequently unaffected by the divestiture decision.

The restructuring of AT&T began with release of its 22 operating companies, which were subsequently reorganized into seven regional holding companies as shown in Figure 6.4. The operating companies even won the Bell

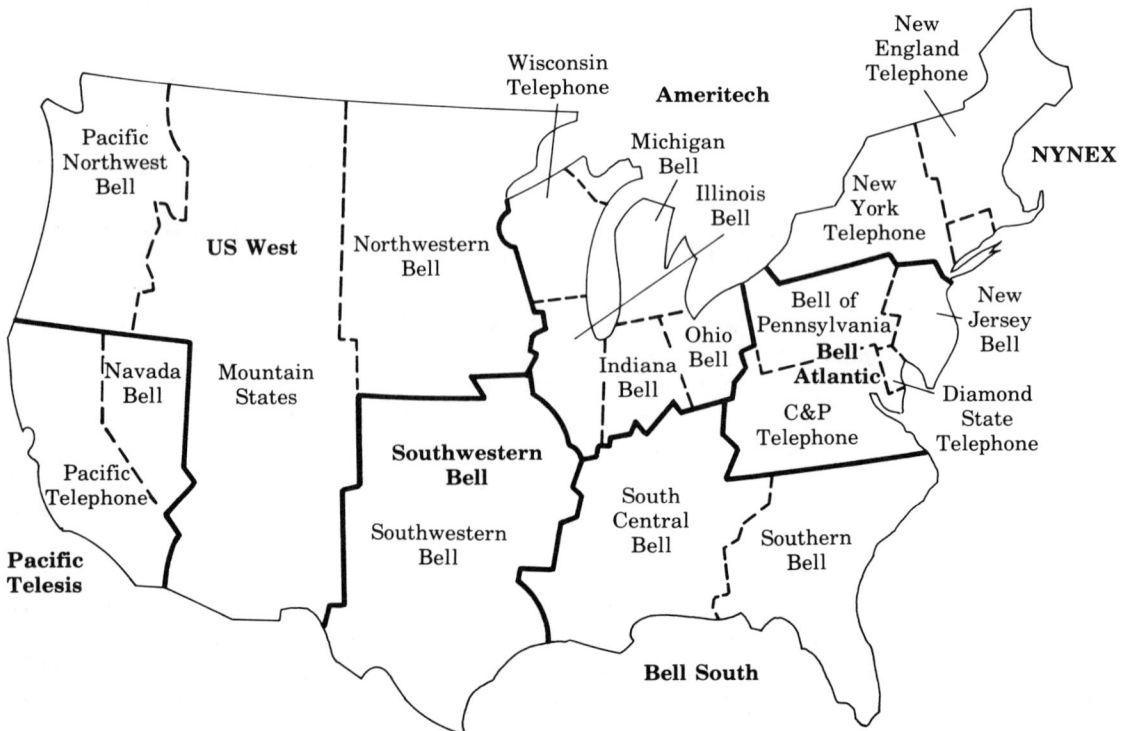

FIGURE 6.4 The regional holding companies

name and logo away from AT&T, except for its use by Bell Laboratories. Beneath Corporate Administration, AT&T is now composed of three major segments: AT&T Communications, AT&T Technologies, and American Transtech (which provides all shareowner services). AT&T Communications includes the former Long Lines and is responsible for all international and long-distance facilities and networks.

AT&T Technologies is an unregulated business which incorporates the former Western Electric manufacturing company and includes (Figure 6.5):

■ AT&T Bell Laboratories, whose responsibilities are to design today's systems and services and to develop the technology base needed to keep AT&T in the forefront of information systems products and services
■ AT&T Network Systems, charged with development, installation, and maintenance of network telecommunication equipment
■ AT&T Technology Systems, whose focus is on Components and Electronics Systems, Computer Systems, and Federal Systems
■ AT&T Consumer Products, for design, manufacture, and wholesale of home communication products
■ AT&T International, responsible for consolidating all overseas operations, products, and services
■ AT&T Information Systems, providing the separate subsidiary that allows AT&T to enter information processing markets on a deregulated basis.

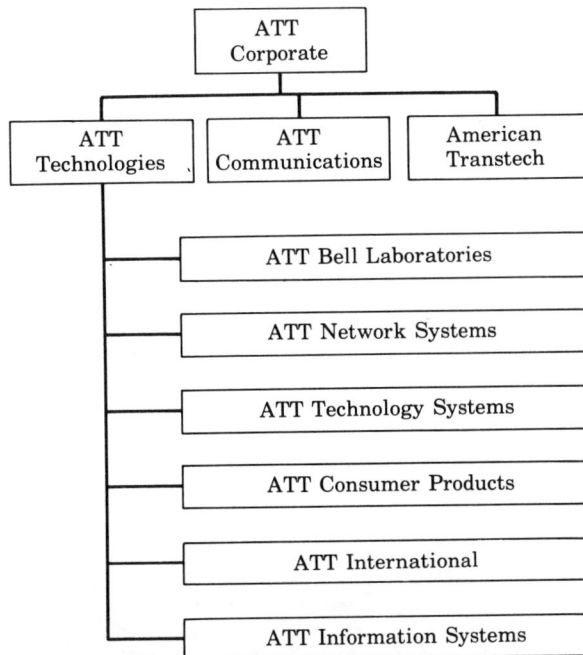

FIGURE 6.5 Reorganization of AT&T as of 1986

Division of the former Bell System assets and revenues was even more difficult than dealing with the structure. The FCC had always allowed AT&T to sidestep division of its revenues and use cross-subsidization to support the tremendous expenses of providing local service. Thus, charges for long-distance service were allowed to be higher than necessary to subsidize lower than necessary charges for local service (so that net company profit remained within the 10-12 percent limit). This enabled the first specialized common carriers to offer long-distance rates much lower than those of AT&T. With divestiture, all of the disadvantages of local service provision were inherited by the BOCs: the labor-intensive operations; the control by often fickle state Public Utility Commissions (PUC); the enormous installed base of difficult-to-maintain, technologically obsolete equipment; and the constant demand for universal service through new (expensive) installations.

To compensate for the disadvantages, the regional holding companies were allowed to keep their monopolies on local telephone service (although AT&T and MCI may challenge this), the revenues from Yellow Pages advertising, and much of the modern AT&T switching equipment. They were also released from the requirement to buy all equipment from Western Electric. In the meantime, they had to divide their regions into local-access transport areas (**LATA**s), within which they could provide short-distance service, but between which they had to allow all long-distance carriers equal opportunity to provide the service (Figure 6.6). AT&T thus lost its near-monopoly

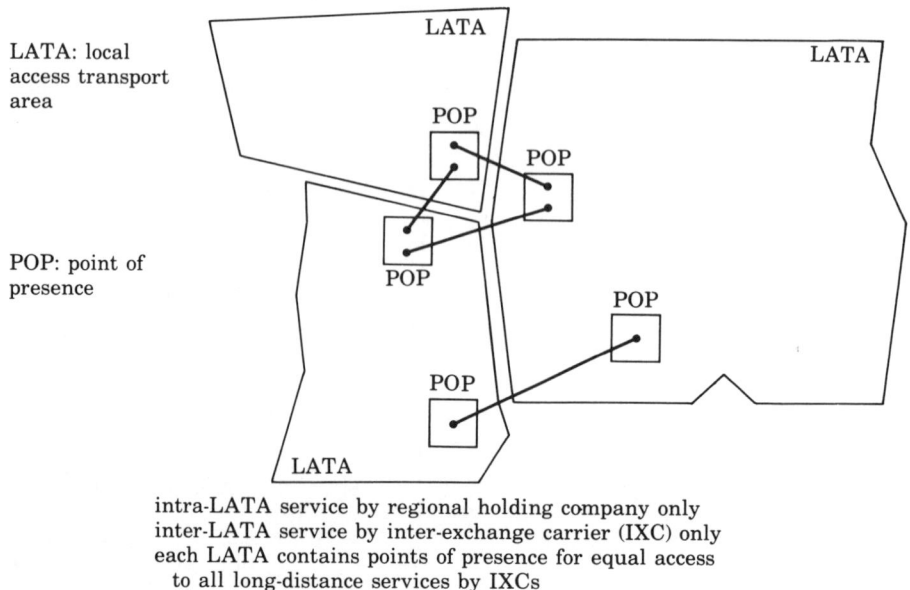

LATA: local
access transport
area

POP: point of
presence

intra-LATA service by regional holding company only
inter-LATA service by inter-exchange carrier (IXC) only
each LATA contains points of presence for equal access
    to all long-distance services by IXCs

FIGURE 6.6 Post-divestiture telephone service

on long-distance service, but could reduce its rates to compete more effectively.

Implications

The details of what divestiture means to data communication users will continue to be sorted out through the next few years. Major concerns include (at least) compatibilities in equipment from a variety of communication vendors, end-to-end quality of services, and ultimately, the costs.

Perhaps the larger impact, however, is the loss to users of the ability to handle all communication needs through a single source or vendor. Large companies in particular have found that they need considerably more staff expertise to coordinate their selection and use of services from an ever-larger community of vendors. At the same time, AT&T has been somewhat slow to reorganize its activities and change its marketing approach to deal effectively with the new competition, and consequently has not always provided the levels of support customers had come to expect.

THE COMMUNICATIONS INDUSTRY

In addition to the common carriers and the network companies providing value-added services, the communications industry consists of segments parallel to the various components of an information system. Types of vendors include the original equipment manufacturers and product creators, companies that add specific communication system value to the products of others, and service organizations whose products are the knowledge and skills of their people.

Hardware

The largest industry segment is made up of the companies that sell hardware components. These products range from the simplicity of cable and serial interface cards to the sophistication of large time-sharing host computers. Modems still represent the largest volume of independent devices sold, closely followed now by the sharing hardware such as multiplexers and switching devices. As more and more microprocessor intelligence is added to these, the distinction among them, cluster controllers, and front-end processors is beginning to blur. Where user programmability is important, a similar loss of distinction between front-end and general-purpose processing is beginning to make it difficult to label some activities as communication processing or data processing.

Terminals and computers are not always considered to be data communication hardware, and are mentioned here for completeness. There are certainly characteristics of each that are important to appropriate selections within a communications-based information system (see Chapter 3). Portable terminals and notebook or lap-top personal computers will continue to be of special interest to users with remote access computing requirements.

Software

Most communication software sold independently of hardware is developed for computers at the ends of communication links. This includes teleprocessing monitors for large hosts, terminal emulation programs for personal computers, and some more generally capable software systems such as those used to interconnect assortments of microcomputers, either to a host or together. Much of the communication software is sold by computer vendors who have developed network architectures largely to interconnect their own brands and models of equipment. To date, there is little or limited compatibility among software products from various vendors.

We include the growing number of firmware implementations of communication functions in the software segment of the industry because they are components that implement specific algorithms rather than being independent devices. Data link protocols, multi-access contention management, and encryption functions are all becoming more commonly available on chips or as chip sets. Hardware designers can select, or software designers can specify dependence on, these particular chips, as appropriate to individual products and applications.

Procedures and Personnel

As in most information systems, the procedures and personnel segments of the communication industry are often difficult to discuss separately. Network management and control, for example, are usually offered by vendors in packages of software and hardware combined. Most buyers want a total approach to monitoring and reporting the network status, along with the ability to make whatever adaptations or modifications of configuration and flow seem appropriate for the traffic loads. Another desirable type of product handles the daily operation and maintenance of a network.

A particularly fast-growing segment of the communications industry recently has been consulting. Activities range from troubleshooting particular traffic problems, to design of communication subnets, to complete information system integration. Immediately following divestiture, demand for data communication specialists or managers of network services far exceeded the available expertise. Consequently, most communication system installations, other than the very largest, have had to depend on consultants at some point. Understanding of the fundamental principles discussed in this text and an appreciation for the complexity of the design issues will continue to assist many managers in selection of assistants and in evaluation of their recommendations.

Data

A value-added network service that can be considered an industry segment of its own is provision for public subscriber access to large, on-line databases, such as those of the New York Times or Dow Jones, or to timeshared hardware and software facilities. For this reason, many value-added networks are becoming more widely known as public data networks (**PDN**s), or information utilities. Data services are usually provided by linking a database or timesharing company host with the facilities of the VAN. Subscribers connect to a particular service by requesting the appropriate destination through the VAN. Charges for the service are usually based on the length of time connected to the data service, the actual database activities or software package requested, the total amount of traffic generated through the network, and whatever translation facilities are requested from the VAN. VAN access is certainly a lower cost alternative to dialing the data service directly and paying telephone system charges for the entire call, but its primary value is in masking any inherent equipment incompatibilities. Standardization of network protocols, such as the CCITT X.25 recommendation, are increasing the viability of large public data networks.

BROADCAST NETWORKS

Up to this point, we have been considering wide area networks that are interconnected by point-to-point links. Taking a multipoint approach, we soon discover that different functions are necessary at the OSI network level. Ideally, broadcast media create a multipoint situation in which:

1. all devices or stations in the network can hear all of the transmissions, regardless of origin
2. simultaneous or overlapping transmissions, called **collisions,** destroy the information content of all the involved signals
3. collisions can be detected so that damaged signals are reliably discarded

Thus, instead of being concerned with path selection and packet routing, broadcast nets must manage mechanisms for sharing access to a common linking medium.

Time-Division Multiple Access

Loss of data through signal collisions can be prevented by use of a sharing discipline. For example, the transmission time can be divided into slots assigned in rotation to different stations in the network. This approach, called time-division multiple access (TDMA) is used for multipoint links rather than the multiplexing discussed for point-to-point links in Chapter 3. TDMA requires accurate clocks to keep the slot times synchronized among all stations, and suffers from the same inefficient use of channel capacity as TDM. Polling schemes are also possible, but are not very efficient for the bursty data traffic typical of networks with many terminal devices.

Aloha

A contention approach was first used instead of TDMA or polling for a broadcast packet network at the University of Hawaii. Radio links connected terminals among the islands to a central computer located on Oahu.

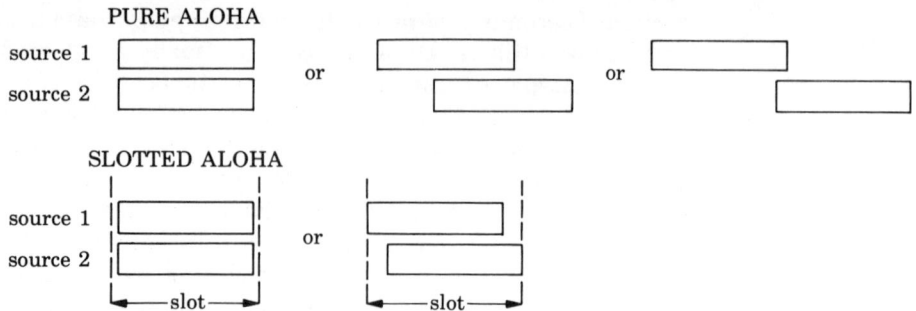

FIGURE 6.7 Packet overlaps causing collisions

To simplify the radio equipment, a single pair of broadcast channels was chosen for all stations, but the geography prohibited some from hearing the transmissions of others. The simplest possible approach to sharing was adopted: terminal stations were allowed to transmit on one channel whenever they had traffic to send to the computer. If a collision was detected at the computer, no acknowledgements would be returned and the terminal stations would eventually retransmit. Different delays for different stations experiencing a collision were built in to reduce the chances of colliding again. This scheme is known as "pure" **Aloha,** and was the first in a series of progressively sophisticated contention schemes. Traffic from the central computer back to the terminal stations needed no special management technique, because the computer was the only transmitter on that channel.

The performance of the Aloha approach was of particular interest to potential users at the University of Hawaii. Mathematical analysis of the probabilities for successful transmission indicated that the maximum channel utilization to be expected was only 18 percent. Beyond that, increased traffic would simply result in more collisions. It was not clear that this would be adequate for busy periods when many of the terminals would be in use simultaneously.

A simple suggestion for improving the performance of Aloha is to combine the contention and TDMA approaches. The idea is to eliminate the collisions due to small amounts of overlap between packets (Figure 6.7). Transmission time is divided into slots, and stations are restricted to begin transmission only at the beginning of a slot. This scheme is known as "slotted" Aloha, and statistical analysis predicts that slotting should double the maximum throughput of pure Aloha. For many systems with predominantly bursty data terminal traffic, this performance level should be adequate.

Satellites

Another broadcast environment having some special considerations is the use of communication satellites to relay microwave signals. Aside from some

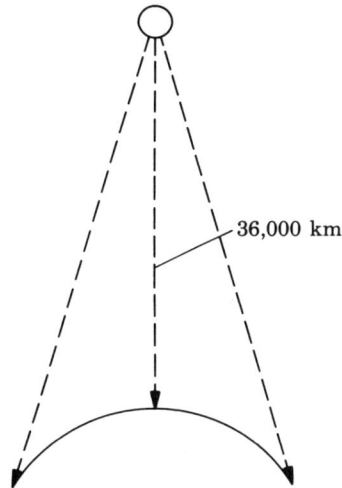

FIGURE 6.8 Geosynchronous communication satellite links

technical concerns over satellite position correction and signal losses due to natural phenomena such as solar transits, the most important characteristic of satellite links is the length of time it takes for a signal to travel from sender to receiver. Communication satellites are usually placed at a height of some 36,000 kilometers to maintain geosynchronous orbits accurately over long periods of time. The minimum transmission delay is thus about 240 to 270 milliseconds, depending on whether the receiver is directly under the satellite or toward the outside edge of the receiving cone (Figure 6.8). At microwave speeds, a number of packets will be transmitted before any is received.

Selection of an appropriate sharing scheme is a primary concern for satellite links. In situations with relatively constant levels of traffic, TDMA can be used effectively. Otherwise, for bursty traffic, the low bandwidth efficiency of Aloha is a deterrent, although transmitters could be required to listen to the results of their own transmissions to detect collisions. Correct reception by the sender ensures no collision could have occurred, but different reception conditions at different receiver locations still require use of some type of error detection and correction scheme. Retransmission is usually considered inappropriate for satellite links because of the large buffers that would be necessary to cover the transmission delay time.

Again, a combination of TDMA and Aloha can be defined to create a better solution. A limited Aloha channel can be set aside strictly for making reservations for slots on the main bandwidth TDMA channel (Figure 6.9). Once a reservation succeeds in getting through without a collision, data packets are guaranteed appropriate transmission capacity. Of course, this

...	d	r	d	d	d	d	r	d	d	d	d	r	d	d

d: data slots (assigned)   time ———▶

r: reservation slots (Aloha)

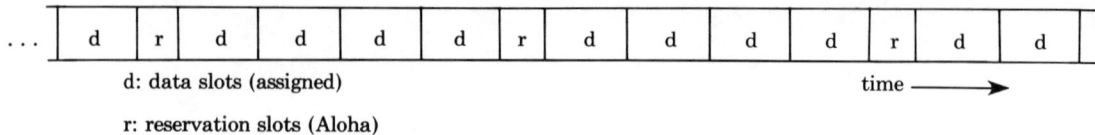

FIGURE 6.9 Combined TDMA and Aloha for satellite channel reservation

requires even more sophistication of the stations in the network as well as of the satellite, or an extra delay for a ground station to handle the reservations.

CHAPTER REVIEW

Capsule

An increasingly vast array of data communication products and services is available to the public and to businesses today, from special uses of voice telephone networks to privately leased satellite links. Public offerings of basic interstate data transport are regulated by the Federal Communications Commission and enhanced services must be presented by subsidiaries separate from the regulated companies. Divestiture of the Bell operating companies from AT&T has been a significant stimulus to competition in both arenas.

Broadcast media provide a different environment for networking from the point-to-point connections of most public networks. A contention approach to multiple access link sharing was developed at the University of Hawaii for its packet radio network. The Aloha technique performs well only at very low channel utilizations. Variations of Aloha have been adopted to deal with the long delay times typical for satellite communication links.

NEW TERMS

Aloha   local loop
BOC   Mbps
central office   PDN
collision   tariff
common carrier   TDMA
conditioned line   trunk
kbps   VAN
LATA

QUESTIONS

1. One concern with pure Aloha is that acknowledgement packets are just as likely to suffer collisions as any other packets. What are some possible alternatives to use of positive acknowledgements?
2. What companies offer long-distance telephone service in your area? How do the rates compare for voice calls? How do you specify which carrier is to handle your particular calls?
3. Random delay times are used by some contention systems to minimize the probability of repeat collisions. What could be done to create a priority scheme instead?
4. What is the current status of the MCI antitrust suit against AT&T?
5. "Access charges" were designed during divestiture to force long-distance callers to help pay the high costs of local service. Large businesses threatened to "bypass" local operating companies completely by connecting directly to the long-distance carriers. Has this threat been realized? What is the current state of bypass technology? What are the governing regulations?
6. Does your area have "life-line" service? If so, how does it work?
7. Find out the current corporate structure for the various components of AT&T. What changes have the FCC's Computer Inquiry III allowed in the original divestiture rules?

7

Local Area Networks

AN ENVIRONMENT

If we narrow our view from the rather broad geographical scope considered in the previous chapter, we find a particular environment that is attracting more and more attention: the *local area*. Local area networks (**LAN**s) are often defined as being of limited geographical extent, typically less than ten miles, and owned by a single organization for its private use. Examples range from connection of several devices within the same room to interconnection through a group of buildings on a campus or in a complex. The importance of the network may be simply to provide data communication among computer devices, or to function as the backbone of a sophisticated information utility, providing access to the many resources required to carry out the activities of the owning organization. As long as a LAN is strictly for private use, it is not subject to regulation by the FCC or PUCs, except that microwave transmission in open air must be licensed as any other radio station.

MEDIA

Twisted-pair Wiring

One of the most popular media for LAN transmission links is twisted-pair copper wire. Much of its attraction is an outgrowth of its use with telephone wiring and two-pair connection of RS-232 terminal devices. Transmit, receive, and ground circuits are required; sometimes dataset-ready (DSR) or data-terminal-ready (DTR) is added to provide more functions. A simple serial connection technique, it can easily span distances of a few hundred feet for direct digital transmission. As with direct connection of terminals, a line driver (modem eliminator) is used instead of the modem pair typical of long-distance connections.

The main advantage of twisted pairs is that many buildings are wired when built with capacity far in excess of the telephone requirements (see Figure 7.1). In such a case, the extra wires may be adapted to data communication use. On the other hand, maintenance of a twisted-pair network interconnecting many devices can be difficult. Keeping track of which wires are used for the different types of interconnections requires meticulous labeling and recording so that faults can be traced or equipment moved when necessary. A large amount of space can be consumed by the pairs, especially as more are added. Within a building, this means that cable trays or raceways tend to fill up, increasing the difficulty of pulling new pairs or tracing old ones. Attention to local and national electrical and building codes is absolutely required. For example, cables are often run in the plenum between the real and hung ceilings of a hallway or room. If this space is also

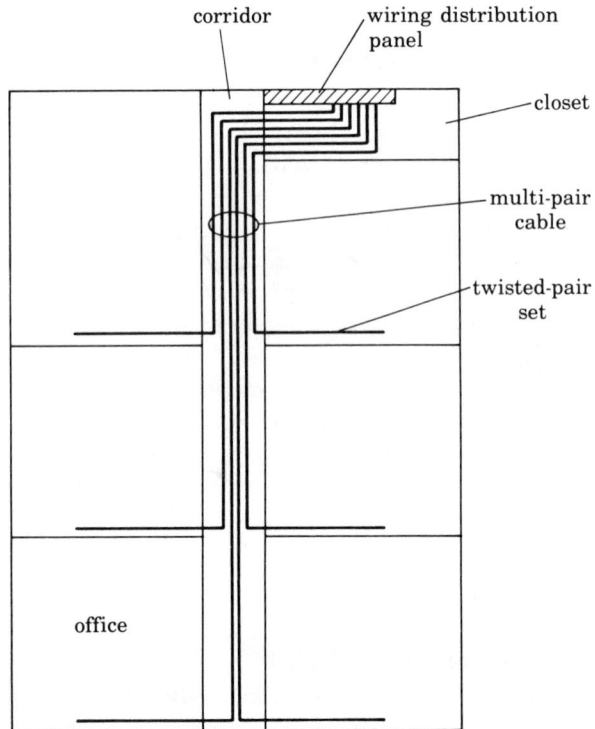

FIGURE 7.1 Sample floor-plan distribution scheme for twisted-pair wiring: one set of pairs per office

used as a return for the air conditioning system, special cable sheathing must be used to satisfy typical fire codes. It is not usually very expensive to do this right the first time, but after installation, corrections can be very costly.

If the network spans multiple buildings, the wire must be properly protected across outdoor runs. This is often handled by running through underground conduit systems that have typically been installed for electrical wiring or to protect steam pipes. Here again, space can be a problem as the conduits fill up. Long outdoor runs of copper wire have a worse disadvantage in areas where thunderstorms are common: they may conduct large surges of current induced from nearby lightning strikes. These surges often do extensive damage to the connected equipment. Even if only the line driver is destroyed, repairs and down-time can quickly escalate costs.

A more recent approach to twisted-pair LANs is to share the use of telephone wiring for both voice and data transmission. This can be accomplished in analog systems with frequency division multiplexing, using one channel for the voice traffic and another for the data. As digital transmission of voice becomes more common, time division multiplexing provides a simpler sharing technique. The data rates supported depend on interleaving with enough voice samples so that the quality of the reconstructed voice signal is maintained.

Coaxial Cable

The second popular LAN transmission medium is coaxial cable. It has a number of advantages over twisted-pair wiring. The most significant are its greater carrying capacity per volume and a wider bandwidth of frequencies for transmission. It is also less susceptible to noise; it is easier to shield, and cross-talk is not the problem that it is with pairs. The difference in typical wiring plans for twisted-pair and coaxial cable can be seen by comparing Figure 7.2 with Figure 7.1.

Maintenance of cable systems tends to be simpler because there is much less cable to keep track of. Design planning is considerably more important than with twisted pairs, to ensure that taps are installed wherever needed or where growth is likely so that additional equipment may be connected without disturbance to the operating network. In such cases, moving equipment from one place to another means simply detaching it, capping the tap, and attaching to the tap in the new location. For an entire campus (group of buildings) having many devices and a high likelihood of equipment moves, cable networks can cost significantly less for new installations and for continuing maintenance. Different types and sizes of cable are also available for various environmental conditions (such as underground or aerial) and installation requirements (such as through conduits or in overhead raceways).

Other

Fiber optic and microwave links will become more important as the technologies are more widely applied and understood. The successful installations

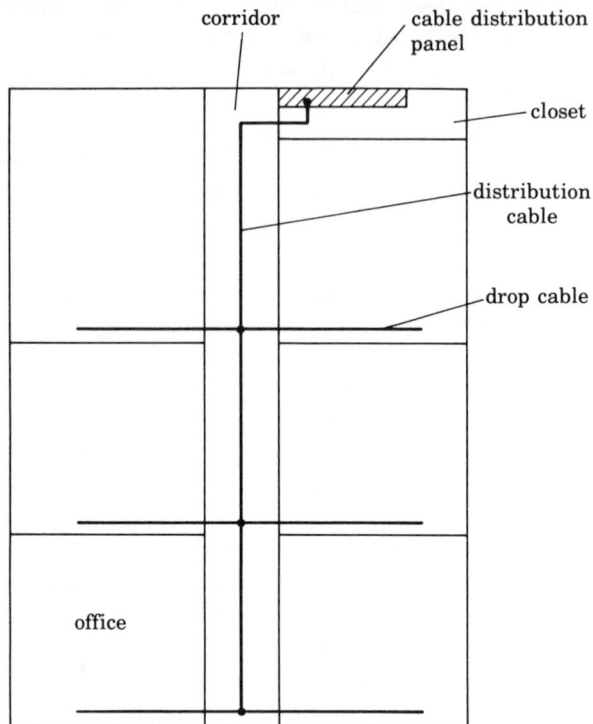

FIGURE 7.2 Sample floor-plan distribution scheme for coaxial cable

in use by various telephone companies will eventually lead to less expensive equipment appropriate for use in local area networks. Current costs and scarce expertise have limited most applications to point-to-point links with special environmental or very high-volume traffic requirements.

Fiber optic cables are particularly useful in situations with special environmental requirements. The carrying capacity for the cable size and weight is far greater than that of coaxial cables. Fiber should be considered for areas with restricted space, such as full conduits, or where weight is a problem. Electrical current surges cannot be induced by lightning in fiber optics and the cables are immune to other types of electromagnetic interference, such as from nearby machinery or power distribution lines. They do not emit radiation that could be detected by an unauthorized listener. Similarly, the fiber optic cables cannot be tapped without immediately being detected.

One disadvantage of fiber optics is the extra care required in handling the cable. It is somewhat fragile, and cannot be pulled as vigorously or bent as easily as most coaxial cable. Splices must be carefully made to minimize transmission losses. Another disadvantage is the size and expense of equipment needed to interface devices at the ends of each fiber. Tapping the cable so that signals can be inserted and removed is also a major problem. Taps are responsible for more signal loss than any other component.

Microwave transmission links are primarily used to connect non-contiguous locations belonging to the same organization. Since this amounts to radio transmission in open air, microwave stations must be licensed by the FCC. Even when channel boundaries are carefully maintained and directional antennae are used, microwave is susceptible to compromise or jamming by unauthorized listeners. Weather conditions or intervening objects such as birds sometimes introduce unpredictable levels of noise, and there is some lingering controversy about the long-term biological effects of the radiation on human neighbors. Nevertheless, microwave transmission is becoming more popular for high-speed, line-of-sight connections where the cost can be justified by the traffic requirements.

TOPOLOGY

Closely related to the issue of selecting an appropriate medium for a LAN is the **topology,** the configuration or shape formed by the interconnecting links.

Star

Most telephone systems are shaped like a **star,** with every device individually connected to a central switch (Figure 7.3a). Each device can communicate with *any* other single device by making a connection through the center, as in Figure 7.3b. This is called **total connectivity.** Communication among multiple devices requires more sophistication at the center. Figure 7.3c shows that a multi-drop connection must be created or simulated and an appropriate sharing discipline enforced. Roll-call polling could be used by the central device to collect a message for transmission, for example, and then selective forwarding to that node's successor could be used to simulate hub-go-ahead polling.

The foremost disadvantage to a star topology is that a failure of the central device disables the entire network; it is a **critical resource.** Only functions that can be handled independently by the individual devices can continue. No other device is critical in terms of the network's ability to operate, although failures of one-of-a-kind devices often inconvenience the users. Protection from failure of a critical resource is usually provided by redundancy built into the device or by installation of duplicate devices. Redundancy increases the device complexity, and often drives the cost up. The number of interconnections for which a central device is responsible makes duplication expensive as well, but at least some fault tolerance is provided (Figure 7.4). Other topologies might be more suitable for applications needing very high reliability.

A second important disadvantage of the star is that the central location can be a bottleneck under high traffic conditions. If many devices are connected, the central switching capacity must be large to keep some connec-

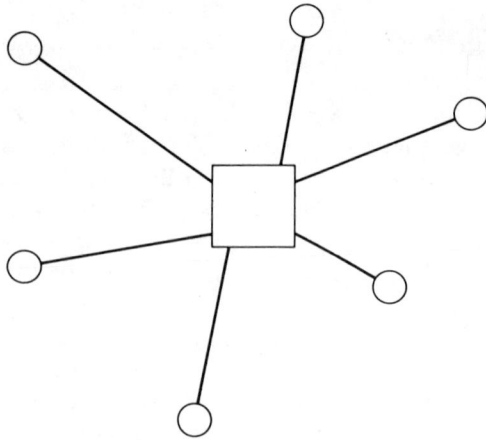

FIGURE 7.3a Example of a star

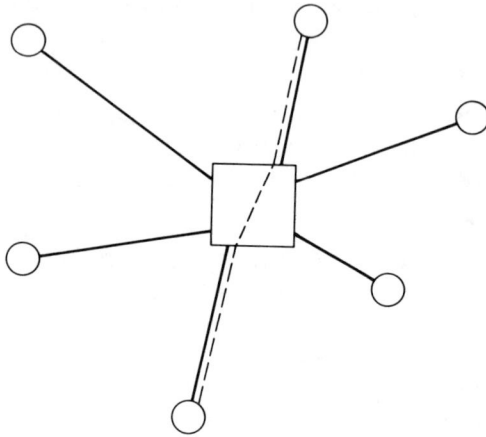

FIGURE 7.3b A star network showing a path for traffic between one pair of devices

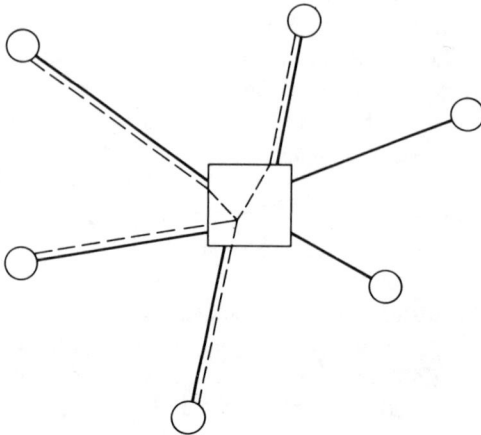

FIGURE 7.3c A star network showing a multi-point path for several devices. This type of traffic requires use of a sharing discipline.

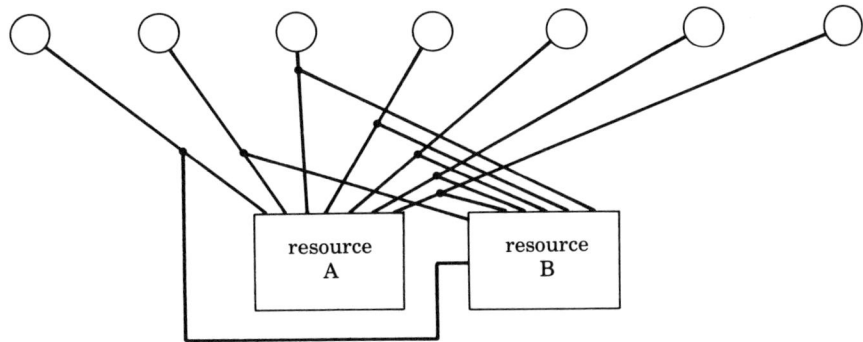

FIGURE 7.4 Device duplication prevents network down-time if a critical resource fails

tions from being blocked when all switch paths are busy. These paths are expensive if they are used only occasionally. If there are fewer paths than possible device pairings, the central device should give users a choice between calling back later or having the call placed in a queue to await service.

Bus and Tree

A **bus** interconnects multiple devices to a single shared link (Figure 7.5). It is particularly popular as an internal connection technique for the various components of computers. Unlike the point-to-point connections typically offered by a star, the bus is inherently a multipoint configuration and requires a sharing discipline. Processor buses typically use a priority scheme to resolve contention over bus access.

For local networks, the layout of individual buildings or groups of buildings may make it undesirable to have only a single piece of cable run through every possible device location. The bus structure can be generalized to a **tree** by connecting multiple buses together on a bus, as though they were branches on a tree (Figure 7.6). This preserves the broadcast nature of

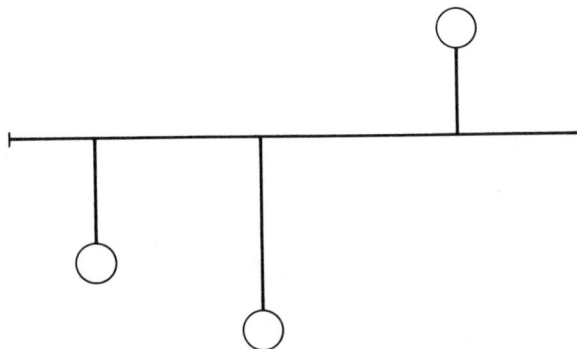

FIGURE 7.5 Example of a bus

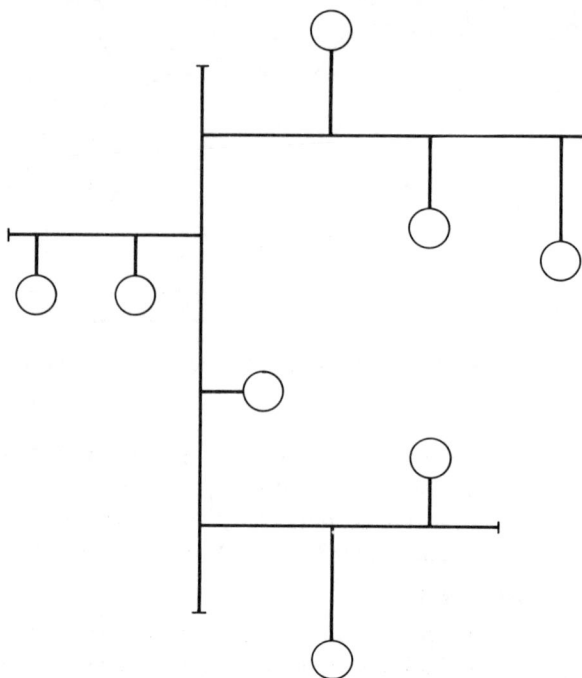

FIGURE 7.6 Example of a tree

the network. Devices are most often connected to buses and trees passively; that is, transmissions propagate throughout the entire network without the help of any device after the sender, as in Figure 7.7. For very long buses, repeaters may be required to amplify the signals enough to cover the distances, but these are considered part of the links rather than the attached devices. The devices simply listen to all transmissions for those signals that are addressed to them; they do not have to actively forward anything. At each end of the bus or the tree branches and trunk, the signals are absorbed to prevent reflection and ensure that they traverse the entire network structure only once.

Unlike the star, where a single central device is the critical resource for the network, the bus itself is critical, even though it is a passive device in this type of LAN. If any attached device fails in an actively transmitting mode, the entire bus or tree is jammed. Breaks in a bus or tree branch may not be as disastrous, because only devices beyond the break are lost. In some cases, the segments on each side of a break can continue to operate independently so long as no data or responses are required from inaccessible devices.

Ring

If the two ends of a single bus are connected together, we have another topology called a **ring**. Because a ring has no ends at which to absorb

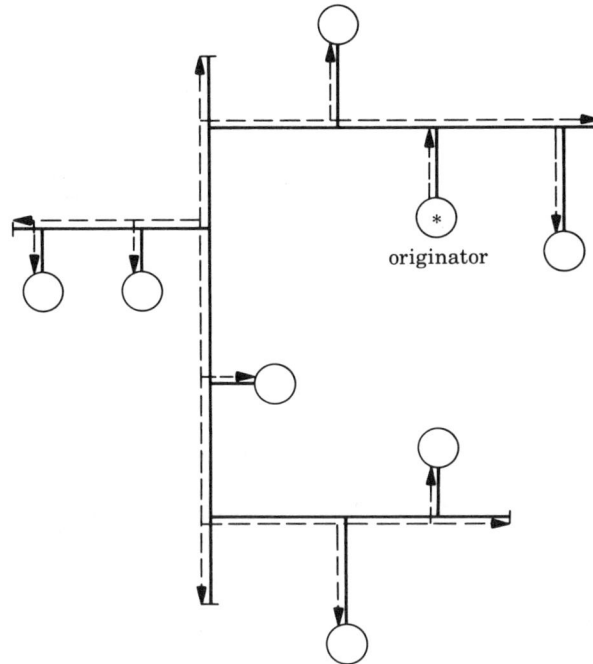

FIGURE 7.7 Signal propagation paths in a tree network

signals, transmission must be limited to a single direction, and the attached devices are required to forward those signals that are supposed to continue. This is more function than is typical of computer communication interfaces, so attachment and forwarding functions are usually isolated in a special ring interface (Figure 7.8).

Depending on the sharing discipline used by the ring, signals can be removed at the destination to simulate point-to-point connections, or the signals can be allowed to make a complete circuit for broadcast connections. If senders take responsibility for removing their messages, they could check returning signals against originals for transmission accuracy, or look for acknowledgement indicators appended to the messages.

Figure 7.8 clearly shows that the ring interfaces and the links between them are both critical to the operability of a ring network. Device failures are well isolated from damaging the network by the ring interfaces. The interfaces themselves, however, must be prevented from failing to pass on a circulating message as well as from failing in an actively transmitting mode. Redundant links are sometimes provided to minimize the chances of network loss from either link or interface failures by allowing reconfiguration as in Figure 7.9.

In most networks, the links are much more reliable than the network interfaces. Consequently, another approach to improving the reliability of

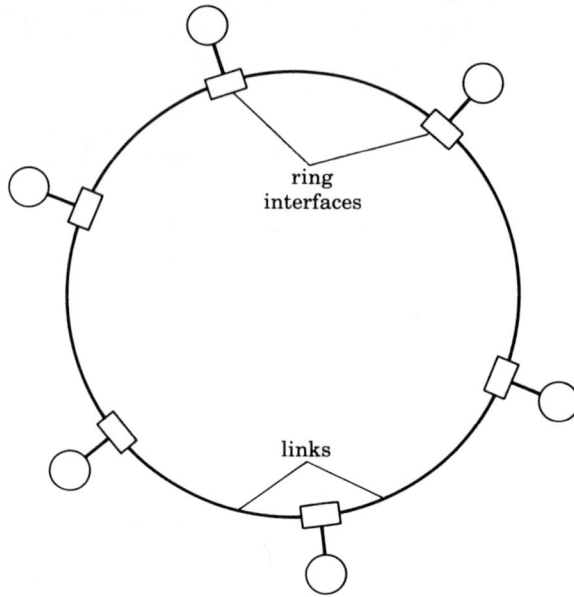

FIGURE 7.8 Example of a ring

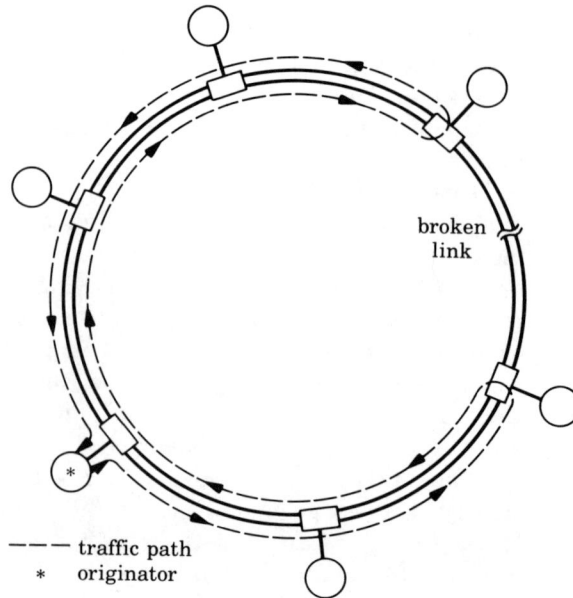

FIGURE 7.9 Alternative circulation in a ring using redundant links

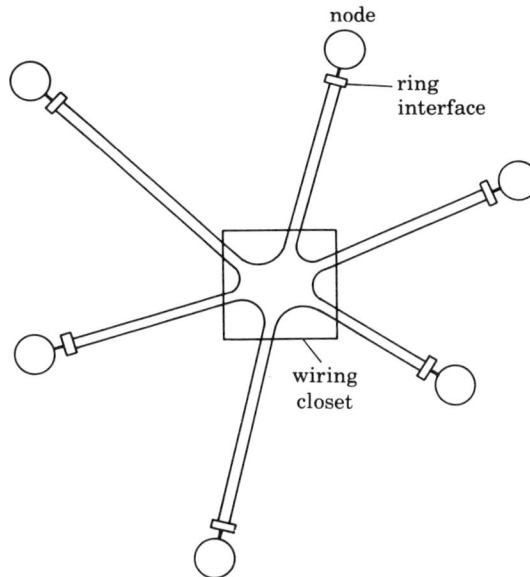

FIGURE 7.10 A star-shaped ring

rings is to localize all interfaces within a central wiring closet, as in Figure 7.10. This reduces the opportunity for interfaces to be damaged or abused out in various network locations and provides central control and maintenance. Several ring network vendors and proponents have taken such a star-shaped ring approach, including Proteon and IBM.

TRANSMISSION TECHNIQUES

Baseband

Two approaches to signal transmission are widely used in local area networks. The first, called **baseband,** uses the entire available bandwidth to form one data channel. The digital signals are serialized and transmitted directly on the link without being modulated onto any carrier frequency. Specific voltage levels are usually chosen to represent one and zero bits, and signaling can be thought of as pulsing the right sequence of voltage levels down the line. Because there is no carrier modulation required, very simple line driver chips can transmit baseband signals on point-to-point links. This approach limits the distance that can be covered without using repeaters to keep the signal level recognizable over the noise.

Baseband transmission can also be used for multi-point networks. Line drivers must be replaced by slightly more sophisticated **transceivers** to ensure proper signal levels can be maintained across the multiple drops of the sharing devices. The Ethernet specification originated by Xerox is a complete physical and electrical characterization of a baseband network using coaxial cable. Distance limitations were imposed to keep signal levels and propagation times within the bounds considered acceptable in support of the chosen sharing discipline.

The advantages of baseband networks are:

1. the drivers and transceivers are relatively simple devices
2. any topology can be supported
3. choices for media include twisted-pair copper, coaxial cable, and fiber optics
4. high data rates can be supported (1-10 Mbps)

The disadvantages include:

1. distance limitations
2. susceptibility to cross-talk and other noises typical of wire and cable
3. the difficulty of making multiple taps from optical fiber

Broadband

The second LAN transmission technique is **broadband,** where the bandwidth is frequency-divided into multiple channels, each of which can be used independently. Coaxial cable is especially amenable to broadband transmission because of its large bandwidth capacity. Radio frequency modems are required to modulate transmissions onto appropriate channel carrier frequencies and ensure they do not interfere with each other. Fiber optics and microwave radio have even broader bandwidths than coaxial cable; each requires different types of transceivers. Few implementations of broadband fiber optic transmission exist outside the laboratory, where devices to do efficient wavelength-division multiplexing (WDM, or the optics version of FDM) are still being investigated.

Community antenna television (CATV) systems have used broadband transmission successfully over coaxial cable for many years. Components are readily available and the technology is well understood. Transmission is unidirectional on each channel (because of the amplifier design) and a variety of amplifiers is available for different configurations. The major difference between CATV and data usage of broadband cable systems is the allocation of channel capacity to the direction of transmission. Most of the CATV channel bandwidth is directed *forward,* or outbound, from the primary transmitter. Very little channel space is allocated for *reverse* traffic. The most popular scheme is called sub-split because the lower frequencies are set aside for reverse traffic.

Single-cable broadband LANs usually employ a mid-split system to assign approximately equal channel capacity to each direction of transmission. Each device on the cable transmits only on a reverse channel and receives only on a forward channel. A frequency translator device at the **head-end** of the cable must take transmissions from the incoming channel and put

central
retransmission
facility

head
end

originator

•••••• reverse channel traffic

— — — forward channel traffic

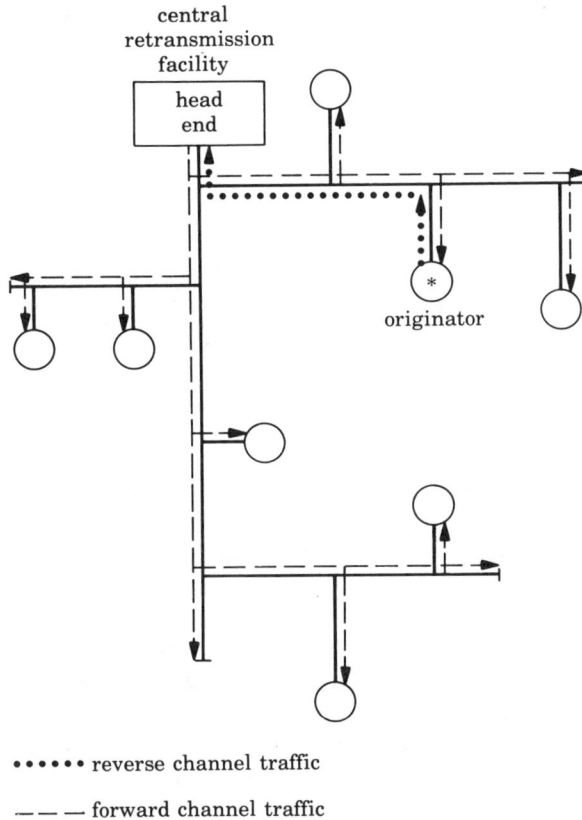

FIGURE 7.11 Traffic flow in a broadband tree network

them on the outgoing channel so they can be received by all devices (Figure 7.11). If two cables are used, one for transmit and one for receive, separate channels and a frequency translator are not necessary. The cables can simply be connected at the head-end location and the transmitted signals will reach all devices on the outbound leg.

The maximum transmission rate of a channel is proportional to its bandwidth, so the total capacity of broadband and baseband should be about the same for the same medium. Actually, we might expect broadband to be a little less because of the guard bands needed between FDM channels. In practice, baseband equipment has not yet been developed to exploit its full advantage. Baseband cable systems have offered primarily 10 Mbps or less capacity, while each 6 MHz broadband channel typically provides a 2.5 or 5 Mbps capability. Thus, the typical 50-channel broadband system could support up to 250 Mbps. Most broadband data network vendors limit their offerings to about six data channels.

The primary advantages of broadband for LANs are:

1. greater overall transmission capacity under current technology usage
2. ability to allocate channels of the same medium to entirely different kinds of simultaneous traffic, such as data, television, and even voice

The major disadvantages are:

1. more design expertise required to ensure the cable network meets the requirements of the various types of transmission components
2. more technical expertise needed to understand and provide maintenance support for the radio frequency components
3. costlier corrections to a broadband network

SHARING SCHEMES

Point-to-Point

Establishing a path between a source and a destination in a point-to-point LAN is usually handled by circuit switching. In a star, for example, the central device must switch traffic coming in from attached devices so that it goes out to the correct destinations. One way of providing connections is by using separate physical paths through the switch for every pair of communicating devices in the same way that a telephone switchboard might work (Figure 7.12). This is called **space division** switching. In older systems, an operator was required to plug wires in manually to complete the proper physical path. Newer systems use electronic methods to make connections automatically, as in telephone electronic switching systems (ESSs) or privately owned automatic branch exchanges (PBXs). A number of companies

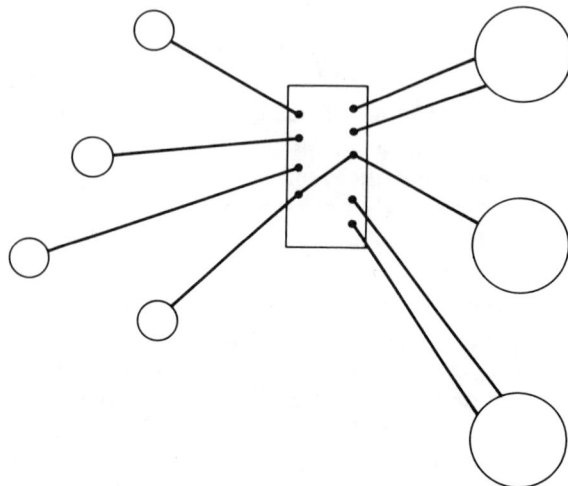

FIGURE 7.12 A space-division switch

offer digital data switching equipment that works similarly to these telephone systems.

Digital technology is becoming more popular for voice as well as data to take advantage of the channel sharing technique called time-division multiple access (TDMA). This is the statistical multiplexing approach by another name. In voice systems, the maximum number of simultaneous users may be limited to ensure an acceptable quality of analog signal is reconstructed from the digitized transmission. Data systems are usually limited instead by the amount of storage available to hold the incoming traffic while multiplexing onto the shared channel occurs. Some PBX switches offer both digitized voice and data transmission in a single system using TDMA.

Multipoint

Multipoint LANs are basically packet-switched, using either contention or polling to share the transmission medium effectively. The most popular contention scheme is an enhancement of the broadcast Aloha approach (refer to Chapter 6) called carrier-sense multiple access (**CSMA**). Devices wishing to send traffic must first listen, by "sensing" the medium, to see if any other transmission is in progress before initiating their own transmissions. This significantly reduces the probability of collisions and subsequent retransmissions. The sender may require the destination to return a positive acknowledgement of correct receipt or a specific request for any retransmission of incorrectly received or damaged data.

If a sender can also listen to the transmission to detect collisions, we get CSMA with collision detection, **CSMA/CD**. When a collision is heard, the transmission is immediately aborted so no signal time is wasted. A brief jamming signal is then issued to ensure that all stations detect the collision. Finally, automatic retransmission can be delayed differently by each sender to minimize chances of a second collision.

It may be useful to illustrate each of these techniques in terms of what would happen at a lively party. For Aloha, anyone with something to say would just blurt it out, regardless of who else was speaking. Interfering or overlapping comments would be discarded by listeners and the speakers would retransmit any unacknowledged messages. With CSMA, people would listen before speaking. If anyone else could be heard speaking, the new speaker would refrain and try again later. Collisions would be limited to people beginning to speak at effectively the same time in the same vicinity. CSMA/CD amounts to having speakers also listen while speaking. As soon as interference is heard, all involved speakers should stop. Each would have a different solution on how long to wait before trying again, minimizing the chance for subsequent collisions. Without imposing some type of sharing discipline, our party would soon grow very noisy as each speaker tried to raise the volume of his signal in order to override all the others.

The polling approach to multipoint sharing is a variant on hub-go-ahead that gives explicit permission to transmit to only a single device at a time.

The passing of permission is accomplished with a special message called a **token.** Every device in the LAN must know at least its own predecessor and successor in the polling list. Cooperation among all devices is needed to ensure that there is only one token and that it does not get lost or destroyed. Token schemes are especially popular for ring LANs because the polling order can correspond to the physical order of the devices in the network.

Performance

Much mathematical analysis and computer simulation has been generated to predict the performance of multipoint LANs under the various sharing disciplines. This has been applied to the potential interconnection of hundreds or thousands of devices such as terminals, workstations, personal computers, and larger computers, as well as to the high-speed interconnection of several large computers. Contention systems generally seem to perform better under light traffic loads, and polling systems are generally better for heavy traffic conditions. Care is needed in applying such simplified conclusions to any specific system without substantial further investigation.

In considering performance, it is also important to notice that different sharing schemes can be implemented on various topologies. Even a star could do token passing if a sophisticated central device used a roll-call approach, as in Figure 7.13, for example. The efficiency of the implementation is a different issue. Performance analysis of LANs in general is a topic for ongoing investigation.

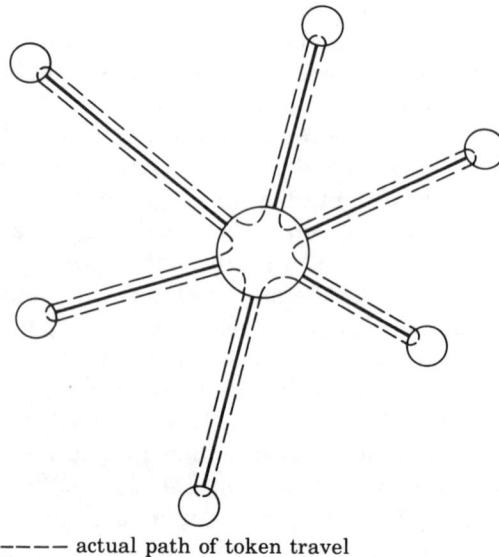

– – – – actual path of token travel

FIGURE 7.13 A logical ring

INTERFACES AND INTERCONNECTIONS

Most local area network products of the early 1980s were designed to provide communication subnet capabilities comparable to the lower three levels of the OSI model. The physical aspects of local networks differ somewhat from the typical long-haul network concern over compatibility with common carrier facilities. LANs concentrate instead on proper grounding and noise shielding techniques while maintaining the right signal levels to reach through the network without overpowering anyone else. Devices for interconnection of LANs operate at much higher speeds than most long-haul network gateways, so specific format and protocol translations are usually hardware supported rather than having a general library of functions available on demand. This often limits the flexibility for connecting a LAN to networks from other vendors.

LAN data link protocols are usually modifications of HDLC that take advantage of the less general structure of LAN topologies. In Ethernet, for example, no flag sequences are used to begin and end frames explicitly because the processes of carrier sense and baseband transmission in the physical layer effectively accomplish the framing. Similarly, the control field is unused by the Ethernet data link layer itself; it is reserved for the coordination of higher levels through value assignments by Xerox Corporation.

It is at the network level, however, that LANs differ most from the OSI store-and-forward model. LANs have little need to deal with routing in stars or inherently broadcast configurations. Instead they must be concerned with sharing access to the medium, flow control to handle congestion, and knowing the status of network participants. Store-and-forward support is usually minimal because of the limited buffer capacity typical of the LAN interfaces. Messaging is more likely to be available only at a higher level (presentation or application), as in electronic mail, for example.

LAN services are usually provided by microprocessor-based interface units. Devices included in a network are attached to an interface box or incorporate an interface board which handles the subnet functions and transmits the appropriate signals onto the LAN medium. Other functions typically implemented in the interface are: finding the right destination by associating names with network addresses, port selection by allowing multiple destinations to have the same name and searching for a free resource, port contention by allowing more potential requests for a destination than there are ports, and automatic queuing of connection requests when all ports are busy. Some network interfaces have also been programmed to include sophisticated higher level services such as congestion control, aliasing (multiple names for one location), session establishment, or virtual terminal protocols.

Connection of local networks to a variety of local, geographic, or public networks is of increasing interest to many LAN users. **Bridges** are devices used to connect similar local networks together. They may be as simple as a frequency translator to tie together channels on the same broadband cable, or more complex, as an interface between broadband and baseband systems. If the complexity or sophistication required increases, as between networks from different vendors or between LANs and public nets, *gateways* are used to make physical and higher level protocol translations.

NETWORK MANAGEMENT

Management of a local area network should encompass effective, efficient communication, reliable operation, and appropriate allocation of resources. These are not actually different issues, but rather different perspectives on getting the job done. Many networks provide for checking the status of interface units and for running diagnostics to isolate faults. They may also monitor performance by collecting and analyzing traffic data and presenting statistical reports. The value of these capabilities increases dramatically as the network becomes busier and the traffic load reaches a significant proportion of the capacity. Examination of the delay statistics, flow and points of congestion, and any patterns in resource usage should lead to formulation of appropriate facilities rearrangement or network growth strategies.

In many LANs where reporting and network software services are important, a special node is designated as the network control center (**NCC**). The NCC is usually given extra storage and peripherals to support its abilities as collector, coordinator, and reporter of the performance data. Data or programs could also be downloaded from an NCC to the network interfaces. This is particularly convenient if modifications of characteristics or responsibilities occur often. In some cases, the NCC is fundamental to the proper functioning of the LAN; it may be responsible for initializing or rebooting the interfaces. Redundancy or complete backup of these NCCs is used to provide the desired degree of fault tolerance for network operation. This prevents the NCC from being a critical resource.

STANDARDIZATION

Baseband Networks

The first attempt at a major LAN standard was a joint proposal by Xerox, Intel, and Digital Equipment Corporations for a baseband approach called **Ethernet,** after an experimental LAN developed by Xerox. The original specification* covered everything from the cable and its electrical characteristics to the details of a CSMA/CD scheme. Lacking other standards and respecting the potential marketability of compatible equipment, a number

---

* "The Ethernet: A Local Area Network—Data Link Layer and Physical Layer Specifications", Version 1.0, September 30, 1980; available from Xerox Corporation, OPD Office Systems Business Unit, 3450 Hillview Avenue, Palo Alto, CA 94394.

of companies began developing products to meet or interface with the Ethernet specifications. This early response to production of "standard" interfaces has given Ethernet a volume advantage which still holds among today's LAN users. The few changes made in later versions of the Ethernet standard have not caused any difficulty for vendors or users wishing to accommodate the revisions.

In the United States, the IEEE Standards Committee 802 has provided the major forum for discussion and acceptance of Ethernet as an industry standard. A baseband CSMA/CD agreement was reached in June 1983 and is well on its way to adoption by most of the major vendors. IBM proposed an alternative baseband approach using a token ring access method rather than contention. The proposal received enough support that a separate standard has been developed. The resulting controversy generated speculation that perhaps LANs were still too new to be subjected to the rigidities of formal standardization. In any case, user pressures for general device compatibilities and network interconnection capabilities continue to motivate standards development. Probably one of the most important standardization forces has been General Motors; their development of the Manufacturing Automation Protocol (**MAP**) has both encouraged many vendors to adopt the IEEE token bus standard and generated much wider commitment to acceptance of the ISO standards.

Broadband Networks

Broadband LANs have a rather different history from baseband. Broadband technology has been well-proven over many years of use by the CATV industry; the cable techniques and hardware are inexpensive and quite reliable. Use of broadband channels for data transmission has only become popular in the 1980s. No single vendor had developed any large body of experimental LAN experience or exposure before offering a product, as Xerox did with Ethernet. Frequency definition of channels was supposed to be adopted from CATV usage, primarily to preserve the potential compatibility for using the same cable to transmit data and video. Several different vendors still managed to define incompatible data channels, and Wangnet expansions have even started to preempt video channels for data use. The mid-1980s has seen much discussion of what and how to standardize in broadband LANs. IEEE 802 is a major arena for competing CSMA/CD proposals as vendors support their own investments. Fortunately, agreement on the token bus standard was reached before too much product development investment had been made.

PRIVATE BRANCH EXCHANGES

Another type of network that is becoming more popular for local area environments is the digital private branch exchange (PBX). The familiar installation and maintenance procedures of telephone systems, the potential for capitalizing on wiring already in place in existing buildings, and extensive network accounting procedures carried over from voice telephone systems have combined with increasingly capable digital technology to make PBXs viable as an alternative to cable-based LAN systems. Some PBXs handle data only, but most interest seems to be in those providing integrated voice and data on a single system with the voice signals digitized right in the telephone. Voice and data are then transmitted and switched in exactly the same way, constrained only by the 64 kbps data rate required to reproduce quality voice signals.

The basic function of a PBX is to provide circuit switching services among all the attached telephones, terminals, computers, Central Office trunks, and any special devices on the network. The PBX assigns paths of fixed bandwidth and delay between any two resources connected to the switch for the duration of a "conversation." Most PBXs use time division multiplexing to move data through the switch on an internal bus. The bus is divided into timeslot units, each one corresponding to a fixed bandwidth path. These timeslots are assigned at call set-up time to serve the circuits created by the switch. The entire switching process consists of some combination of space switching between external ports and the internal bus, and time switching so that connected devices transmit and receive on the bus during their assigned timeslots. Today's PBXs use digital computers to control their internal functions for economic, performance, and flexibility reasons.

The major elements of a digital PBX are shown in Figure 7.14. Key concepts include:

- *port*-the physical connection point for the wires from any external device attached to the switch
- *conversation*-interconnection of resources (e.g., telephones, terminals, trunks, or computers attached to the switch) so that traffic can flow
- *timeslot*-the mechanism for providing a pathway through the switch
- *cabinet*-a physical package with shelves containing cards on which ports are located
- *node*-an independent unit containing the capabilities expected of a PBX; several may be linked together to form a larger system

PBXs fall into three major architectural classes. The first is called centralized because it consists of a single, large node (Figure 7.15). All of the switching functions and the network control for call processing and resource management are contained in one central location. The other two classes are both distributed systems, made up of several distinctly independent nodes linked together with activities coordinated to give users the appearance of a single large system. These two classes differ in the manner of linking the nodes: all nodes can be attached to a single shared resource (Figure 7.16), or a mesh of interconnecting links can be provided (Figure 7.17).

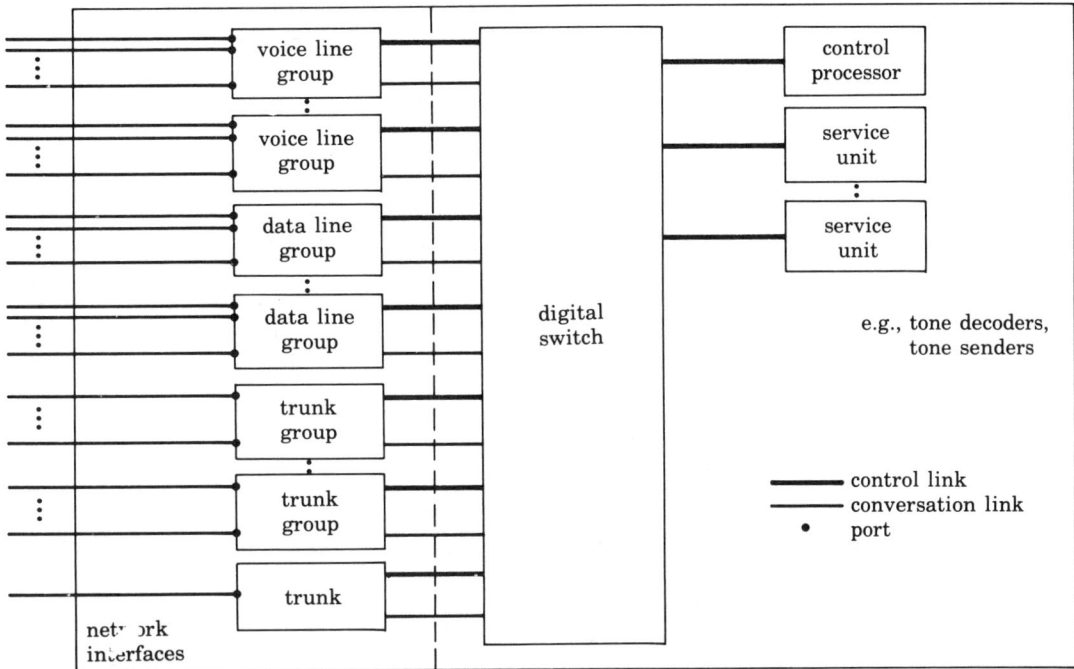

FIGURE 7.14 Elements of a voice/data PBX

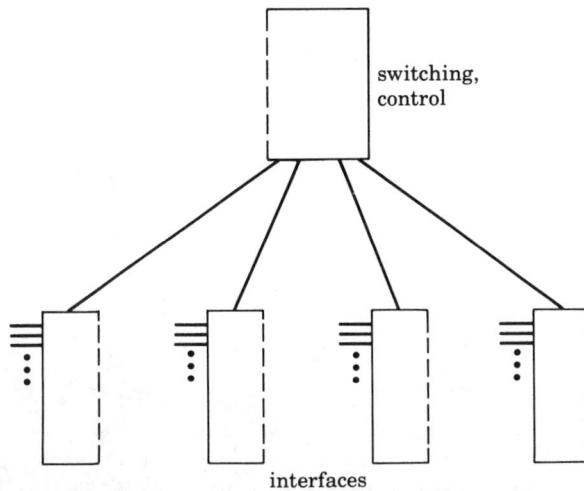

FIGURE 7.15 Centralized PBX architecture

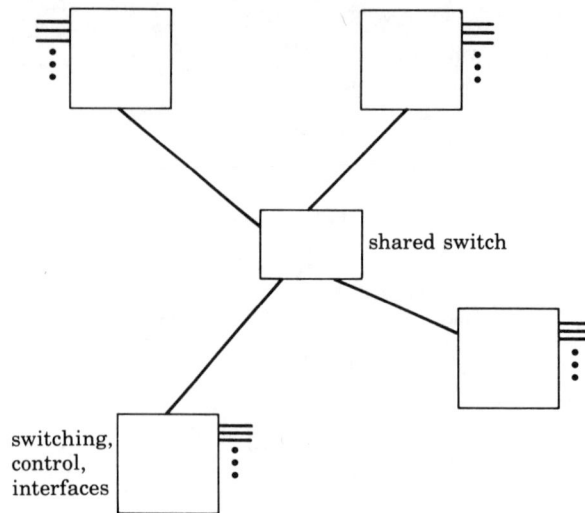

FIGURE 7.16 Distributed PBX architecture: shared resource

A key issue in the application of PBXs to local area networking is their switching capacity. The first concern is how many voice and data conversations can be in progress simultaneously. This depends on the total number of pathways available through the switch (Figure 7.14). Two timeslots are needed to handle a conversation, one to carry traffic in each direction. If there are not enough timeslots, some call attempts might be "blocked" for lack of sufficient pathways. In older voice telephone systems, a high degree

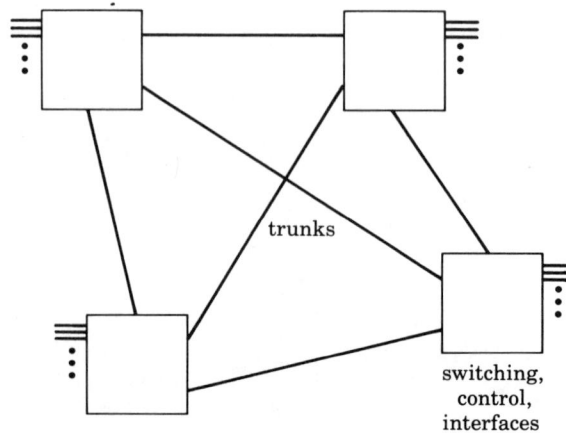

FIGURE 7.17 Distributed PBX architecture: mesh network

of blocking was acceptable because simultaneous call attempts by more than a small fraction of users was very rare, and because people were willing to try their calls again later. With data calls typically lasting much longer than voice calls, however, it would be too easy to completely fill up the capacity of a blocking switch PBX. Newer PBXs tend to provide non-blocking switches.

One major factor for the increased interest in PBXs as alternatives to cable-based LANs is the sophistication of PBX network management and accounting tools. PBXs keep track of certain types of calls (e.g., long-distance) for billing purposes, as well as providing mechanisms for allowing or prohibiting particular telephones or users from making those types of calls. Integrated voice and data PBXs apply the same techniques to data calls for a level of accounting detail not yet available in any LAN. Another bonus for PBXs is the increased security inherent in circuit switching as opposed to the broadcast nature of the packet switching in most LANs. In the final analysis, however, a decision between cable-based LANs and digital PBXs will require consideration of an entire range of issues, including at least applications, environment, technology, and costs.

CHAPTER REVIEW

Capsule

Local area networks are a special application of data communication techniques within a limited geographical extent and owned by a single organization. Baseband systems are good for high-speed interconnection of computers and terminal devices. Broadband systems are good when many devices must be connected and when it is desirable to use the same cable for different types of transmissions (data, video, voice). Performance is largely a matter of which access method is used to share the transmission capacity. Much work is still being done on definition of standards at the subnet level; higher levels are only just beginning to be tackled. In cases where telephone systems must be replaced during the same timeframe as a data network installation, digital PBXs may offer a cost-effective alternative to cable-based LANs.

Project

We wish to expand the supermarket information system to include two computers in each store. One will be responsible for all data and operations associated with inventory and orders; the other will handle accounting, payroll, and customer credit. The intelligent cash registers may have to interact with both host computers during a single customer checkout. Data about the items purchased are sent to the inventory computer so that quantities on hand are updated. Authorization for the customer to pay for purchases by check is obtained from the accounting computer. Let's investigate the possibility of using a local area network to facilitate such interactions.

1. Check payment authorization is a transaction process to be handled in real time as requested, while the inventory updates could be batched together and submitted at the end of each customer checkout or on a polling command from the inventory computer (assuming the register has enough local memory). Would a data PBX be a good approach to networking the registers and computers? Explain.
2. Assume that the twisted-pair cable plant connecting the registers and other terminal equipment with the computer room is to be re-used for the network. Choose a suitable LAN (using product literature or information from a source like DATAPRO). Describe what requirements the wiring must satisfy and how each type of device will interface with the network physically and procedurally. Describe any software changes that will be required in the registers and the host computers. State your assumptions.
3. If we are not constrained to use the existing wiring for the LAN, what medium and LAN products would you recommend? Why?

NEW TERMS

baseband	PBX
bridge	port
broadband	ring
bus	space division
critical resource	star
CSMA	TDMA
CSMA/CD	token
Ethernet	topology
head end	total connectivity
LAN	transceiver
local area	tree
NCC	

QUESTIONS

1. What transmission and sharing techniques are actually being used in the new telephone systems that offer simultaneous voice and data communication? Find a product announcement or advertisement that supports your answer.
2. Where would international standards such as X.25 and X.75 be appropriate in a LAN environment?
3. Using double cable links between nodes on a ring, how could you continue to have a ring if one ring interface failed entirely without any effective bypass?

4. What is the minimum delay between successive token acquisitions by the same node in a ring? the maximum delay? How could these limits be used to detect a lost token? What coordination would be needed before generating a new token?

5. One disadvantage to CSMA/CD is the unpredictable delay which may be experienced by a message in the face of collisions. Give an example of a situation where knowing the maximum possible delay, as in token passing, is definitely preferable to unpredictable delays.

6. How could the logic of token passing be implemented in a tree network? Draw a diagram to illustrate your answer. Do the token bus products advertised follow your suggestion?

8

Distributed Processing

DEFINITIONS

In our discussion of computer networks up to this point, we have been primarily concerned with the effective, efficient interconnection of nodes. We concentrated on the lower layers of the OSI model, simply mentioning some possibilities for the presentation and application layers. **Distributed processing** concentrates on the upper layers by enlarging our view of the entire network of connected resources to that of the whole as a single system. Then, as we discover what jobs are appropriate for such a complex system, we can discuss the definition, assignment, and coordination of subtasks among the interconnected nodes and components.

A **distributed system** usually grows out of two practically opposite situations: (1) previously independent systems are interconnected where it is desirable to share programs, data, or hardware among them; and (2) a single, large, central host system is outgrown, with planned expansion using additional processors to share the load. In both cases, communication is required among the processing nodes to coordinate the sharing. The basic technology and techniques of computer networking, then, are the underlying foundations of distributed processing.

Definitions for "distributed" systems abound. Vendors have created multiple variations that showcase the particular qualities of their own products, and user groups have tried to encompass ever more integration and sophistication. Now it is finally becoming more common to discuss how distributed a system is rather than whether or not it fits some particular definition.

CHARACTERISTICS

Recalling that a processor is one of the key elements of any data processing system (Figure 8.1), we begin our discussion of a distributed system with interconnected multiple processors. We want to think beyond simple multiprocessor systems (Figure 8.2), however, where extremely close coordination is required (each always has access to the exact status of every device and job in the system, for example). In fact, some of the difficult problems of distributed processing are encountered precisely because the knowledge and coordination of such tight coupling are given up. In a distributed system, the processors maintain some independence of each other in the sense that they do not share *all* the same primary memory, secondary storage, and other peripherals.

One way to characterize independence is to consider the degree of *functional completeness* of the processors: each should have at least its own central processing unit (CPU) and enough primary memory to execute its own programs. Another possibility is to look at the *significance* of the processing. An intelligent disk drive, for example, may be controlled by an internal microprocessor that executes its own programs to store and retrieve material on the disk efficiently. These are certainly important activities in the system, and the program to optimize disk activity may be quite sophisticated. But the programmability of the microprocessor is for developmental and implementation convenience, rather than being crucial to the system's operation. In other words, having multiple processors is a necessary element of a distributed system, but is not enough to make a system distributed.

Another characteristic of distributed systems is *interaction* among the processing units, with how much, and the level, of sophistication contribut-

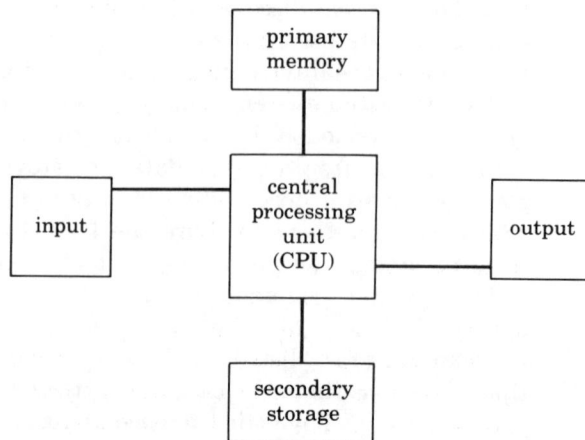

FIGURE 8.1 Elements of a data processing system

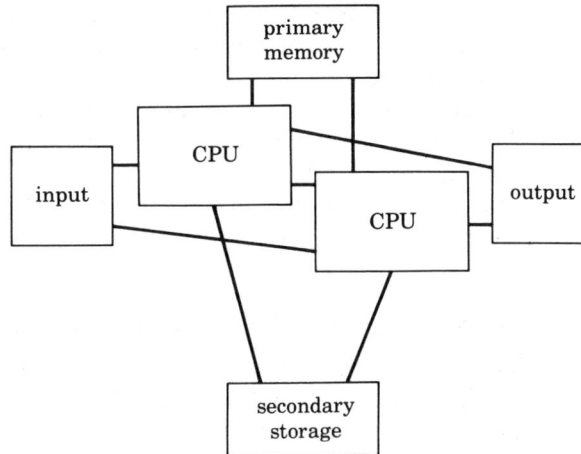

FIGURE 8.2 A multi-processor system

ing to the measure of distribution. A computer network certainly has inter-connected multiple processors. These may simply forward occasional remote job requests, or perhaps minicomputers in several retail stores periodically dump sales summaries to a regional headquarters, for example. Such inter-actions would more likely be called message switching instead of distributed processing. On the other hand, a point-of-sale terminal processor which han-dles pricing, discounts, and tax calculations might have to request a credit authorization from a regional billing center to complete a purchase transac-tion. Clearly, both processors participate in the activities required for the single task, and we consider the interaction significant. If such cooperation is needed only once a month, we probably would still not think of the sys-tem as very distributed. The important factors are the levels and types of exchanges taking place as well as the amount of interaction.

A third important element of a distributed system is the *view* presented to the user of the collection of resources. If the user (either a person or an application program) must specify each host computer location of the de-sired programs, data, or devices, then the total system would not be consid-ered very distributed. If a service or resource can simply be requested ge-nerically or by name, and the system does all the necessary searching, assignment, and coordination of resources, then that system would be quite distributed. Uniformity of the user view across the various resources may also be considered: access procedures and specifications should be the same regardless of the user's location in the network. Giving all users a single, uniform view is usually called *transparency* or a *single systems image*.

Did you notice that there are two rather conflicting characteristics of node behavior in a distributed system? We have discussed both independence and cooperation. Independence is required to get beyond the tight coordination of multiprocessing, yet some of that independence is given up to achieve cooperation. This emphasizes the approach of distribution coming in degrees rather than absolutes. Different balance points between independence and cooperation will be appropriate for different systems, according to the applications being supported. In any case, the benefits of cooperation should outweigh the cost of lost independence if distributed processing is to be worth the effort invested in it.

DIMENSIONS OF DISTRIBUTION

The question of how distributed a particular system is can also be answered by classifying it along three possible dimensions of distribution: **function** is essentially the assignment of tasks to processing units, **data** are inherently distributed whenever multiple processing units have independent memory units, and **control** primarily allocates and monitors resources.

Function

The idea of distributing function in a data processing system is not at all new. Special-purpose processors have been dedicated to input and output tasks from the days of IBM's first Attached Support Processor (ASP), and I/O channels are a well-accepted part of large mainframe architectures. Special-purpose floating-point and array processors are also commonly available for attachment to minicomputers. These examples, however, do not satisfy our definition of independence. The additional processors either share memory with the main CPU, or their ability to do work is tightly coupled to it. Even though they execute their own specific programs, they are totally controlled by the main CPU and act only under its command. The communication paths and patterns are more similar to those of *multiprocessors* sharing a single set of system resources than to interconnected multiple processing systems that cooperate on tasks.

The next degree of distribution (Figure 8.3) beyond multiprocessing is a *functional specialization* of the processors in a network. A large-inventory database might be maintained and managed by a single node and accessed from other nodes. A large financial planning and modeling software package might be located and executed only on one particular node, even if the data came from other nodes. A laser printer might be attached to one node to serve the large-scale printing requirements of the entire network through spooling software. A banking system might have one node responsible for all savings accounts and another for all commercial loans. These are just some of the many examples to be found of functional specialization.

The next degree of distribution is to have *completely general function* at each node of the network so that each node has every capability any other node has. Task execution could occur at any node once programs and data

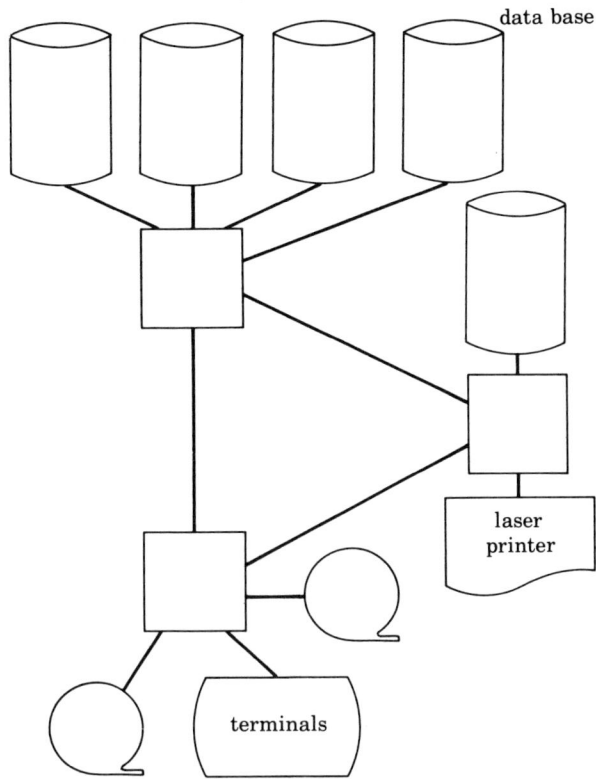

FIGURE 8.3 Functional specialization of multiple processors

were collected there. The system would locate the necessary components and choose an appropriate site for execution. In Figure 8.4 for example, X submits a request for data items A, B, and C to be manipulated by program P. One approach would be to move all the data and the program to node X. Another would be to move just the data to the program site and have the result sent back to X.

Sophisticated algorithms are required to analyze data requests for item locations and create optimal move strategies. The cost of the analysis itself should be balanced against the higher communication cost potential of suboptimal moves. Furthermore, if a task could be split up to run at whatever nodes held appropriate parts of the software and data, we could even have distributed execution as in Figure 8.5. The problems of recognizing subdivisions and choosing strategies have not been solved in much generality, although progress has been made on approaches to specific problems in data management. There are few examples of general distributed systems in the early 1980s where the user truly sees a set of services or resources that can

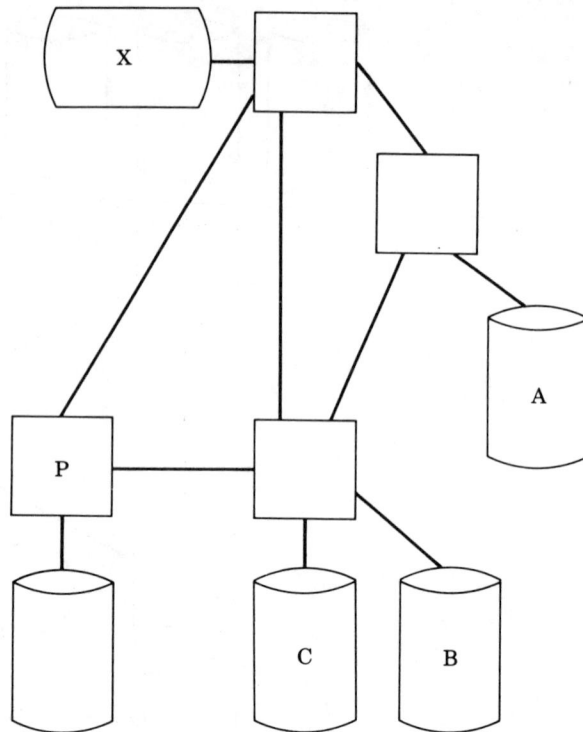

FIGURE 8.4 General functionality at multiple processors

be coordinated by the system to accomplish a variety of general tasks. The end of this chapter presents an example of one vendor's approach to a real distributed system.

Data

There are two extremes in distribution of data: complete duplication of every item, called **replicated** data; and no duplication whatsoever, called **partitioned** data (Figure 8.6). In practice, most systems are hybrids, having some uniquely located data and some items with copies at several nodes. Collection of distributed data for processing by an application requires first locating all the items and then developing a strategy for movement that will satisfy some criteria for efficiency. Maintenance of distributed data can be slow if items are widely scattered, and requires special attention if copies are to be kept consistent.

Management of distributed data belongs in the presentation layer of the OSI model as a generally useful function. A distributed database management system (**DDBMS**) must be more sophisticated than an ordinary

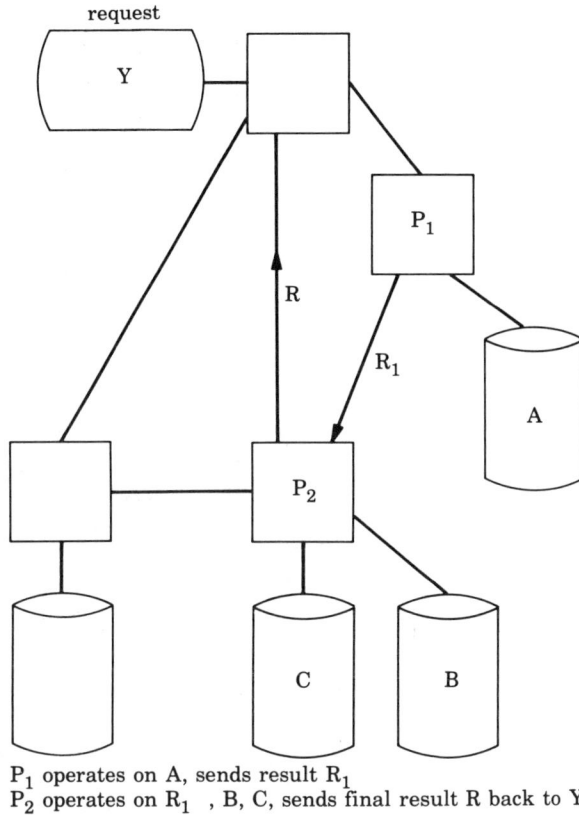

request

P_1 operates on A, sends result R_1
P_2 operates on R_1 , B, C, sends final result R back to Y

FIGURE 8.5 A distributed execution

DBMS to manage multiple copies of data and communication delays among nodes. The difficult areas include:

- *integrity*–the correctness of individual data items in the context of the whole database as a model representing some enterprise
- *organization*–the location and arrangement of data and directories to facilitate efficient responses to user requests
- *security*–the protection of data from accidental or malicious corruption and unauthorized access
- *data incompatibility*–the limitations on data usage because of its structure or representation
- *reliability*–the availability, failure recovery, explicit indications of database status with regard to individual operations, and prevention or reduction of situations where data are inaccessible
- *implementation*–the experience of building systems for actual use in real environments

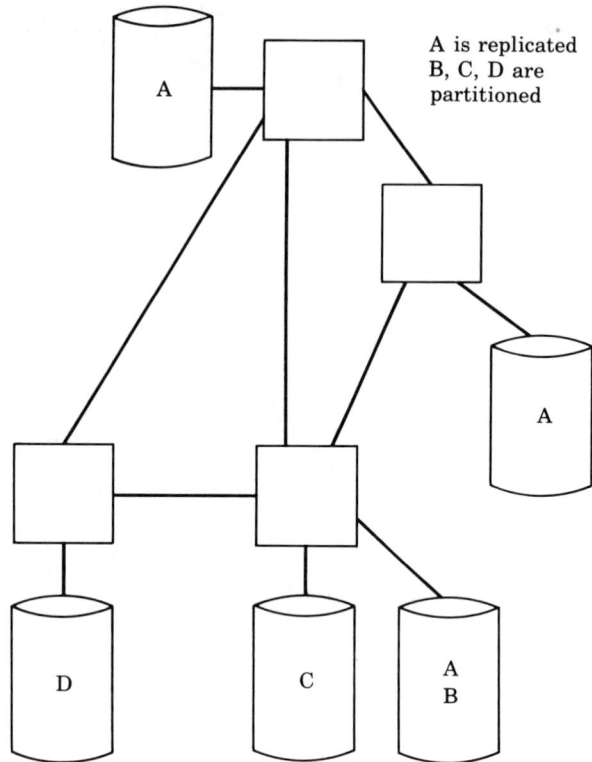

FIGURE 8.6 Replicated vs. partitioned data

A few experimental systems have been built, and several of these issues are still areas of active research.*

Control

Essentially, control involves making decisions about the use of resources in a system. Data about the capabilities and status of each resource are needed, as are programs that use the data to make the resource allocation decisions. Control is effective if the decisions are enforced on, or at least adhered to by, all of the users. Specific control objectives can be diverse and sometimes conflicting. It may be desirable to minimize communication *costs,* by delaying high-volume data traffic until low-rate periods, such as transmitting summaries of a day's sales transactions after midnight. Certain users might need *priority* access to some resources, regardless of the cost of making other users wait: if a submarine cannot launch a missile to prevent

* See for example: L. Svobodova, "File Servers for Network-Based Distributed Systems," *ACM Computing Surveys,* vol 16, no 4, December 1984, pp. 353–398.

its own destruction, refinement of its position and speed calculations is not ultimately useful. In other cases, *fairness* to all users might mean sacrificing some efficiency to the overhead of sharing, as in stopping one user and saving intermediate results so that another user can have a turn.

Complicated control programs may be required to keep track of distributed resources and resolve conflicting requests quickly. The time taken to circulate status requests and control messages can create appreciable processing delays, especially if the system covers a fairly large geographic area or carries a great deal of communication traffic. Furthermore, it is extremely difficult to distinguish between an unexpectedly long communication delay because of heavy traffic, and no answer because a remote resource has failed.

A **centralized** system does not distribute control at all. Requests for service are forwarded to a single, specific location where resources are identified and allocation decisions made. The simplest case of centralized control is a single processor with a set of peripherals and terminals all connected directly to it in a simple star configuration (Figure 8.7). The processor holds all of the data and programs needed for control and provides the only access paths to the resources. Resolution of conflicting requests or control objectives is straightforward because there is only one decision-maker and the

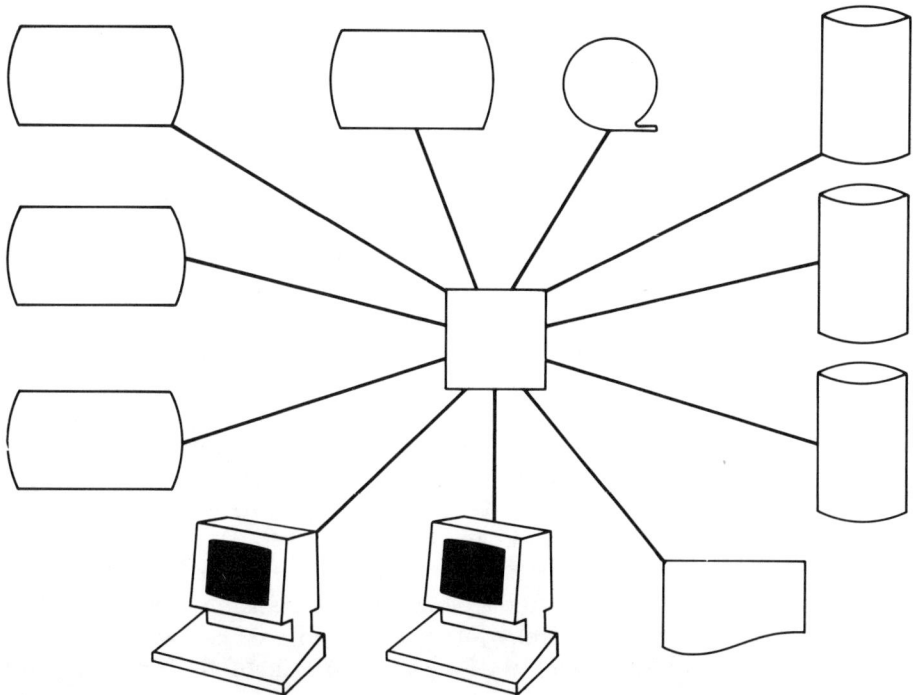

FIGURE 8.7 Centralized control

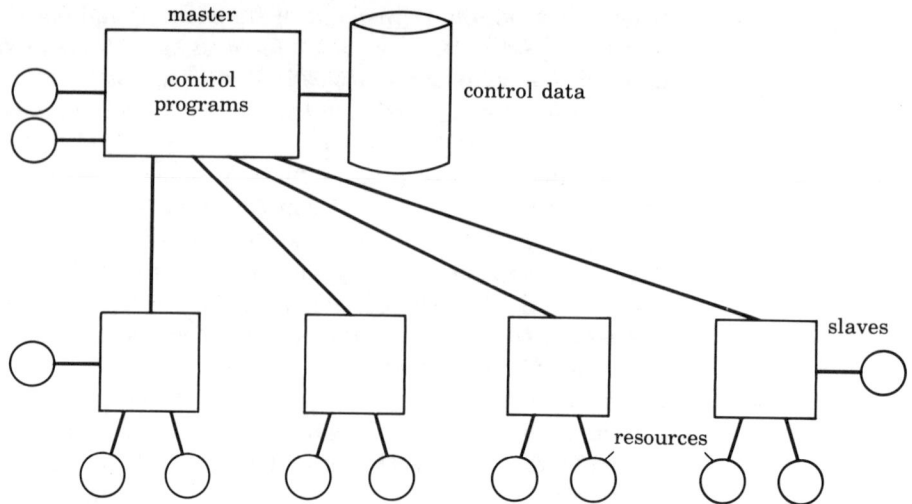

FIGURE 8.8 Master/slave control

data are all simultaneously available and accurate. This is also the greatest vulnerability of centralized control! The processor is a critical resource: if it gets busy, the whole system slows down; if it fails, the entire system is inoperable and all resources are unavailable.

An extension to the centralized control philosophy that takes advantage of multiple processors is called **master/slave** control. Requests for service are accepted by slave machines and forwarded to their master, where all of the data and programs for control are held (Figure 8.8). Resource allocations are decided and all the slaves are notified so that execution can proceed. The master is thus still a critical resource, but a slave could be used as a back-up to provide a measure of fault-tolerance (Figure 8.9). If the master waits for concurrence from the back-up before disseminating decisions to the community of slaves, then the back-up would have all the information necessary to take over as master if the original master failed. Redundant communication paths are also desirable to minimize the possibility of losing more than one node when a node fails. The back-up approach does not improve the potential bottleneck problem of centralized control. In fact, extra traffic is generated for the master and back-up to maintain concurrence.

In a network where the processors all have similar capabilities, we might consider regularly alternating the role of master, much as hub-go-ahead polling alternates permission to transmit. Under this **explicit permission** type of control, every node would need control programs and, at least, access to the appropriate data (Figure 8.10). This is like the logical ring again; every node has a predecessor and a successor in a permission list. Here the forwarding of requests to some other location where decisions are made is

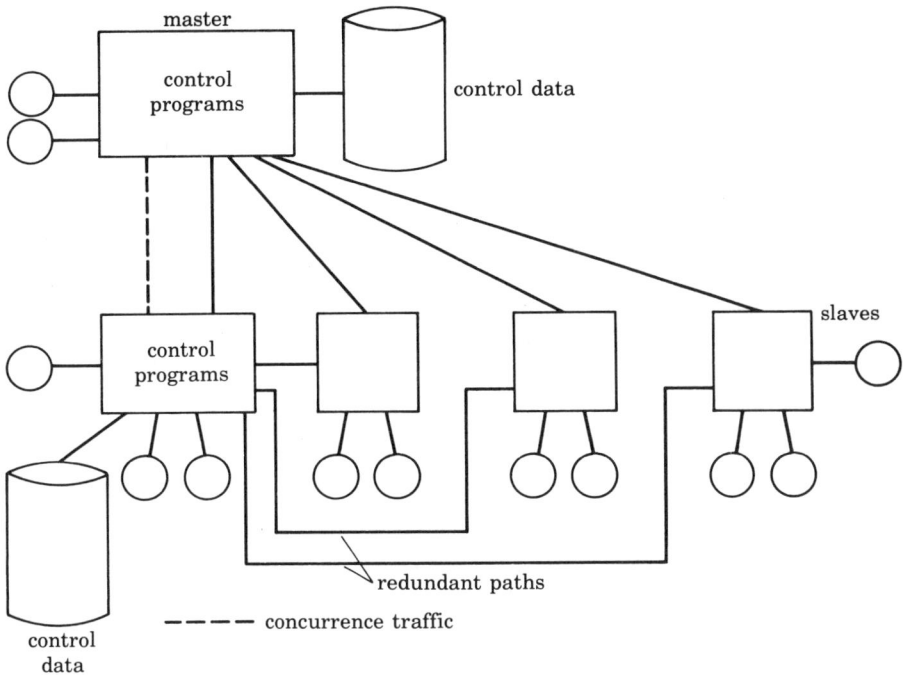

FIGURE 8.9 Master/slave control with back-up

replaced by simply waiting a turn to become the controller. All nodes must participate in providing fault-tolerance for the network. If a node fails, either its predecessor will be unable to pass the permission (token) or its successor will never receive it. Special care is needed to prevent duplicate tokens from being generated by different nodes after a failure occurs.

A **peer cooperation** approach to distributing control expands on the idea of the participation of all nodes. Is it possible to put programs and data at each node so that only one decision is reached for the network, based on the individual local decisions contributed by the nodes? If a request is determined to have no conflict with previously granted requests, then resource allocation proceeds without problems. If any node finds a conflict, then the request could be deferred until the conflicting allocation has been completed, or it could be rejected and the user decides whether later resubmission is appropriate. It is difficult to demonstrate or prove that suggestions of this type will operate correctly. Several peer approaches have been proposed for distributed database management.* Lack of implementation experience is also a hindrance in these schemes.

* See, for example: W.H. Kohler, "A Survey of Techniques for Synchronization and Recovery in Decentralized Computer Systems," *ACM Computing Surveys,* vol. 13, no. 2, June 1981, pp. 149–183.

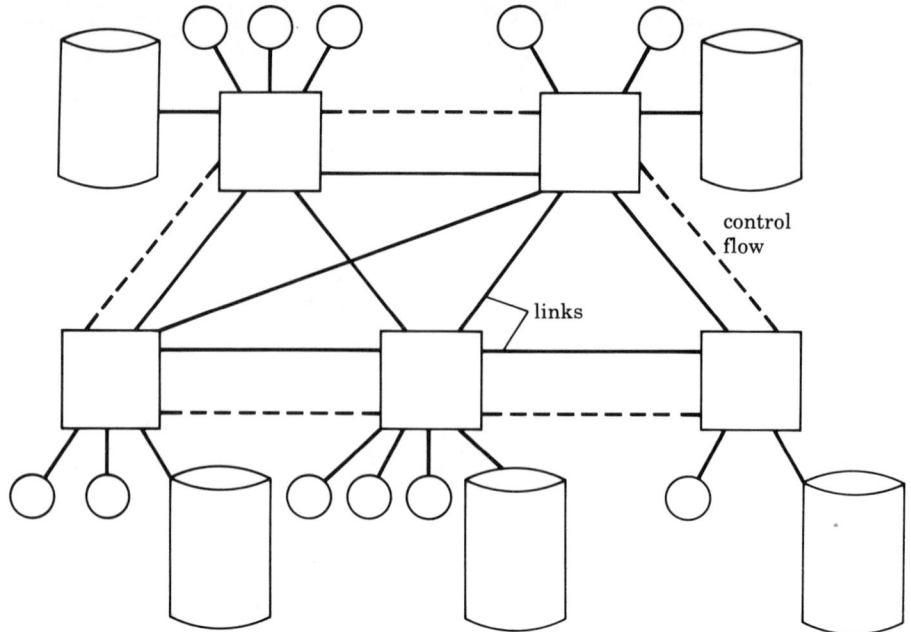

FIGURE 8.10 Control by explicit permission

Issues

The major advantage of a distributed system is that it has multiple resources of various types: processors, memories, peripherals, and communication paths. It could potentially create a total system more reliable than any single component by using backup to continue service even if some component fails. The extra reliability of such continued service is called **fault-tolerance,** and, as with distribution, it should be characterized by degree rather than considered in absolute terms. A centralized system where the processor is a critical resource may not be fault-tolerant with respect to that processor and may still be reliable if the processor and interconnections are reliable. If the processor fails, the system becomes unavailable. A master-slave system would be more fault-tolerant if a slave is used as backup. If a number of slaves were chained behind the master to participate in control (Figure 8.11), an even higher degree of fault-tolerance is possible. Notice that the cost of redundancy and the overhead of concurrency are being traded off in favor of the higher reliability.

As we discussed earlier, it is often difficult to distinguish between failure of a resource and a response that is delayed for some reason. If you telephone a friend and get no answer, for example, you cannot tell whether

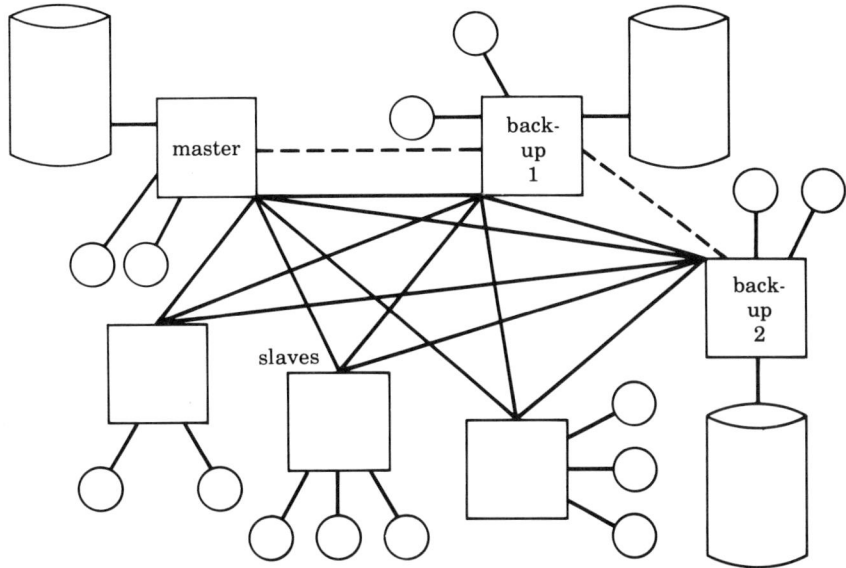

FIGURE 8.11 Master/slave with chained back-ups

there is no one home or your friend simply did not manage to pick up before you hung up. No matter how many times you let the phone ring, there is no sure way to distinguish between these reasons for no answer. Distributed systems, especially geographically dispersed ones, suffer from the same problem. Just as you might hang up after letting the phone ring a reasonable number of times, timeouts are often used to prevent a system from getting stuck when a resource actually does fail. Control software must be smart enough to do the right thing if it encounters unreasonable delays or discovers failures that block communication flows.

One issue that is particularly important in distributed control is the handling of **deadlock,** a situation where multiple executions get stuck because necessary resources cannot be made available. In Figure 8.12, resource Q has been allocated to process A and resource R has been allocated to process B. If process A cannot complete (thus releasing Q) without the use of R, and B cannot release R without the use of Q, deadlock has occurred. In centralized systems, the single decision-maker tracks all allocations and requests, so the problem can be prevented (deadlock avoidance) or recognized (deadlock detection) and resolved. A distributed system has the potential for simultaneous requests and allocations in different places, and delays in disseminating status data are inherent. This makes the coordination needed for avoidance cumbersome, and detection time-consuming and difficult. In addition, more complex deadlocks such as the chain in Figure 8.13 are possible.

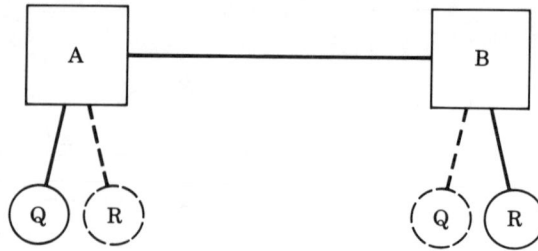

FIGURE 8.12 A simple deadlock situation

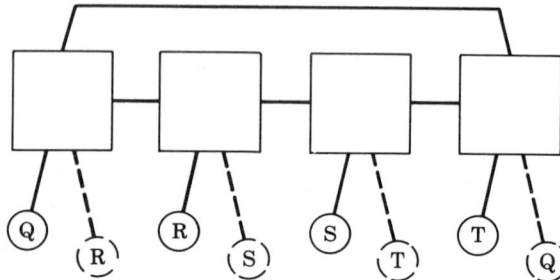

FIGURE 8.13 A deadlock chain

Choice of control strategies is also affected by communication costs. While the cost of processing power has been decreasing at a dramatic rate, communication costs have decreased far more slowly. Decisions about coordinating the resources of a computer network into a distributed processing system must take into account the types and amounts of traffic to be expected, especially if links are being leased from common carriers. Communication costs must be balanced against the cost of the software complexity required to minimize control and data flow or against the potential losses of looser coordination. No one answer or approach seems to apply in general; the specific objectives of each organization creating a system must be examined to determine the appropriate selections.

DISTRIBUTION VS. DECENTRALIZATION

It has been said that *distribution* applies to design and implementation strategies, and **decentralization** is an issue of management style. It is somewhat unfortunate that the word for describing the alternative to both is the same: centralization. In some ways the distinction between distribution and decentralization is an extension of the jump we made from distribution of function (primarily hardware) or data to the distribution of sys-

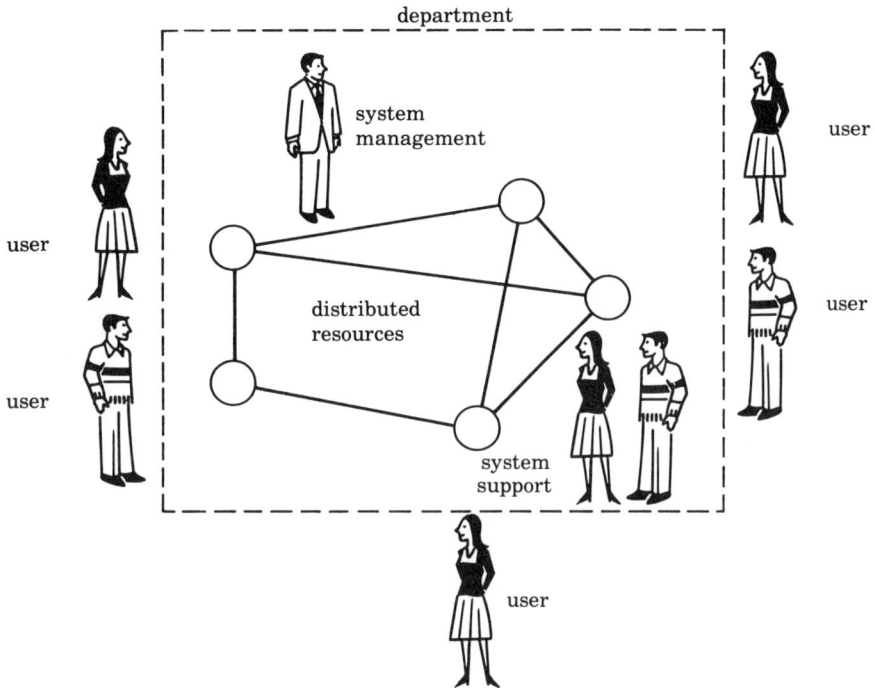

FIGURE 8.14 A centrally managed distributed system

tem control (software). A computer network inherently encompasses a dispersed set of resources that amounts to distribution of both function and data, but it is only in the control software and the application of the network that we achieve distributed processing. Thinking beyond the hardware and software to the operating procedures, the personnel, and their roles in an organization, we move from distribution into issues and degrees of decentralization.

A distributed system could be considered in its totality as a single organizational resource and have all of its support and management concentrated in a single department. The application users would always request and gain access to services through that one department (Figure 8.14). Such an arrangement would certainly be centralized as opposed to decentralized. The degrees of decentralization could range from simply moving operators into the remote equipment locations or programmers into user departments, all the way to having equipment selected, paid for, operated, maintained, and programmed directly by application users (Figure 8.15). To be manageable, extreme decentralization would require creation of and adherence to some organizational standards for physical interconnection and software interac-

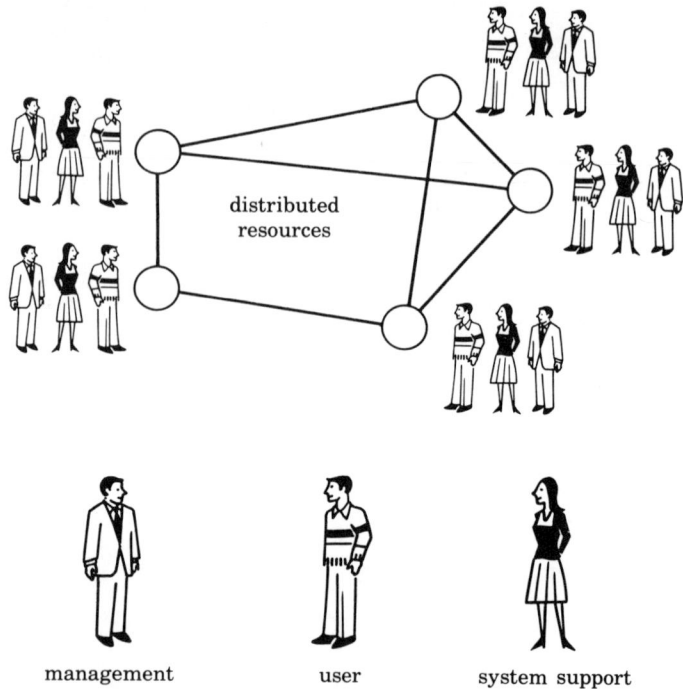

FIGURE 8.15 A decentralized, distributed system

tion. Otherwise, the system would quickly be totally out of management control and could not function with the cooperation necessary for distributed processing.

Neither distribution nor decentralization should be considered in isolation during a design process, because the success of any system in supporting the goals of an organization depends greatly on the ability to provide timely, cost-effective service. Not all combinations of distribution and decentralization will even have compatible definitions of service, much less be able to offer the right tools and support to the right people.

APOLLO DOMAIN

The DOMAIN (tm) system from Apollo Computer, Inc., "is an architecture for networks of personal workstations and servers which creates an integrated distributed computing environment."* It is one of the few commercially available systems that can be characterized as highly distributed, and is marketed as the next technological advance beyond time-sharing.

---

* P.J. Leach et al., "The Architecture of an Integrated Local Network," *IEEE Journal on Selected Areas in Communication,* vol. SAC-1, no. 5, November 1983, pp. 842–57.

Hardware

The major components of a DOMAIN system (Figure 8.16) are:

- highly capable processors to perform significant computational tasks
- a high-speed, high-performance local area network for communication
- a sophisticated graphics display subsystem to support interactive users

We will discuss only the communication aspects.

Apollo's LAN is a 12-Mbps token ring. Ring controllers are the interfaces that attach host devices to the ring; they provide each node with a factory-assigned unique identifier. Reliability is ensured through use of bypass relays so that traffic continues on the ring even if a host crashes or loses power. Each ring controller can also detect loss of signal from its physical predecessor such that broken links are quickly detected. The controller's broadcast capability then aids in determining the ring topology so that the order in which the nodes occur is re-established. The star-shaped ring con-

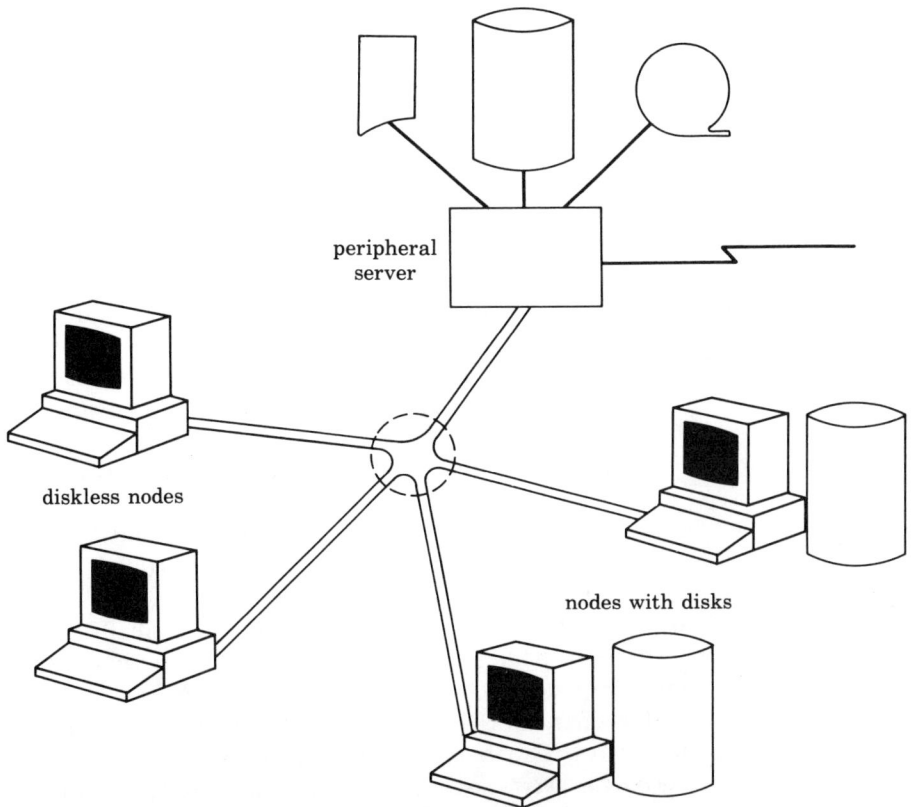

FIGURE 8.16 A sample DOMAIN network

figuration and special "quick-disconnection" hardware promote speed and
ease in network maintenance.

Data

The ring controllers support a maximum packet size of 2048 bytes. Packets
can be modified by a controller as they are received, to provide status information at the hardware level that may be used to improve transmission
efficiency. An "early ACK" field (immediately following the destination address in the packet) has a special bit that is set by a receiver if it attempts
to receive that packet. A transmitter, seeing the early ACK without the bit
set, aborts transmission to save bandwidth by eliminating non-useful traffic
from the ring. The "ACK" byte at the end of a packet has two special bits:
a "copy" bit to say that the destination received the packet correctly, and a
"wait acknowledge" bit to say the packet was seen correctly but could not
be processed on that pass around the ring. These two together are used by
the originating transmitter to adjust its packet timeout value dynamically
to get the best match with the processing condition of the destination receiver.

In the DOMAIN architecture, the idea of an "integrated distributed"
architecture means that each node remains highly autonomous, but when it
is desirable to take advantage of sharing or cooperation, the system mechanisms are in place and appropriate support policies can be selected. Transparency is a particularly important feature provided by DOMAIN through
uniform naming and access mechanisms, regardless of an object's location in
the network. In fact, "objects" are the key concept of system storage as
general containers for anything which might be accessed, including programs, text files, mailboxes, directories, devices, and files organized in records. Every container, or object, is addressed by a unique identifier (UID)
and has an associated content type descriptor, an access control list, a disk
storage descriptor, and other attributes, which are each contained in an
appropriate type of object.

Objects are managed by a network-wide "single-level store" (SLS) that
accepts requests for objects by UID and then maps the object into the
requesting program's address space. Consequently, the distinction between
local and remote objects is completely invisible to user programs that are
willing to assume the possibility of operations failing due to communication
failures. Performance is enhanced by dynamically copying pages of an object on one node to the node of the requestor, where they are saved in local
memory (cached). An important feature of SLS is thus a concurrency control mechanism to coordinate the temporary copies across multiple requesting nodes. This network-transparent access mechanism is not intended to
become a network-wide shared memory along the lines of a multiprocessor
configuration, as programs must assume objects are non-local in order to
ignore the distinction between local and remote.

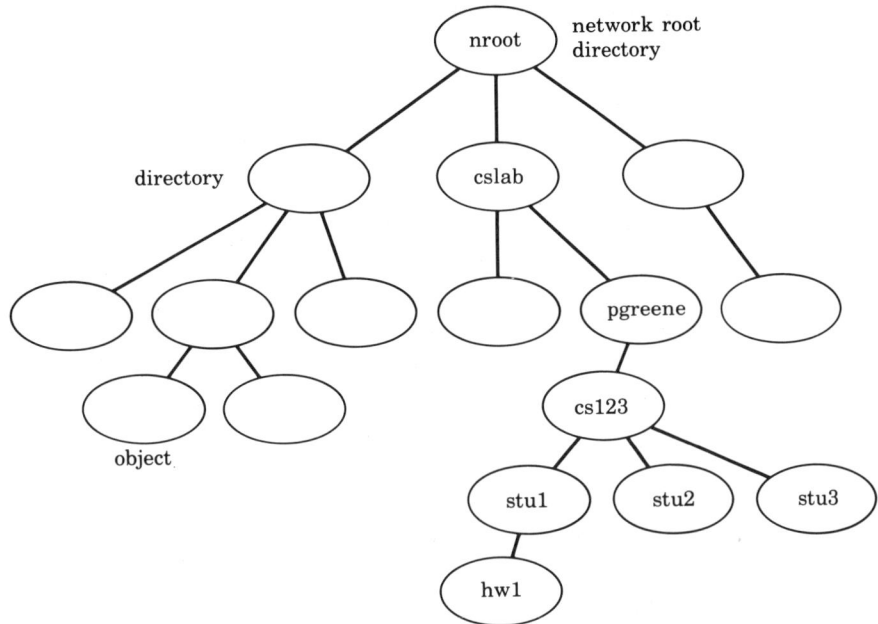

FIGURE 8.17 A sample directory tree

Object access is facilitated by a naming service to translate textual object names into UIDs. A network-wide tree of directories (a directory is itself an object, of course) organizes naming in a convenient way (Figure 8.17) so that user groups and naming abbreviations can be implemented. The complete name of an object might be something like

//nroot/cslab/pgreene/cs123/stuname/hw1

if the directories indicated organization by subnetwork location, instructor, course, student, and file. It would be possible for the student to be logged directly into the

//nroot/cslab/pgreene/cs123/stuname

directory, however, so that this prefix is implied by all accesses to the object with abbreviated name "hw1".

Software

Because the LAN is an integral part of the DOMAIN system, Apollo has customized its communication software to minimize the processing time necessary to send and receive messages instead of trying to minimize the network traffic. The full layering approach of OSI is thus too cumbersome. DOMAIN takes advantage of the reliability of a LAN environment and provides instead an inexpensive datagram delivery service. Remote operations are expected to implement their own tailored, "problem-oriented protocols" on top of the datagrams. Message formats and reliability enhancements are thus specific to particular operations. End-to-end acknowledgements are introduced when necessary.

Experience

The long-term success in the marketplace of Apollo's DOMAIN remains to be established. However, its position as the first commercial system to implement some of the important mechanisms underlying distributed processing cannot be overlooked. DEC has not been nearly so open about the internals of their VAXcluster system, so it is difficult even to begin to compare the two approaches. It will be interesting to see what other products develop out of the various dimensions of possible distribution.

CHAPTER REVIEW

Capsule

Instead of looking at computer networks as the interconnection of individual nodes or systems, a view of the whole as a set of accessible resources leads us to consider integrating the various capabilities into a distributed processing system. Different degrees of distribution can be considered along dimensions of function, data, and control. Networks with more than one computer automatically exhibit some degree of distribution in function and data. The amount and location of software control over resources currently distinguishes networks from distributed systems. In the context of the OSI reference model, a distributed system is created by presentation services and application programs at the highest level. Networks, however, tend to coordinate resource usage at the lowest levels of device drivers or file management systems.

Project

Consider our supermarket system expansion from the preceding chapter (inventory and ordering computer, payroll and credit computer). Once the local area network is in place, we can consider graduating to a distributed system. The two computers provide some redundancy of capability that might be advantageous should one become overburdened or even fail. What additional hardware would be required to allow each computer to provide back-up for the other? What additional software? How distributed would you consider such an arrangement to be, and how would you characterize it according to the discussions of the chapter?

NEW TERMS

centralized

control

data

DDBMS

deadlock

decentralization

distributed processing

distributed system

explicit permission

fault-tolerance

function

master/slave

partitioned data

peer cooperation

replicated data

QUESTIONS

1. Give another example of multiple processors in a system where the processing would not fit our idea of significance.
2. Consider extending a file system so that if a search in the local directory fails, some network searching is initiated. Describe how this might look with a master/slave approach. What issues would have to be tackled to implement a peer-cooperative approach?
3. How would your solutions to the file system extension above destroy or support a single system image for the users?
4. Find a product announcement for a distributed processing system. Categorize it according to the characteristics and dimensions of distribution discussed in this chapter.
5. Centralized control would be straightforward to implement in a star network. Describe how master/slave and peer cooperation could work using only the connecting links of the star topology.
6. What would be the data and control flow for master/slave control of a ring? of a tree? State any assumptions.
7. Discuss deadlock in a token-passing (explicit permission) ring: is it a problem? under what conditions?
8. It has been said that the success of a distributed system depends greatly on how well it mirrors the structure of the organization being served. Do you agree or disagree? Give a specific example to illustrate your answer.
9. The VAXcluster is a sophisticated product from Digital Equipment Corporation. How does it fit our characterization of distributed systems? Discuss the types of distributed control mechanisms used (e.g., lock manager).

9 Network Management

BACKGROUND

Historically, networks have progressed through increasing levels of sophistication and resource distribution, as seen in Figures 9.1 through 9.5. The first "networks" were single host processors with some directly attached terminals. It wasn't long before remote terminals were added, first by extending the length of direct connections, and then by inserting communication links with modems. Distant locations often grew into remote job entry stations with their own card readers and printers, as well as the terminals. Eventually, multiple hosts were interconnected in the various configurations we call networks.

The responsibility for, and the complexity of, managing these "networks" grew in the same way as the networks themselves. The major areas of concern have always been:

1. *Control* defining the characteristics and configuration of devices belonging to the network, and managing the operation of the network by starting and stopping devices and activities appropriately
2. *Observation* collecting data about activities in the network, including traffic flow, errors, and significant events
3. *Diagnosis* detecting failures or problems in the network and determining their causes
4. *Planning* using information from all of the other activities to study the effectiveness of the network in serving its users and plan for changes or growth

161

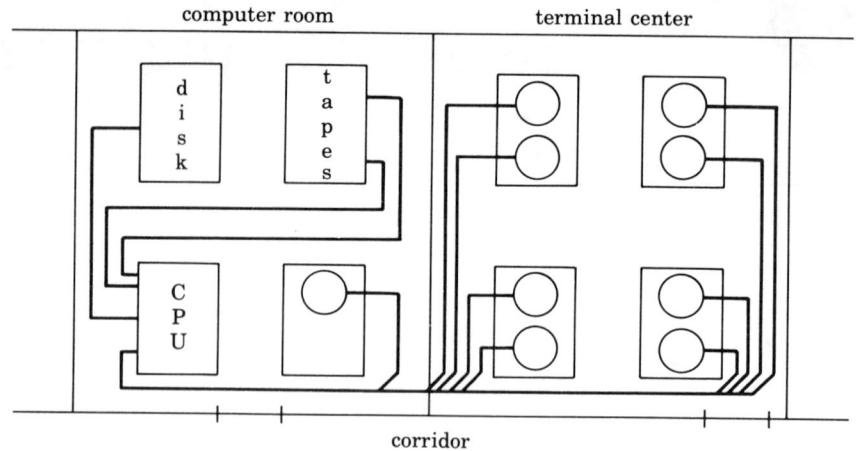

FIGURE 9.1 A simple network of host and local terminals

When "networks" consist of a single host with a few local terminals (Figure 9.1), operators and technicians can easily perform the management and maintenance tasks required to ensure everything is working properly. For example, the operator can run test programs against each terminal and observe the results. Similarly, the technician has access to every line and termination to ensure physical and electrical continuity.

As teleprocessing encourages the geographic distribution of more terminals, and as host capabilities grow to handle multiple applications (Figures 9.2, 9.3, and 9.4), more sophistication is needed to manage and maintain the various pieces of software and hardware. Multiple vendors are usually involved, including at least a computer company and a communications company. Costs also need to be managed more carefully to be kept under control. With the potential for finger-pointing ("it must be *their* problem, my part works just fine") in a multi-vendor environment, the causes of any problems need to be generally identified before vendor service departments are called. Otherwise, much time can be wasted without actually solving the problem.

Incorporation of multiple hosts (Figure 9.5) and further decentralization of resources usually increases the likelihood of multi-vendor networks, with an attendant increase in finger-pointing. More important, multiple operators and technicians are likely to be needed to cover each host processor site, and the distribution of terminals dramatically increases the amount of wiring to be maintained. In addition, increasingly complex communication software and user applications make fault detection and isolation more complicated.

The rest of this chapter is an overview of network management functions and an introduction to some particular implementations. In general, we can

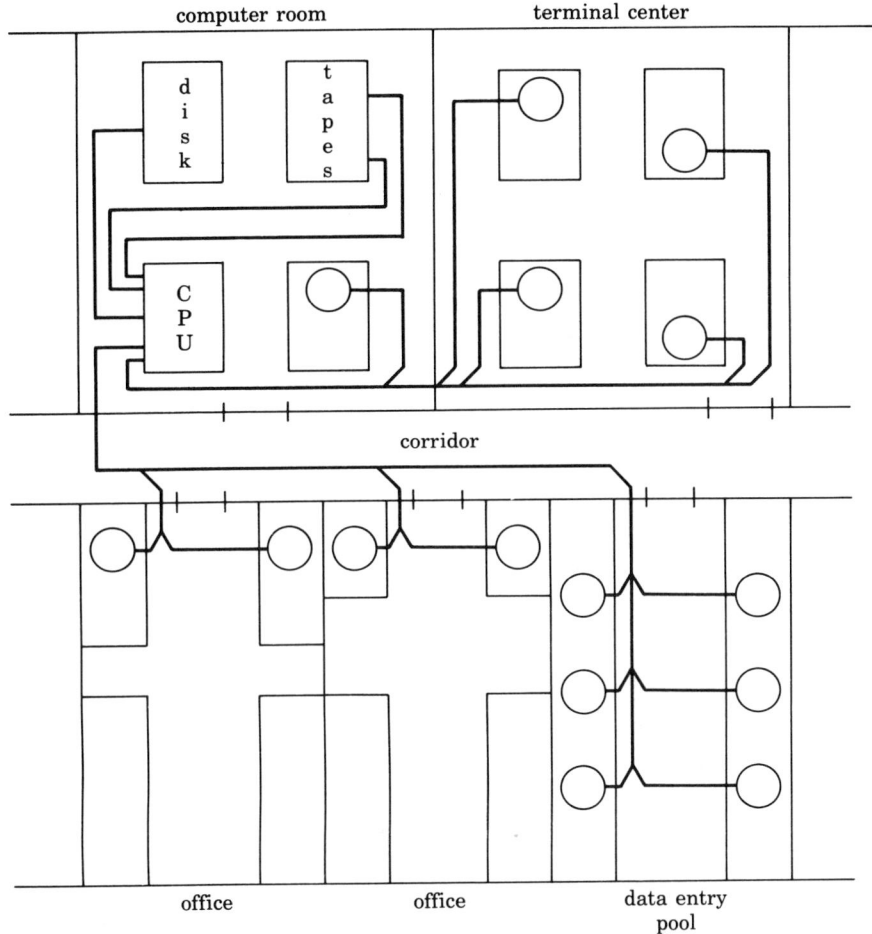

FIGURE 9.2 A simple network of host, local and remote terminals

think of network management as a special application distributed throughout the nodes of the network, as in Figure 9.6. The network manager (person) has access to the management functions (provided by the agent modules) through a terminal interface at some location in the network. As more control and monitoring functions become automated, programs will take over more of each manager's duties.

CONTROL
The first responsibility of network management is to provide the detailed information necessary to set up and operate the network. Some of this infor-

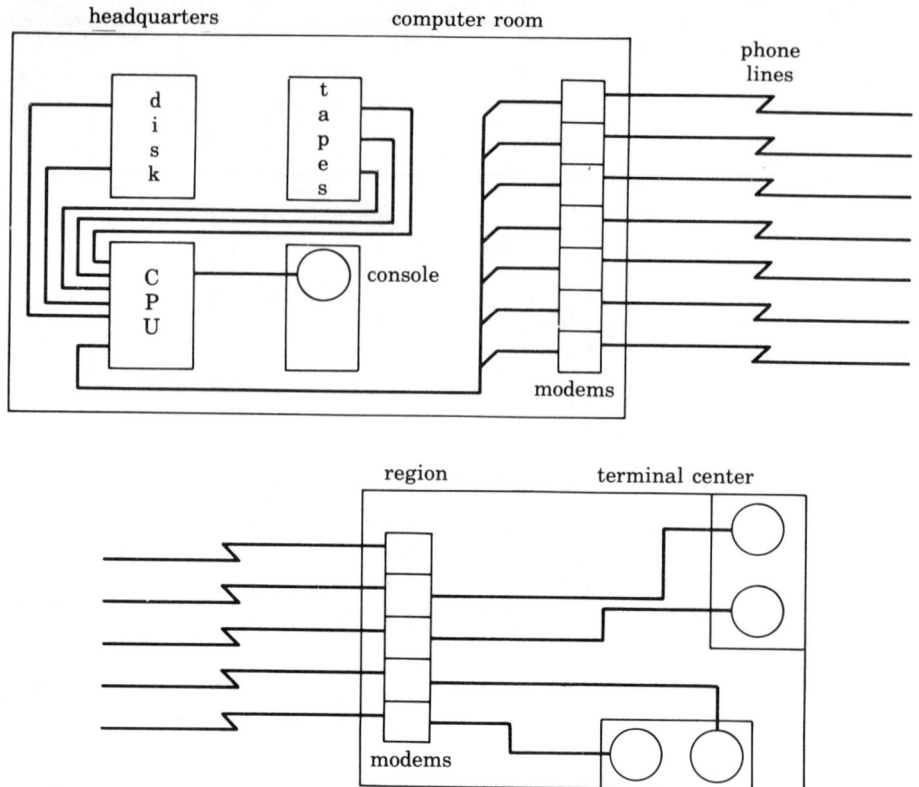

FIGURE 9.3 A telecommunications network of host and remote terminals

mation may be entered during software system generation (such as specification of alternative routing paths to a particular destination, or the characteristics of each communication link). Other parameters may be supplied during network initialization; that is, right after powering up (for example, which nodes are in operation and which terminals are to be activated). Typically the start-up dialogue is automated so that the appropriate data items are retrieved from a file specified by the operator rather than having to be individually entered. Any changes required since the last network start must have been edited into the specified file, unless there is a way to insert them dynamically during the intialization process.

Once all of the necessary parameters have been initialized, most networks are put into a test mode to verify that the components are working properly. This includes at least loopback tests (Figure 9.7) to check hardware interfaces, modems, and communication links, and may also involve the passing of test messages between software modules to ensure proper sequencing, flow, or even buffer allocations (Figure 9.8). The nature and extent

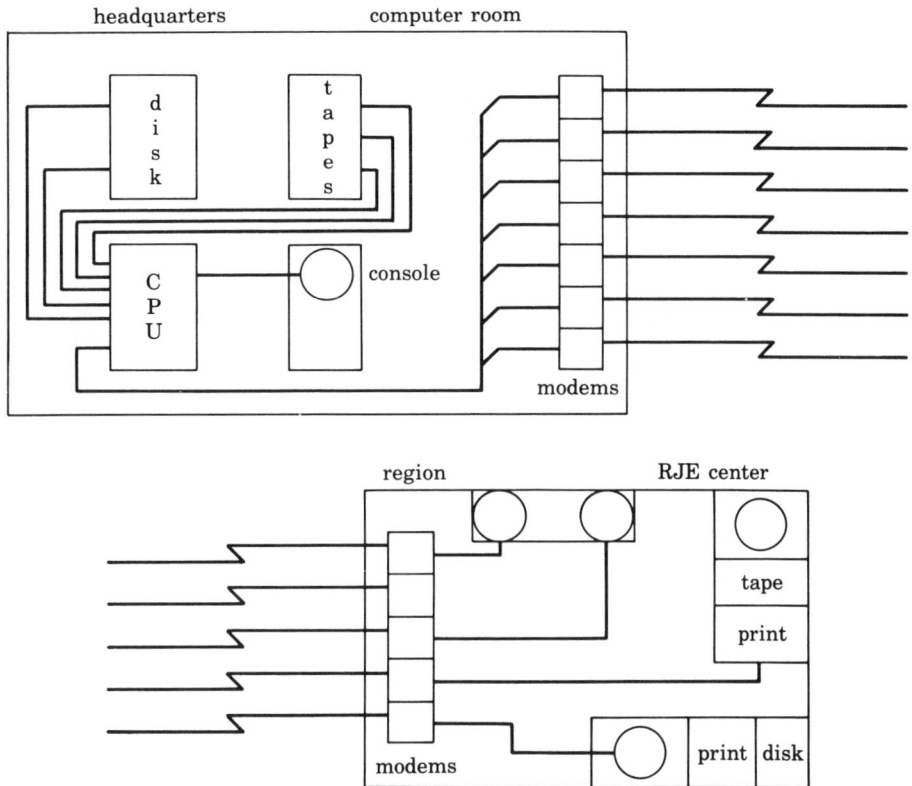

FIGURE 9.4 A telecommunications network with remote job entry (RJE)

of software testing depend on the communication services provided. In a datagram network, for example, explicit acknowledgement of test messages must be provided to verify delivery. This is different from the standard lower-level datagram service assumption of best-effort delivery. Testing must be performed at a higher level where appropriate acknowledgement *is* supported, or the datagram service has to recognize and handle test traffic differently (not usually a desirable complication).

Ordinarily, a network manager prefers to delay user traffic until testing is completed successfully, so that test traffic encounters no competition, and users do not depend on a network that has not yet been proven reliable. This means the manager must be able to issue commands for initializing and testing the network separately from starting its normal user operation. Otherwise, users may not be very happy with the level of service provided, or worse, may initiate critical operations without an appreciation for the potential risks.

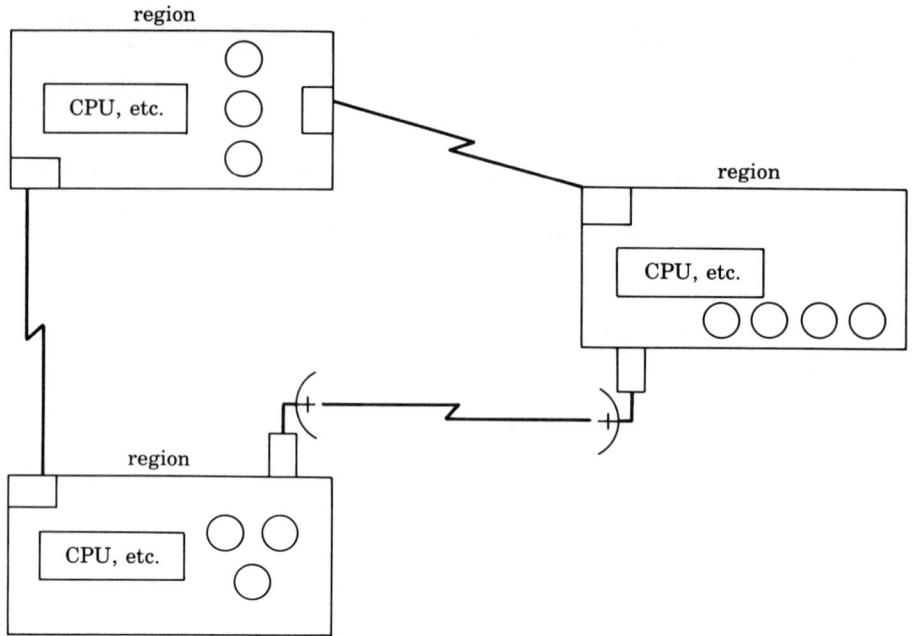

FIGURE 9.5 Multi-host network

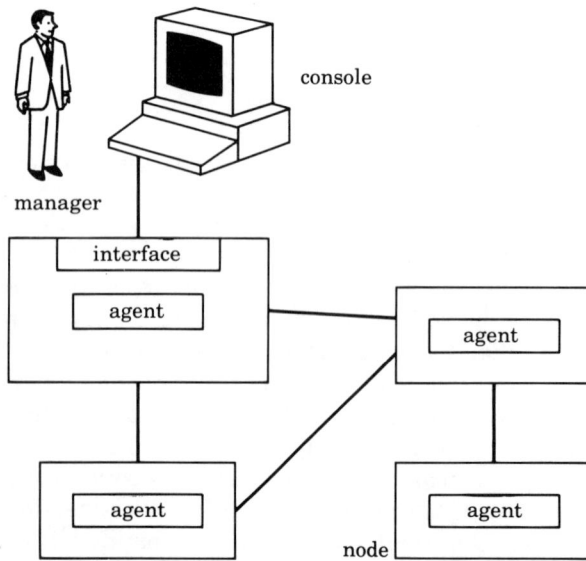

FIGURE 9.6 Distribution of network management components

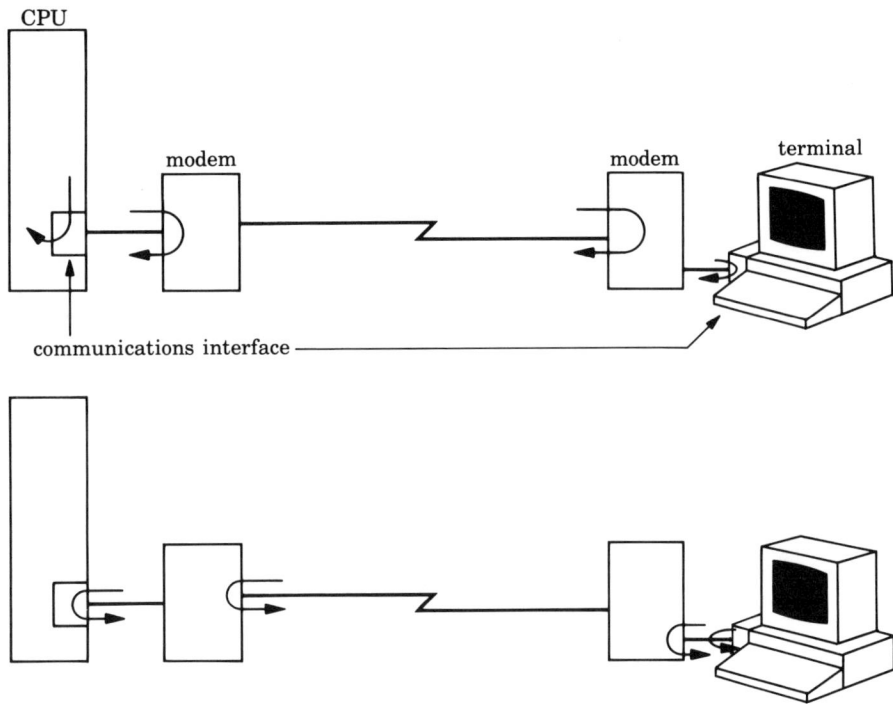

FIGURE 9.7 Loopback testing with signals returned at various points

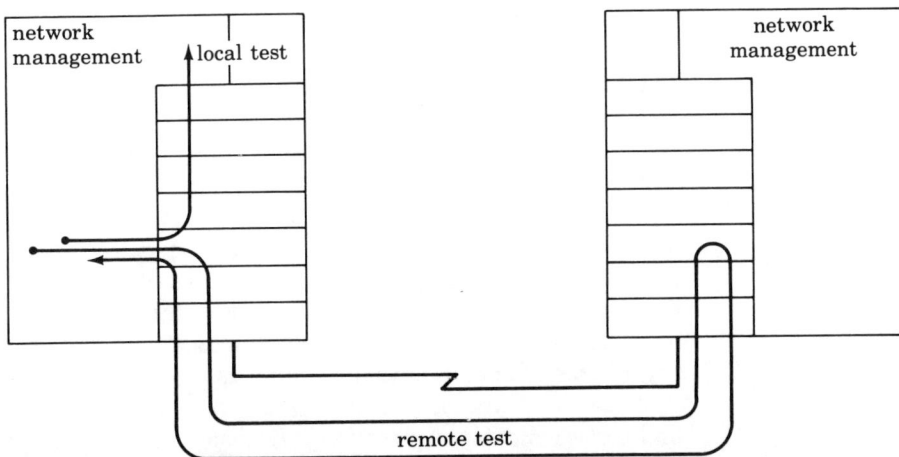

FIGURE 9.8 Software testing

Once the network has been successfully initialized and enters normal operation, the network management control function allows a manager to modify the configuration dynamically. Nodes, routes, links, and other entities can be added and deleted, or have characteristics modified without stopping the network. This is particularly important in large networks or organizations that depend heavily on continuous network operation. Most network management change facilities assume that a terminal operator has access to a set of management commands to specify details. Additional support is usually provided for changes saved as initialization file modifications so they are automatically incorporated into subsequent network start-up operations. As you can see, the operator's network management command interface must be quite powerful to control the network. At the same time, the potential for wreaking havoc is also great. Even the least sophisticated network management systems take pains to provide enough security so management access can be limited to people with suitable training and authority.

OBSERVATION

The observation functions of network management usually require local data access, a communication protocol for remote data access, and mechanisms that provide for either terminal display or file storage (Figure 9.9). Typically the network manager uses a command language to enter requests from a terminal for *display* of network activity information or network components status. There may also be a *logging* function to facilitate automatic data collection periodically for historical purposes or subsequent statistical analysis.

Display

Network activity data are generally available to a network manager as counts of events that have occurred in the network since the last counter reset command or since the last request for that data. If the counters are not reset often enough, an accumulated count can exceed a counter's capacity, wrapping around to look like zero again. This results in a returned value ambiguous by some multiple of the maximum counter capacity, a condition often difficult to detect. Useful counts typically reflect the flow of traffic (both routed through and destined for a particular node), the errors encountered at various levels of processing, and interesting event occurrences (logins, link failures, etc.). See the discussions of DECnet and SNA at the end of this chapter for more specific examples.

Network status data includes information about the network hardware and software components. Typical device information covers details of parameter settings or characteristics, such as a particular link interface being on/off, set to transmit serially at a certain speed (e.g., 9600 bits per second),

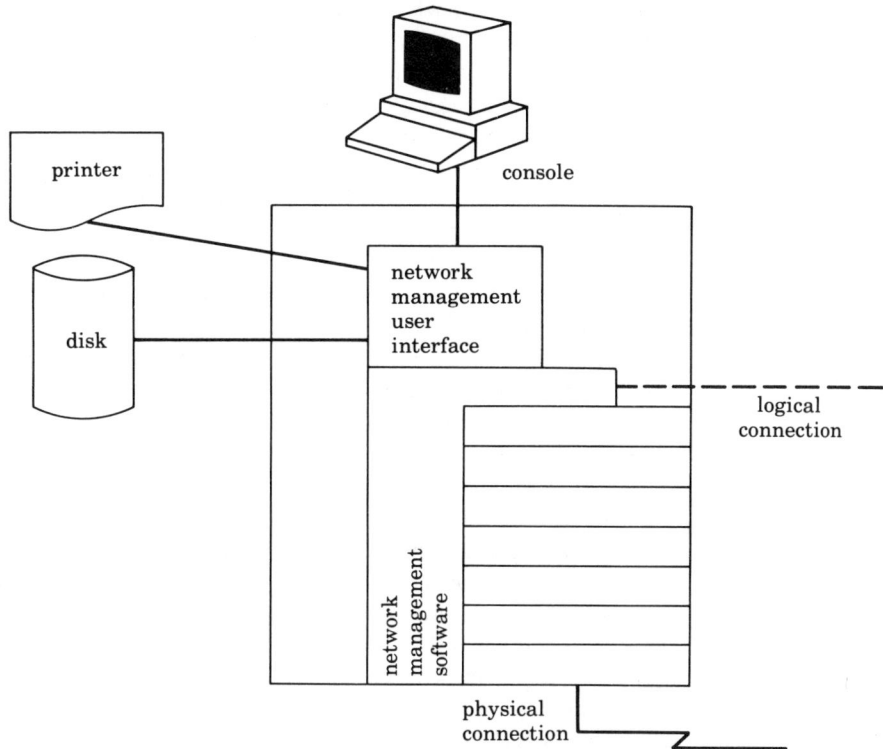

FIGURE 9.9 Network management support of the observation function

using a specific transmission mode and interface (asynchronous, RS-232), in a specific frame format (e.g., flag bits inserted first, and a cyclic redundancy check appended), and with a certain buffer capacity. Typical node information might include active/inactive, accessibility according to current routing information, current operating system identification, network name, number of active sessions, and number of active links. Other types of component information could be version identifications for software elements, last round-trip delay time observed, timer values, threshold settings, and connections currently active.

Logging
In order to get more than just an instantaneous snapshot of what's happening in the network, a record or **log** of event occurrences and periodic counter values is desirable. The network manager specifies the types of events to be logged, such as link failures, testing messages received, routing updates received, congestion detected, no buffers available. In the case of counters, either threshold values or periodicity for recording can be specified, so an

event is generated whenever the threshold is exceeded or the timer expires. Error counters usually have associated threshold values; transmit and receive counters are dumped periodically.

The network manager also specifies what device is to receive logging information: a management console, an operator print device, or a disk file. Filing the data is particularly useful for later processing by statistical analysis programs. Special routines are usually needed to map the logging file data into the input file format expected by a statistical package, unless custom analysis is being done. Logging thus provides the raw data that eventually contribute statistical information used in the network manager's planning activities.

In addition to recording certain events, a network management system usually provides a method of classifying them according to how seriously they affect the operations of the network. Various alarm conditions may be generated by event occurrences in the different categories. Critical alarms, for example, might result in printed console messages plus audio (e.g., buzzer) or visual (e.g., flashing light) alerting mechanisms. Failure of a highly multiplexed link could be damaging enough to produce a "critical" alarm so that a network operator would begin diagnosis and fault isolation procedures immediately. Less serious events would produce less demanding alarms (perhaps only console messages), such as reporting every tenth request for retransmission over a particular link. The network manager is then responsible for periodic examination of the alarm records and for choosing when to initiate corrective actions.

DIAGNOSIS

Problems with the operation or facilities of the network are usually "detected" when a user calls the network manager to say something doesn't work, observations indicate a pattern of unusual behavior of some component, or an alarm provides notification of unsatisfactory performance. Before corrective measures can be undertaken, the network manager must isolate the cause of the problem to identify what service is required. Many networks offer commands and test procedures as tools for use in discovering faulty components, but personal intuition and experience often still produce the quickest results.

Individual tests of the types mentioned for network intialization (loop tests and special test messages) are usually coupled with device controls (turning things off and on, changing parameter settings, etc.) to isolate the cause of a problem. Suppose, as a simple example, a user sits down at terminal "3" attached to node "mkt" in Figure 9.10, turns it on, presses a key for attention, and nothing happens. We might first attempt to verify that the terminal is working properly by placing it in local mode to see if the user could type successfully. If the terminal is indeed operating, we would turn

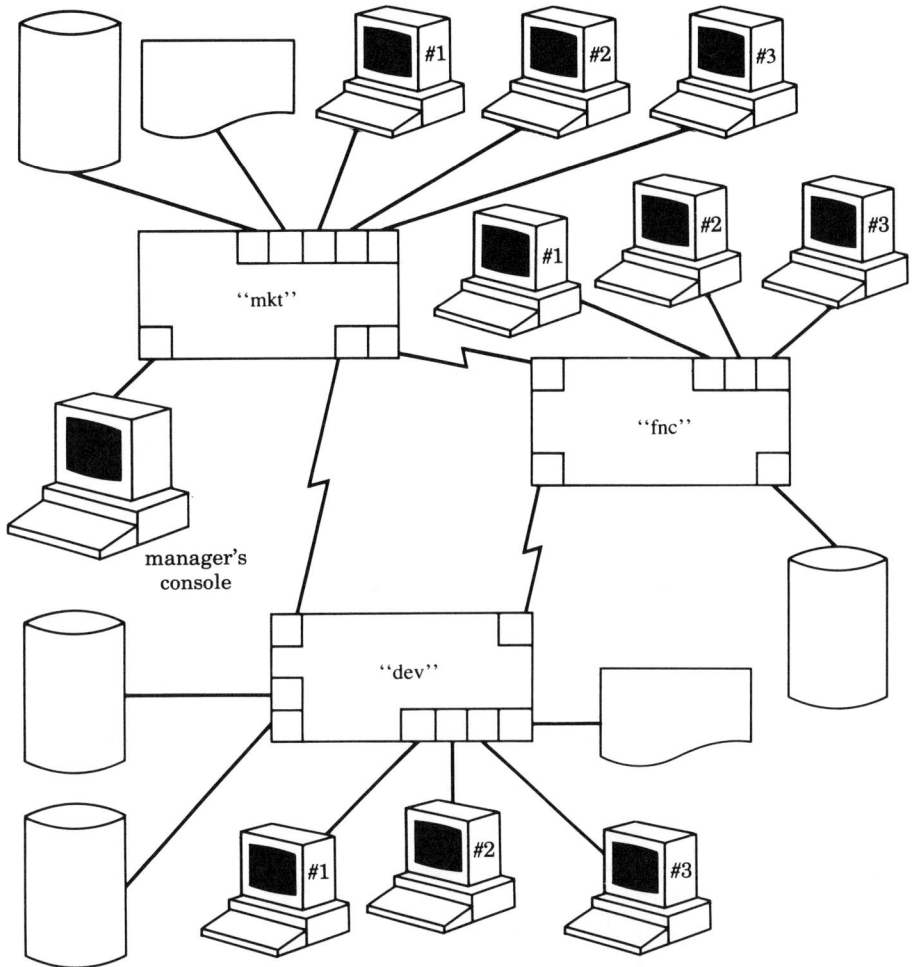

FIGURE 9.10 A sample network configuration for diagnosis

our attention to the elements of the network. From the network management console attached to node "mkt", we have the option of testing from the outside in (terminal to host "mkt") or the inside out (host "mkt" to terminal). Thus, we might first attempt to establish a connection all the way from our console to the terminal. If that didn't work, we might try a series of loop tests as in Figure 9.11, first through the network interface to which the terminal is directly attached, and then through the network interface at the host end of the link. If the loop test through the terminal interface works, we would dispatch a technician to check the terminal's connection to that interface. If the terminal interface test fails but the host interface loop works, we know only that either the terminal interface or the link has a problem. Of course, it is possible that both have failed, but double failures are rare. If the host interface test fails, then we have gained no additional information and manual procedures should be initiated. This probably means sending a technician with screwdrivers, pliers, a voltmeter, and a test set (a piece of equipment that can find and generate test signals on various sub-circuits of an RS-232 interface), to manually test points similar to the ones in our automated tests.

The testing procedures for the same problem would require more sophisticated network support if the terminal with difficulty in Figure 9.11 were

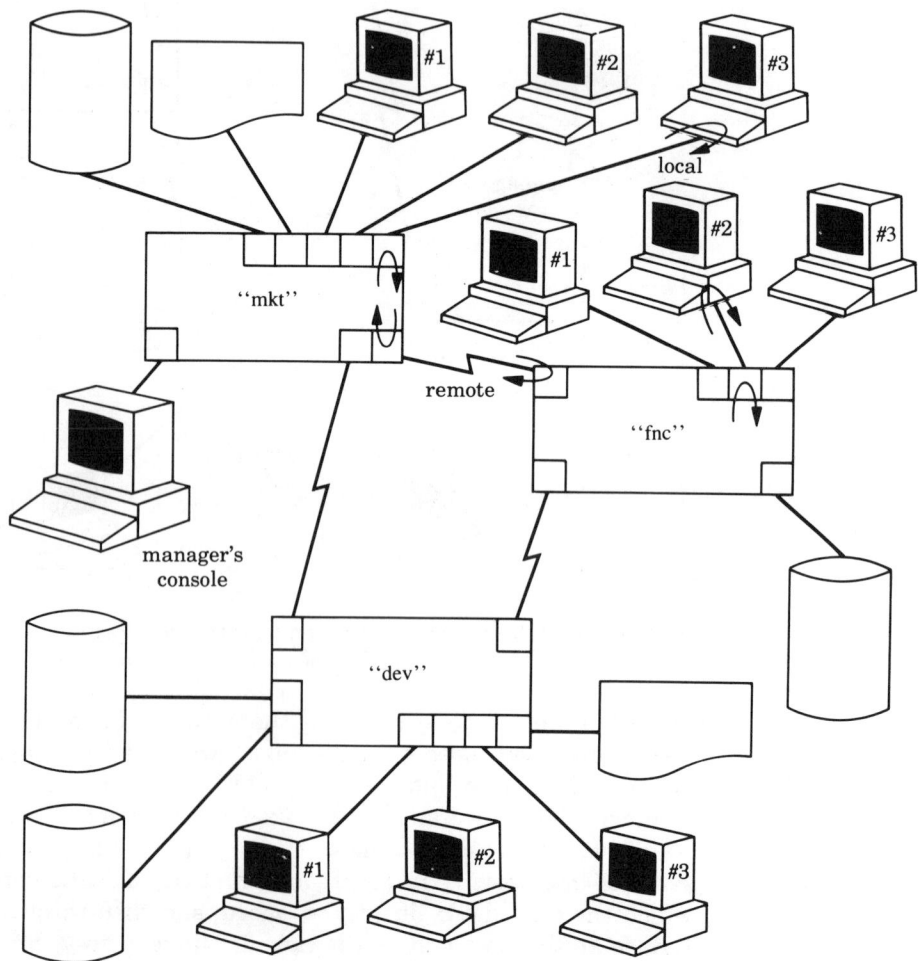

FIGURE 9.11 Loop testing in the sample network

"2" attached to node "fnc". Now the testing commands must be forwarded from node "mkt" (which hosts the management console) to be performed at node "fnc" (which hosts the terminal experiencing the problem), and results must be reported back. As the problems become more complex, such as terminal "2" on node "fnc" not being able to log into an application on node "mkt," the tools for testing must become correspondingly more sophisticated. The software components and hardware elements must be tested along the problem path. In general, large networks can be difficult to diagnose, even when appropriate sequences of loop tests are generated automatically.

PLANNING

Network planning is probably the most difficult network management activity to characterize in a general way. Responsibilities and expectations depend very specifically on the background, topology, and purpose of the network, as well as on the network manager's position in the company organizational structure. If the network was established to meet specific requirements for services and performance, observations should be set up to collect data that verifies or denies that the network met its goals. Traffic projections could be developed on the basis of a historical performance record to predict whether the current network would handle expected future growth. Most network management systems simply provide the data collection capability. Deciding what data will be needed or is useful, analyzing it, interpreting it, and then presenting the results, are all still tasks relegated to humans.

EXAMPLES

The structure and sophistication of a network management system depends on the vendor and the types of services provided. Two very different examples are presented to illustrate how different goals and philosophies can influence both features and capabilities: SNA began with a very centralized approach to network management in reflection of the highly hierarchical network structures supported, while DNA's network management has always been highly distributed to better serve networks more typical of a minicomputer environment.

Systems Network Architecture (SNA)

With the introduction of SNA, IBM networks began to deal with the sharing of communication links and display terminals by multiple applications. As SNA grew to include multi-host systems and an ever-greater variety of devices to be supported by the communication functions, it required a new consolidation and integration of management function into the supporting

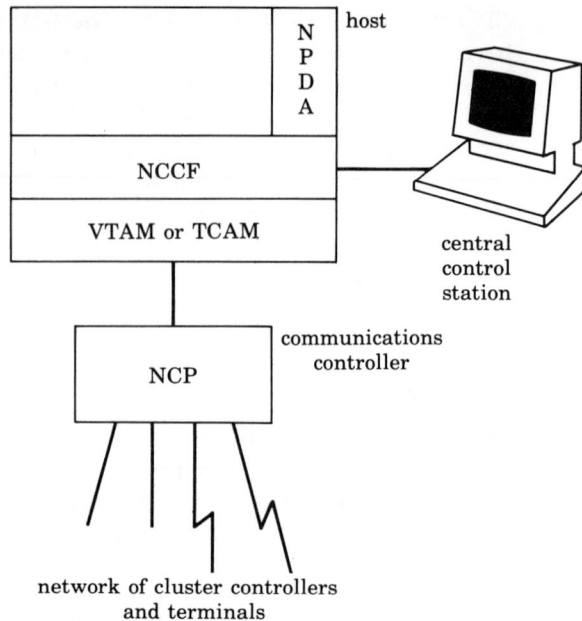

FIGURE 9.12 Early SNA network management components

networks. The basic approach was to give a network manager control over the resources of the entire network from a centrally located operator terminal. In this position, the manager would have access to data about the network elements, and could use the network itself to access remote resources for operational information. Figure 9.12 shows the relationship between the network management and communication components of SNA: the access method (TCAM or the new VTAM) and the Network Control Program (**NCP**) provide the operational communications capabilities, with the Network Communications Control Facility (**NCCF**) and the Network Problem Determination Application (**NPDA**) stacked on top for management purposes.

NCCF was designed as the fundamental mechanism giving centralized operator control over the access method and basic application program environment to the network management applications. NPDA, for example, would use the services of NCCF to allow the central operator to detect errors and isolate their causes anywhere in the network. Other IBM program products, and even user application programs, could also take advantage of NCCF's capabilities. Basically, NCCF allows an operator or a program to issue operator control commands to a local or a remote (multi-host networks) access method. The only constraint is that the command must be in the proper syntax for the intended target; that is, for TCAM or VTAM. Additional NCCF services include file support for sharing and storage of network information, display screen management so that multiple messages can be sent to the same terminal, and some operating system-independent functions that allow the network manager to customize the control environment.

Observation and diagnosis of an SNA network are provided by NPDA, which allows data to be collected, monitored, stored, and displayed on a central or remote NCCF operator terminal. Statistical data can be collected from particular devices, such as IBM communication controllers or microprocessor-based modems, either automatically or on operator demand. This includes results of specific device tests ordered by the operator and maintenance records kept by the controllers. Displays are presented in a hierarchical format intended to assist an operator in following a logical progression of tests to isolate problems to specific physical components. Of course, the operator may need to view a variety of data and test results before coming to a conclusion, and NCCF supports this flexibility.

As the complexity of SNA networks continued to grow, and especially as distributed processing was incorporated, extensions and enhancements of the original network management capabilities were required. First, data had to be collected from resources that were not directly known to the System Services Control Point (SSCP) of the host access method supporting the central network manager. In Figure 9.13 the subnetwork of terminals downstream from the distributed processor is not visible to the management host.

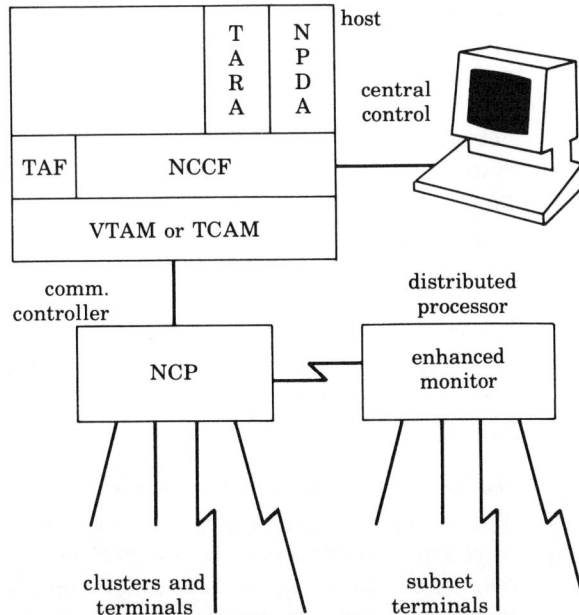

FIGURE 9.13 Enhanced SNA network management components

Consequently, NCCF must be able to interact with the processor monitor in a new way, to control both its operations and those of its subnet. In addition, the distributed processor must forward or return statistical data about the subnet as well as its own locally connected devices. To prevent burdening the network with extra traffic and overloading the operator with detail, some provisions for filtering and summarizing the total network data are also desirable.

The enhancements shown in Figure 9.13 include the Threshold Analysis and Remote Access program (TARA) for NPDA and the Terminal Access Facility (TAF) feature of NCCF. TARA supports collection of data from the "downstream" network, both on direct operator command and automatically through special timer facilities of NCCF. Data are displayed in a hierarchical format as a consistent extension of prior NPDA displays. Thresholds may also be set to ensure generation of operator alarms from anywhere in the network. TAF, on the other hand, extends the accessibility of network management functions to various display-oriented tools within specific host software environments, such as IBM's Customer Information Control System (CICS) or the Information Management System (IMS). This requires special support to manage the multiple screen requirements of simultaneous applications and to swap conveniently between operator control and application modes.

The other major enhancements in SNA's network management capabilities include extension of alarm generation to downstream elements, summary capabilities in NPDA to limit the operator's view of data to a particular area of concern in the network, and a Network Logical Data Manager (NLDM). NLDM enables NCCF applications to recognize SNA sessions, rather than just view the physical components of the network. This extends the diagnostic capabilities to handle logical errors and failures at higher network layers, such as discovery of broken or "hung" sessions. Session activities can be traced and data collected about protocols and message flows to provide an operator with a much narrower view of network activities useful for certain types of problem-solving.

Network management has thus grown considerably in SNA, from dealing strictly with the physical components of the network to handling higher-level elements. Future versions will almost certainly continue to expand the software management capabilities. Planning applications will probably continue to be custom-built by individual organizations on the base provided by the IBM program products.

Digital Network Architecture (DNA)

The basic structure of the network management components of DNA are shown in Figure 9.14. The vertical arrows represent a standard flow for messages sent into the network to another node. The horizontal arrows represent control interfaces for the express purpose of interacting directly with the local layers of communication software. Network management is the only application allowed to differ from the hierarchical flow restrictions of the basic OSI reference model. The control interfaces are for management of the local node. Interaction with other nodes for management of the complete network is accomplished using the Network Information and Control Exchange (**NICE**) protocol, whose messages are sent through the standard vertical communication interfaces.

The control functions of network management in DECnet include loading remote systems with software or data, configuring resources, setting parameter values, and starting and stopping network functions and operations. For example, to prepare for maintenance on a local link, the network manager might first "SET LINE fnc3 DOWN" to force Data Link Control to make link 3 from node "fnc" unavailable and get all traffic transferred to another link before 3 comes out of service. As another example, a manager across the network might "SET NODE mkt ACTIVE" to add a node to

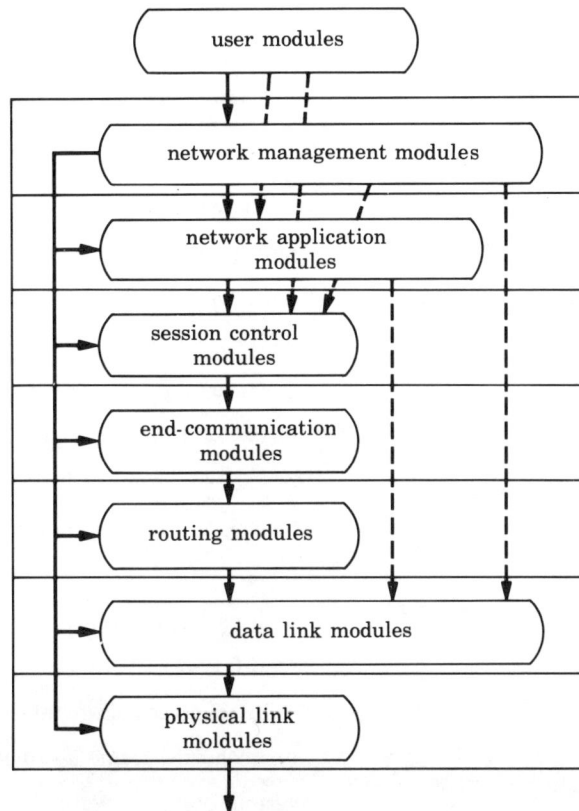

FIGURE 9.14 Network management components in digital network architecture

those actively participating. In the case of an unattended remote node, the network manager can load new versions of software or different configuration parameters from a central location, rather than sending an operator to the remote site.

The observation functions in DECnet include dumping memory from remote systems; examining parameters, configuration status, and operation status; and collecting performance data. These are handled mostly by the display commands (for status, parameters, counters, etc.) and the ENABLE/DISABLE logging command. "SHOW KNOWN NODES SUMMARY" will give the status of all network nodes known to the local node, including whether each is accessible (can be reached currently by a route from the local node), how many links are active, and what the last transmission delay experienced was (the number of links traversed). "SHOW KNOWN LINE COUNTERS," on the other hand, might give a whole list of values as in Figure 9.15.

seconds since last zeroed

data blocks received

multicast data blocks received

receive failure

bytes received

multicast bytes received

data overrun

data blocks sent

multicast data blocks sent

blocks sent, multiple collisions

blocks sent, single collision

blocks sent, initially deferred

bytes sent

multicast bytes sent

send failure

collision detect check failure

unrecognized frame destination

system buffer unavailable

FIGURE 9.15 Show known line counters

When a network failure makes some destination in the network inaccessible, a DECnet manager can use loop testing to pinpoint what has failed. Looping is tried first at the physical level (modem loopback), and then at successively higher levels of network function. The first loop that does not successfully return the special test messages is considered the point of failure. Figure 9.16 shows some of the looping that can be specified. Testing of a link at the physical level makes it unavailable to carry user traffic during the test, while a node loop test simply adds to the total load of network traffic. If a remote node fails and looping does not uncover the trouble, memory dumps can be commanded for manual examination. Many DECnet failures can thus be readily diagnosed during continued operation of the network. This is an advantage when large numbers of minicomputers are interconnected to support distributed applications.

The planning aspects of network management are not directly provided within DECnet. The basic data can be collected with periodic displays of status and by setting up logging of appropriate events to a disk file. These

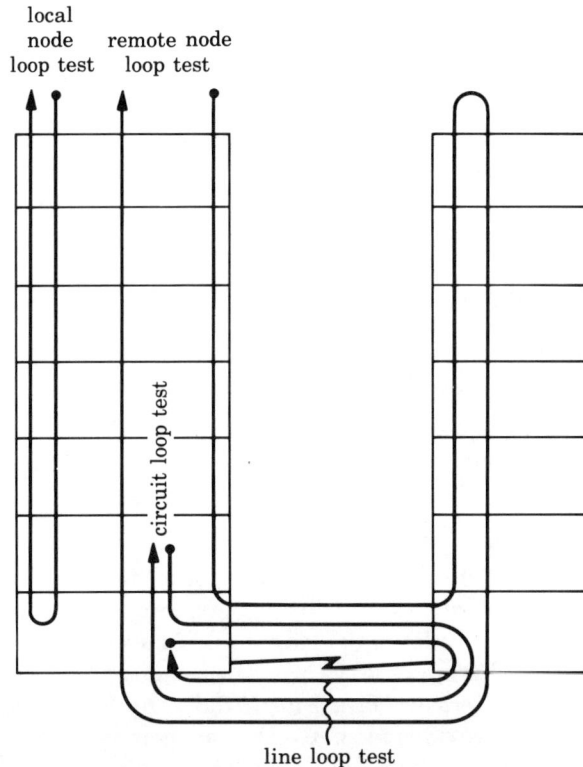

FIGURE 9.16 DECnet loop tests

must be analyzed by applications written for the purpose, and interpreted by someone familiar with the goals and budget for the network. Much attention has been paid lately to companies that include their communication capabilities in their business plans and strategies. Since large communication networks usually require significant capital investments, organizations that find new ways to generate business and income through communications are bound to improve their overall viability. It will be interesting to see how companies such as Sears Roebuck, American Express, and Aetna Insurance pursue their network investments in the post-divestiture (of AT&T) years.

CHAPTER REVIEW

Capsule

The major responsibilities of network management are for control of the network operation and resources, observation of its status and performance, diagnosis of any problems or failures, and planning for growth or service adjustments. As networks have grown in size and complexity, management responsibilities have also grown, requiring that more tools and capabilities be built into the network hardware and software. Vendor proprietary networks (such as DECnet or SNA networks) often include sophisticated features for use by network management personnel, but the support does not usually extend to or encompass components from other manufacturers. Heterogeneous networks are often left to the users to figure out entirely.

NEW TERMS

alarms	NCCF
control	NCP
diagnosis	NICE
display	NPDA
log	observation
loopback test	planning

QUESTIONS

1. Find an advertisement for a bit-error rate monitor. What does it do? Where does it fit into our discussion of control, observation, diagnosis, and planning? How could you plan to use it most effectively?
2. Excelan makes a product called the Nutcracker. From the product literature or a *DataPro* description, explain what capabilities it provides for network management of Ethernets.
3. How does IBM's Netview product differ from previous network management programs?

10 Design Techniques and Issues

GOALS AND SPECIFIC OBJECTIVES

As with any computer system design, analysis of the organizational context within which a data communication system must operate is an extremely important preliminary step. This involves identifying the problems to be solved by the new system, understanding how the work has been handled, and establishing the information flow required to get the job done.

For example, an on-line, remote order entry system may be desired to reduce the amount of time between placement of customer orders and scheduling the factory production cycle. Orders may have been written by traveling sales personnel and mailed to the home office for verification, data entry, credit checking, and correlation with orders from other regions. Batches of orders would then be sent to the factories for production scheduling, with all status information maintained by the home office where subsequent inquiries would be phoned in and answered by clerical personnel. In this case, the flow of data from the salespeople to the home office to the factory is adequate (Figure 10.1) but could occur more rapidly with on-line data communication. In addition, on-line order status might allow for faster response to inquiries (Figure 10.2).

Once the general organizational goals for the system have been established, more detailed communication objectives can be articulated. This should allow specific design alternatives to be developed for review.

System Capabilities

One requirement common to most data communication systems is provision of access to an entire set of resources in several different locations. Simple

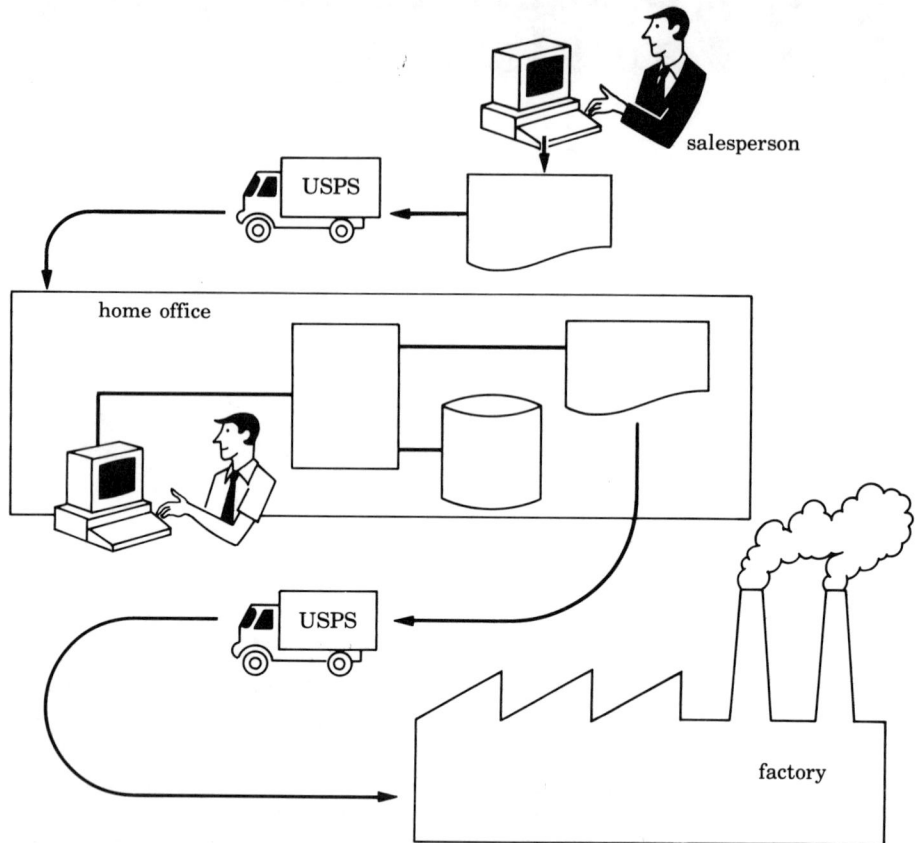

FIGURE 10.1 A simple order entry system

terminal-to-computer connections usually fall into this category, as does access to special devices such as laser printers. These can be characterized more generally as a desire for *resource sharing:* terminals share a host's computing capacity, several hosts share access to a specific database, or a technical editor shares text on-line with authors.

If sharing of specific resources is a system objective, then disciplines and protection must be among the design criteria. Some device resources are suitable for use by only one request at a time: printers and tape drives will give strange results if the work of several users is intermingled. It is highly desirable for the system to have software that tracks requests for single-user resources and allocates the devices appropriately. Other resources, such as disks or certain types of programs, may easily be shared, as long as the system tracks whose turn it is and prevents errors from damaging the work of other users.

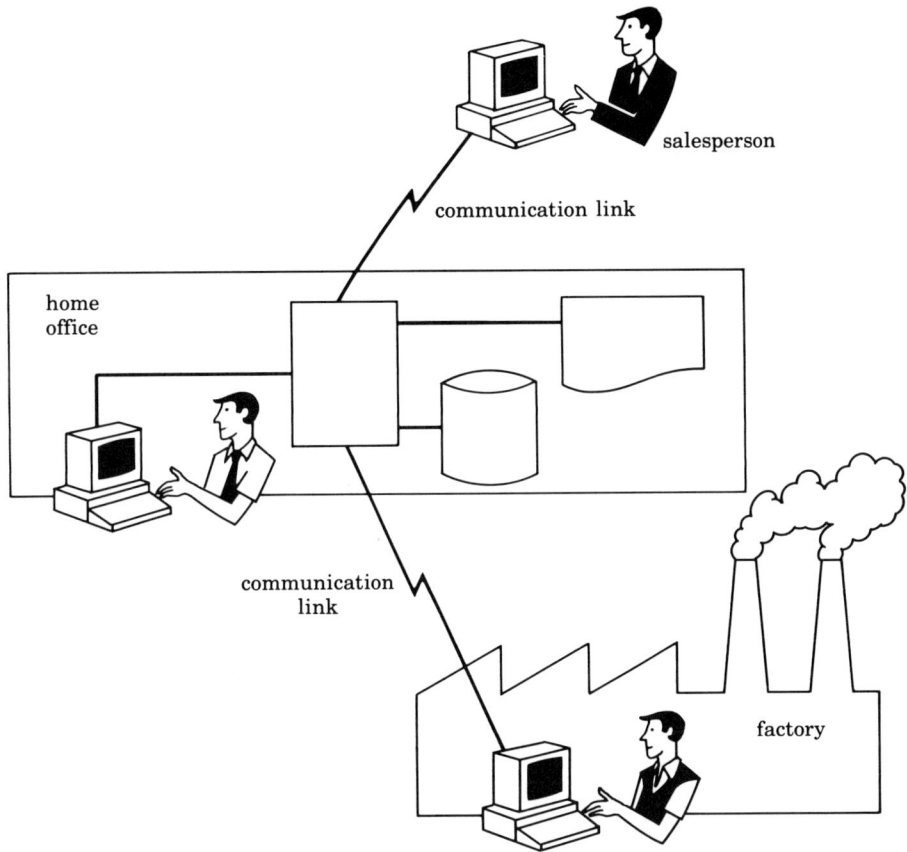

FIGURE 10.2 An on-line order entry system

Connectivity may itself be an important objective of communication systems. In the remote order entry example, putting the salesperson in direct contact with the data entry programs not only makes the entry process quicker, it also eliminates some potential for errors in the data flow from person to paper to person to keyboard. Similarly, connecting the factory's production operations to the order system allows more detailed status information to be kept for timely response to customer inquiries.

Consider a larger operation than our previous order entry example: numerous regional offices generate orders, the factory has its own computer to manage production, and several warehouses handle product distribution (Figure 10.3). Connecting the warehouses to the home office would facilitate scheduling of deliveries and maintain better order status information (Figure 10.4). Even more interconnection, such as among offices or warehouses (Figure 10.5), might ensure quick response on orders for popular items.

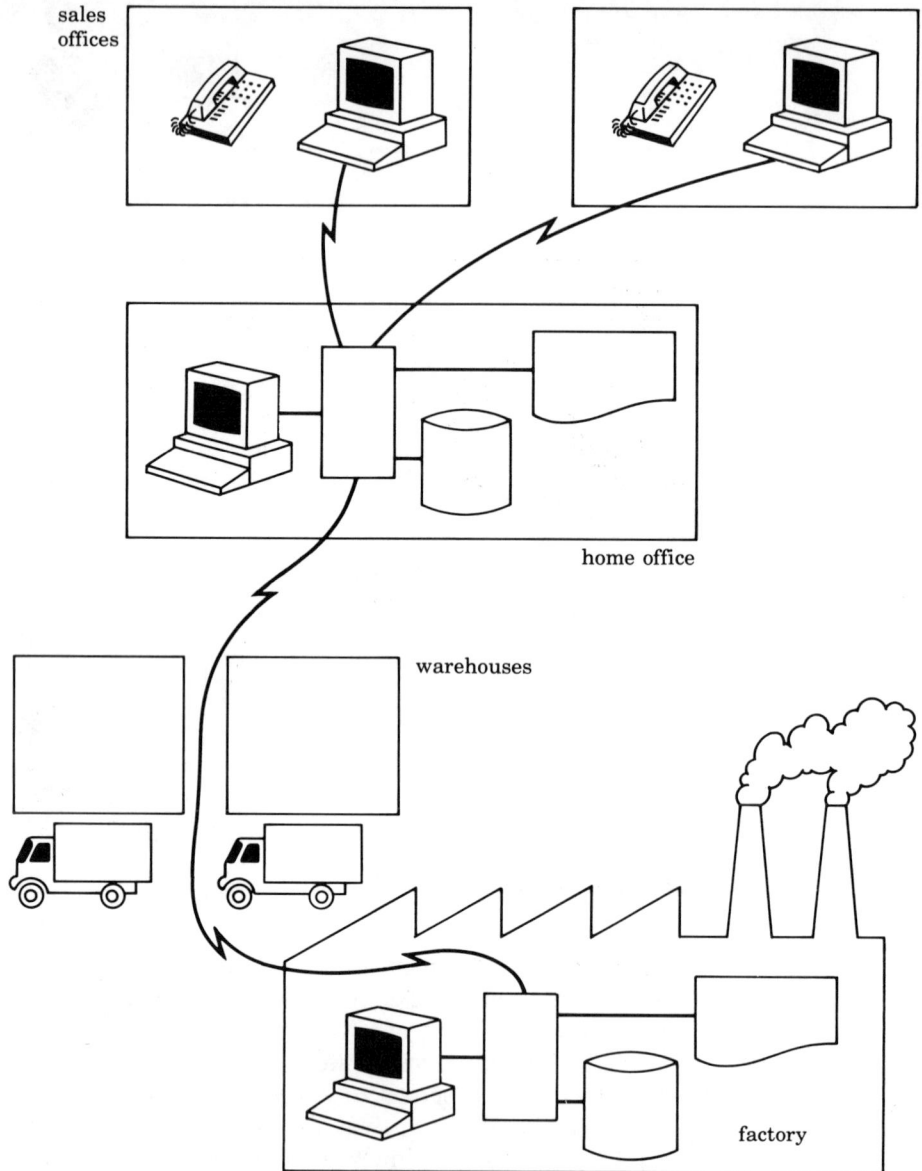

FIGURE 10.3 A large company on-line order entry system

In a local area network, communication among many of the devices might be important, as in the office system of Figure 10.6. A broadcast approach might be better than a fully interconnected point-to-point network, depending on the number and location of devices as well as on the projected growth patterns.

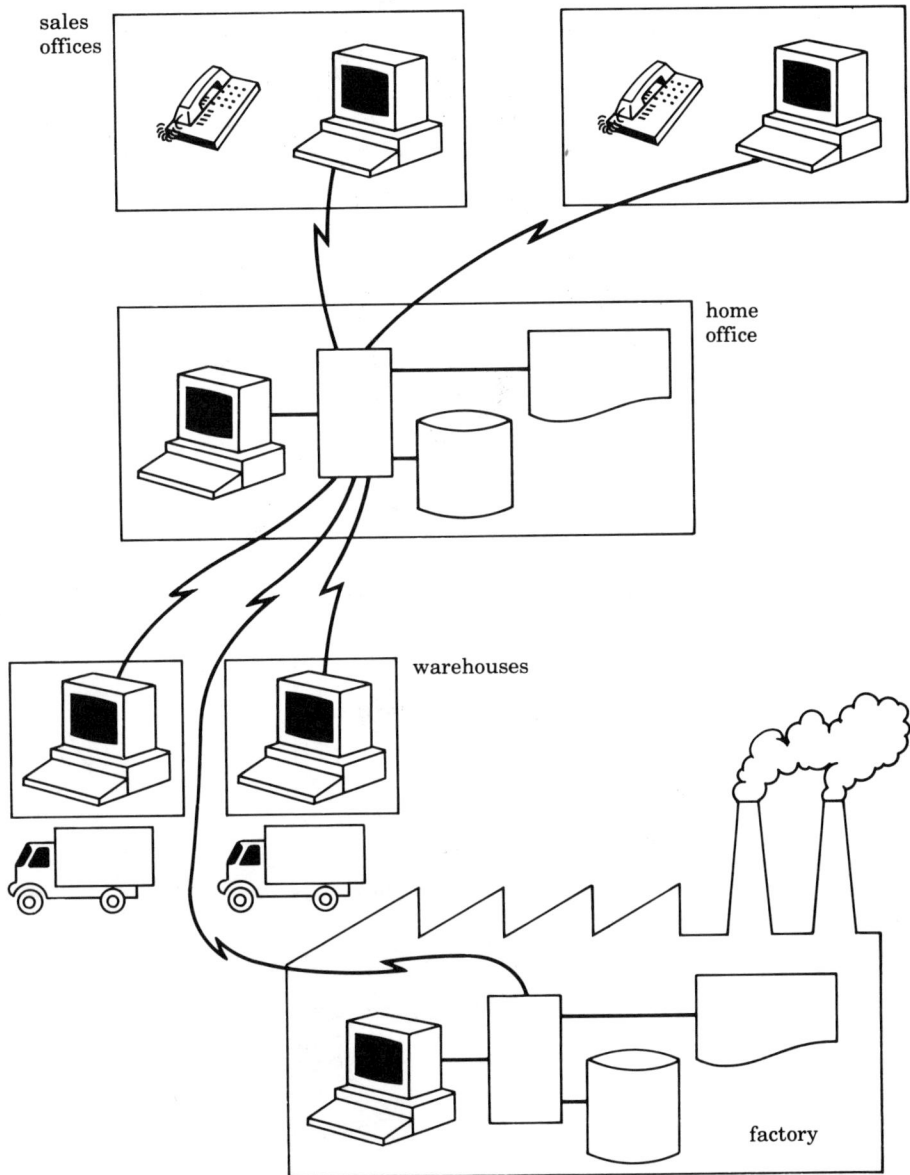

FIGURE 10.4 More connections for on-line order entry

Another desirable communication system objective may be *simultaneity,* either real or apparent. A single time-sharing host gives the illusion of simultaneous processing to numerous terminal users, for example, by switching among them quickly enough that no single user notices any delay. A communication network could give simultaneous operation to multiple users

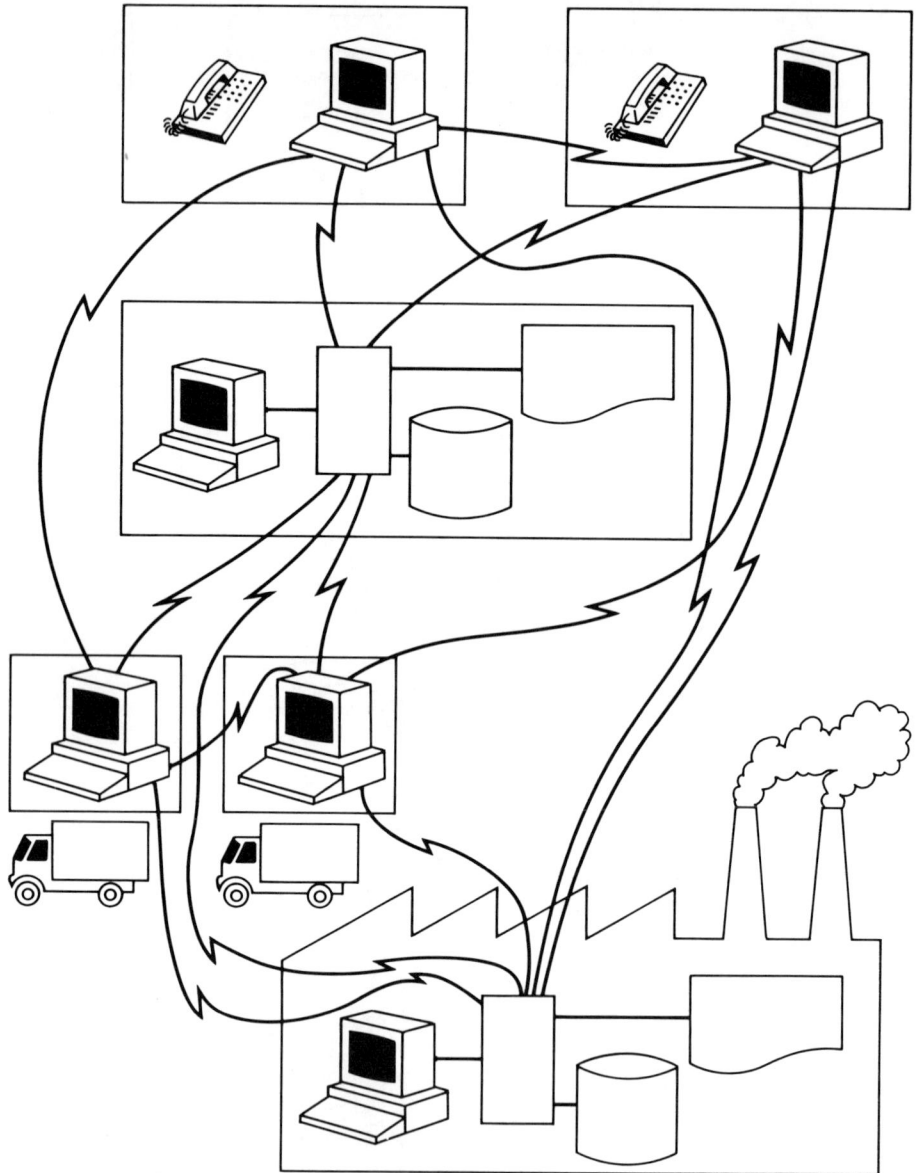

FIGURE 10.5 Interconnected order management system

by directing their traffic to a second server (such as a printer or a host computer) that was not currently busy (Figure 10.7). In our simple order entry system, this could mean connecting multiple terminals in each warehouse for printing shipping orders, or giving each warehouse its own processor for inventory management.

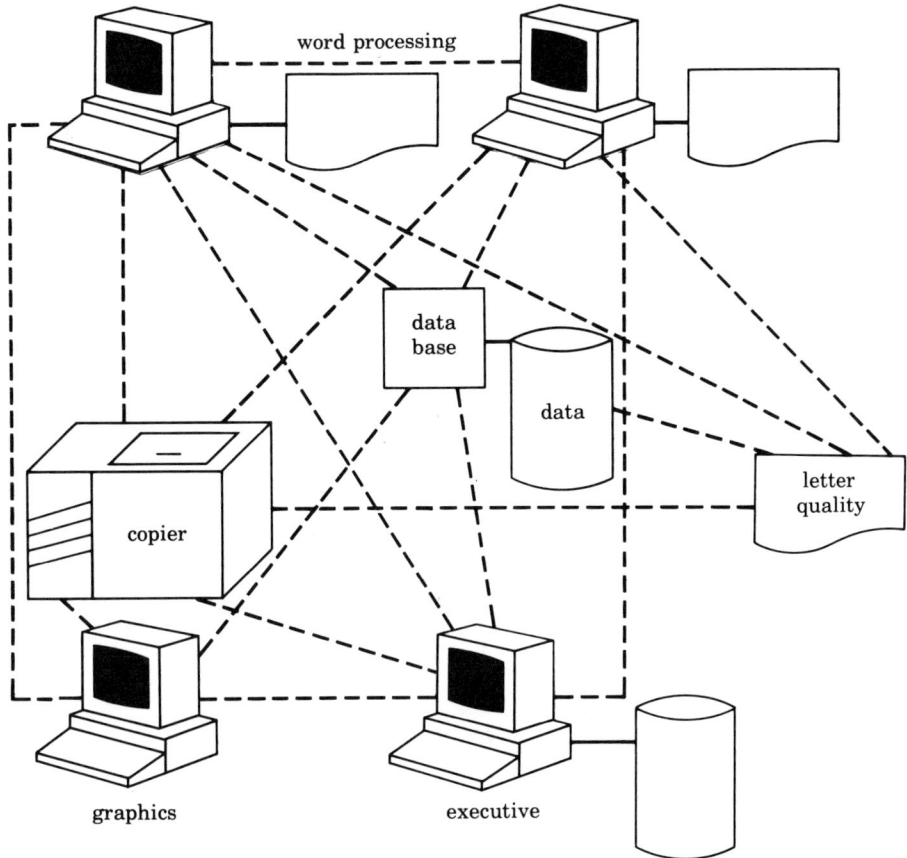

FIGURE 10.6 Desired communication flow in an office system

Performance

Once we establish the components and connections required to *do* a job effectively, we can consider how *well* they do it. Such performance objectives are often qualitative, but analysis is easier if they are quantitative. Specific values and tolerances should be developed whenever possible and justified according to individual application requirements.

One of the most common performance objectives is **response time,** which should be considered in two parts: the reaction time of the system to a request, and its completion time. The reaction time should be reasonably short and, ideally, uniform throughout the system to prevent user frustration. The interval to completion depends on the complexity of the activity and how busy the resources are. Consequently, specification of a short response time has a significant impact on the type and amount of equipment

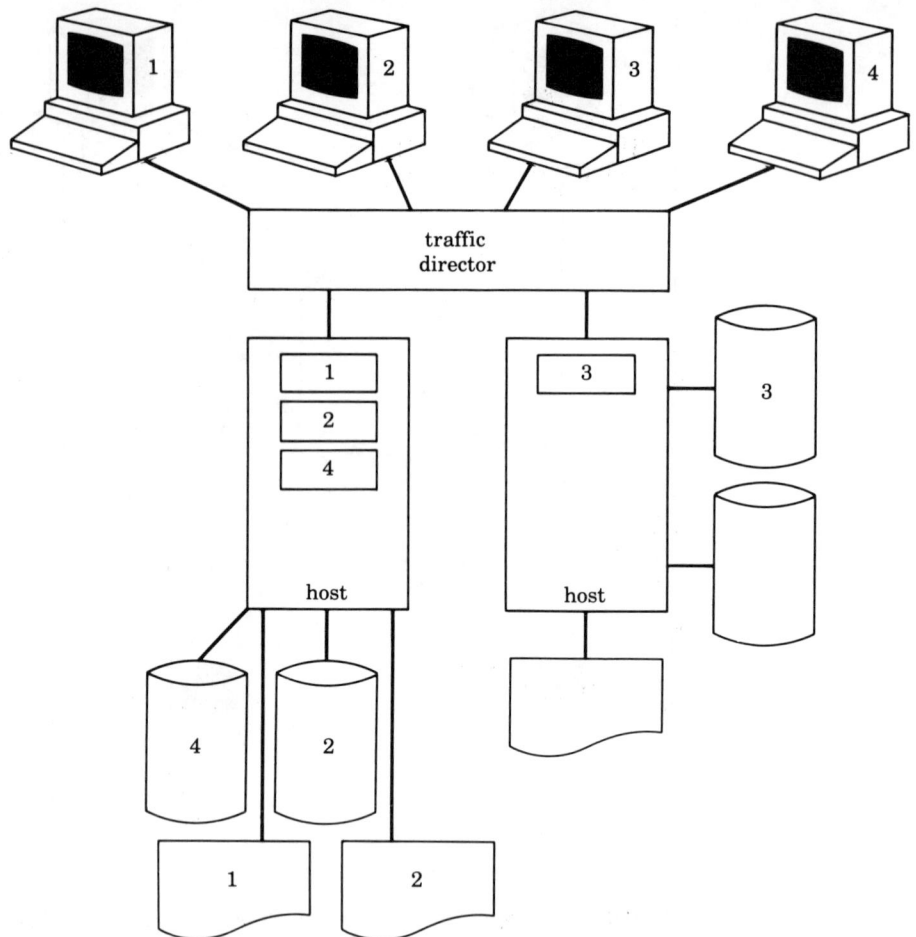

FIGURE 10.7 Multiple resource usage for improved simultaneity

selected. Typically, multiple resources tend to reduce the interval to completion at the expense of more complex coordination requirements.

In the sales order entry system, for example, a response time of a few seconds might seem reasonable. In breaking this down, however, we would probably want the system to react quickly (in less than one-half second, perhaps), but complete verification and placement, or processing, of the order could take even five to ten seconds while the clerk exchanged pleasantries with the customer. Where response times are not critical, they are often specified probabilistically: two seconds or less 50 per cent of the time, or less than three seconds 75 per cent of the time. Where response time is critical, in medical or military systems for example, it may dictate the entire system design. In these cases, it is especially important to distinguish between the communication (usually the reaction) and computational (the processing) responsibilities in meeting the response time requirements.

Another important performance objective is **availability** of the resources when work is requested. First, the components must be operating, and second, they must not be too busy. Availability has a direct impact on response time: busy resources will at least prolong the completion interval and extend the response time; failed ones may make completion indefinite, if not impossible.

As with response time, availability requirements vary greatly according to the application context. Banks that transfer millions of dollars a day cannot tolerate an unavailable system. If operations are not timely, their customers will go elsewhere! A small business, on the other hand, may not be able to justify the cost of a highly available system. In this case, it may be more cost-effective for resource-consuming operations (such as inventory updates or sales reports to the home office) to be held off until evening so that resources are available to applications that must run during business hours (such as order entry and verification).

An issue closely related to availability is **reliability:** can we depend on the resources to operate correctly, and recover if something fails. Transmission links are sometimes specified by their maximum expected error rates, for example. Hardware manufacturers usually characterize reliability by how long the equipment can be expected to work (mean time between failures, **MTBF**) and how long it will take to fix it (mean time to repair, **MTTR**). During repairs, of course, the specific resource will be unavailable. Often a network of resources is no more reliable than its least reliable component, although redundant elements may be incorporated to ensure availability through back-up or alternates. If we consider the probability that a desired combination of resources will be working properly, we see that the aggregate can be less reliable than the individual parts (Figure 10.8). In practice, evaluating the reliability of a system is complicated by a lack of accurate component data. State-of-the-art components inherently have no history of operation on which to base MTBF information. Manufacturers tend to give estimates based on experience with other equipment, but these should not necessarily be treated with confidence.

To a large extent, the degree to which a system is available and reliable depends on what the owning organization is willing to pay. This is clearly the case when redundant hardware and coordinating software are included in a system. For availability, the system must be able to detect and remove a failed component (either hardware or software), substitute a working one, and then shift the traffic to take advantage of the alternate. For reliability, more money is often paid for components with internal redundancy and diagnostics or with alarm notification and back-up capabilities. Uniformity of approach throughout the system should be examined carefully, however,

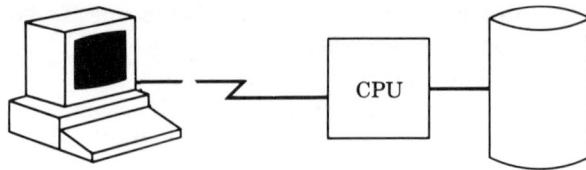

—individual probability that resource
will work properly:

terminal	96%
link	90%
CPU	99%
disk	94%

—aggregate probability = product of
component probabilities

$$.96* .90* .99* .94 = .80$$

probability that system will work
properly is thus 80%

—even if all components are 99%
reliable, the aggregate is only
$(.99)^4 \rightarrow 96\%$

FIGURE 10.8 Reliability of a system based on component reliabilities

to prevent needless expense. For example, a network with only single access links to a particular service office may not be able to take advantage of the greater reliability offered by multiple intermediate transmission links (Figure 10.9).

The influence of cost on availability and reliability is also evident in typical maintenance contract arrangements where the cost is a function of

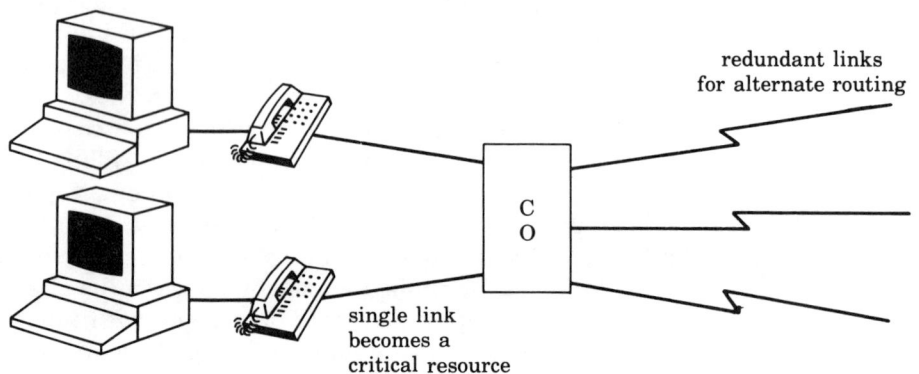

redundant links
for alternate routing

single link
becomes a
critical resource

FIGURE 10.9 Non-uniform redundancy may give non-uniform reliability

the level of service. If down-time is costly enough (business cannot be conducted during the failure), expensive service arrangements are justified. These may be specified in terms of the maximum time it will take for a repair technician to arrive. On-site personnel may be specified to ensure quick reaction if the service organization does not have a large local force. Availability of spares and procedures for problem-solving escalation may also be specified in a maintenance agreement. For example, the local technician might be given one hour to find the cause of a problem. After that, a higher level of expertise must be available (e.g., a regional service representative). If that person cannot solve the problem within another two hours, assistance from the national service group might be required, and so on, perhaps as far as involving the design engineers. Both the level of expertise required and the specified timeframe will contribute to the cost of a maintenance contract.

In comparison with hardware, software reliability is even more difficult to characterize. We seldom think of programs "breaking" or of data "wearing out" the way that hardware can. However, complex software is almost never exhaustively tested or proven to operate correctly. Consequently, there is always some probability that unforeseen situations will arise or error conditions will be encountered that cause a program to do something inappropriate or fail altogether. It is then necessary to fix the program and also to recover from the results of the wrong or incomplete activity.

Recovery in general is a difficult problem. Detection of the failure must first be possible, such as noticing that a particular device fails to respond or that the result of a data manipulation is not sensible. Some types of fault-detection that can be built into hardware include control signals to ensure proper event flow (no data are transmitted unless the data terminal ready signal is on, for example); timeouts, which tacitly assume that correctly operating devices will always be able to respond within a set time limit; and redundancy that is checked by comparison logic for identical results. Software can be built to include such features as checks on manually entered batch totals or independent modules that do computations for comparing results. In any case, it is difficult to establish confidence (much less a numeric probability) that all possible error and failure conditions have been anticipated.

Once a failure has been detected, recovery is still difficult. Any errors and ill effects must be corrected and cleaned up. Failures that occur in the middle of an activity present the most difficult recovery problems. If a payroll program fails after some of the checks have been printed, it should have a restart mechanism without printing duplicate checks. A virtual circuit severed in the midst of a session should have some way to determine where the conversation left off in order to begin again. If it is not possible to pick up the flow of activity from where it left off, then there must be a way to undo the portion that was begun, such as voiding the paychecks written so that the checkbook balance is restored properly before restarting. Sometimes this can be done by backing up to a previously known correct state; other times it is necessary to keep a record of all operations so that their effects can be reversed one by one. Automatic recovery is preferable, but procedures should always be available for manual recovery. At the very least, some network authority should be notified of failures and apprised of corrective actions.

Constraints

In Chapter 8 we suggested that the most successful systems support their organizations by mirroring the organizational structure and objectives. Consequently, organizational geography and application requirements will have a large effect on any data communication system design. For example, the topology will be constrained by the configuration of nodes and links required. In our order entry system of Figure 10.5, the geography (locations and separations) of the factory, warehouses, home and regional offices has as much impact on the selection of links as does the placement of the processors in the home office and the factory. Large distances are not usually handled with rings, for example; tree or interconnected topologies are preferred for their shorter transmission delay times.

Data must also be gathered about the flow and amount of traffic expected throughout the network so that a selection for overall topology will make sense. Then, consideration of traffic patterns, such as peak times or loads, can be added to response time requirements to determine transmission speeds for links, the adequacy of processors and peripherals, and whether extra equipment is needed to ensure resource availability. It is unlikely that consideration of such a variety of factors would progress sequentially. Design development is most often an iterative process involving specification refinements as their interactive effects are discovered.

One of the most difficult factors to specify accurately about any system is expected growth. The very success of a system seems to stimulate additional users, new applications, or requests for new, more, or different capabilities and resources. Underestimating the growth potential means the system runs out of capacity or capability too soon; overestimating usually means inappropriate (from an organizational point of view) allocation of funds. Deliberately making the system big enough to handle growth projections also increases maintenance costs—unused parts still have to be exercised and kept up to date. In fact, by the time the system's growth actually requires excess capacity, those components could even be inferior to newer models, or worse yet, obsolete. Designers must always be aware of the total life cycle of a system (Figure 10.10) when presenting a plan to management, and ensure that constraints and assumptions are clearly stated. Otherwise, assessments of the cost-effectiveness of building a particular system may be misleading or inaccurate.

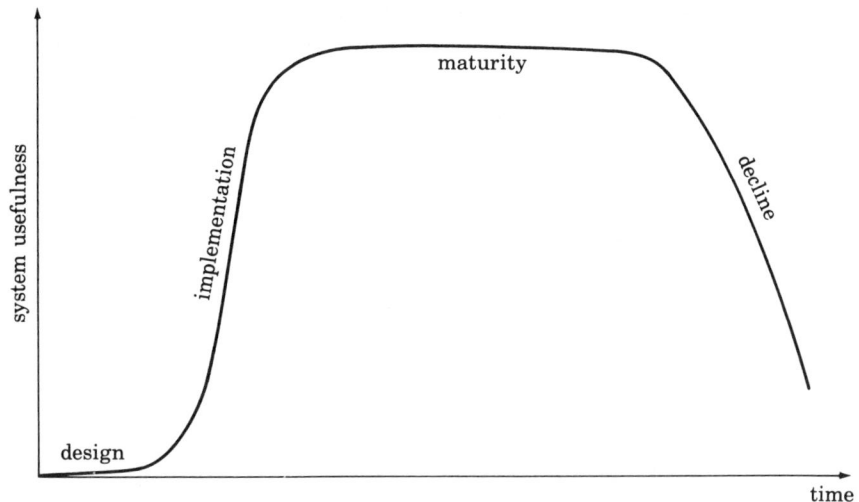

FIGURE 10.10 Stages in the life cycle of a system

SUBNET DESIGN

Communication systems are often designed with an outside-in approach that starts at the top with the application layer and at the bottom with the physical device requirements, and then proceeds from both ends toward the middle. The application can have a significant influence on the hardware devices required at the various nodes. The physical characteristics and organizational geography influence linking decisions, and then the network and transport layers are determined from the desired service and management characteristics.

Physical Level

Near-universal acceptance of RS-232-C as the standard specification for physical level interconnection often limits our concerns over hardware. Devices that adhere to the standard will simply have to be checked for compatibility among the individual circuits and subsets. Organizational goals should also be checked for possible hardware impact or support requirements. If a host computer, for example, can effect a highly desirable automatic disconnect when DTR (data terminal ready) is dropped, all terminal wiring should include that signal on the proper pin.

Specification of the types of devices in the network is usually followed by consideration of an appropriate transmission medium. For transmission facilities to be acquired from a common carrier, the class of service, error rates, signal levels, and noise tolerances should be specified. For facilities to be installed locally or on-site, the primary criteria are the available paths and likely interference. Indoors, for example, electrical and building codes, proximity to power cabling or electrical machinery noise, and availability of cable trays behind dropped ceilings can be important. Outdoors between buildings, consideration is likely to include underground versus aerial paths, potential for interference with or from neighbors, possibilities of damage from lightning, and biological side effects of electromagnetic radiation. Electrical requirements of the medium, such as grounding or shielding, are as important as the propagation characteristics. The final physical concern is over appropriate interfacing of the devices with the medium; that is, the required signal conversion.

Data Link Level

The primary consideration in linking the node or device locations is the information flow needed to support organizational requirements. In fact, this is where flow and geography combine into a first suggestion for topology. The types of devices determine the prevalence of asynchronous or synchronous transmission. The data link framing approach can be chosen on that basis also, or according to the support requirements of a particular vendor's products. Now that a number of data link protocols have been implemented in chips rather than in software, the choices are well defined and the tradeoffs depend largely on the vendor.

A cost issue that is not always obvious is the trade-off between quality of the transmission link (higher quality service costs more) and effective use of the data link error control mechanisms (refer to Chapter 5). It may be more appropriate in certain applications to trade occasionally lower throughput due to error correction against the overall lower cost of lower-quality transmission link service.

Network Level

The first decision at the network level is whether to use point-to-point or multipoint links. Store-and-forward techniques are necessary in all point-to-point configurations except fully interconnected ones, and link sharing requires multiplexers or concentration. Multipoint configurations must choose a link-sharing discipline from the polling and contention variations. Hybrid networks having both point-to-point and multipoint links must have nodes sophisticated enough to handle the differences between incoming and outgoing links.

A major concern in store-and-forward networks is routing. Incoming traffic must be examined and sent out on an appropriate link according to its destination address. Each node usually contains a table or directory that specifies what links are to be used for what destinations. **Fixed routing** puts all traffic for a given destination on a single specified link. An unavailable node or a broken link means traffic cannot flow and must be stored or rejected. If the network could discover or be informed of lost nodes and links, the tables could be updated so alternative links would be selected. This is called **adaptive routing.** A more sophisticated approach also uses traffic information to minimize congestion.

In multipoint networks, a sharing discipline must be chosen rather than a routing algorithm. Polling can be centralized or distributed (token passing); contention choices range from Aloha through CSMA/CD. Selection depends on some combination of end-to-end propagation delays, whether the medium supports broadcast, expected channel loading, and any preference for bounding the time waited for access.

Both point-to-point and multipoint networks are concerned with flow control so that incoming traffic won't overflow the receiving buffer space. Selection of buffer sizes is a major responsibility for network designers: too small means extra delays or lost traffic, too large means wasted resources.

Design Tools

Several techniques and tools have been developed to deal with the complexity of design choices for communication subnets. Circuit analysis verifies signal levels and component selections at the physical level, especially for coaxial cable networks. Graph theory has contributed greatly to techniques for construction of routing tables. Path costs, delay times, or other criteria can be minimized under certain types of constraints. Statistical analysis has been used extensively to predict traffic flow and congestion for particular network configurations and sharing disciplines. Most techniques are being automated in computer programs using sophisticated modeling and simulation approaches and numerical solutions. This is especially useful for examining the effects of small changes in parameters.

Most of the design tools available are oriented towards wide-area voice networks using public and private telephone links. Unfortunately, voice and data networks differ significantly in a number of important design criteria, including length of calls, transmission speed required, tolerance for errors due to noise, and response times (did you ever notice how distracting the delay due to a satellite link is on a telephone conversation?). Thus, tools designed primarily for voice do not usually work well for data networks. Even the tools developed for data are often limited to only one of the following network types, making comparison of alternatives very costly: private lines, multipoint private lines, concentration and backbones, or packet-switching.

Much of the effectiveness of these telephone network design tools depends on a built-in database of tariff information. Since divestiture, such data has changed rapidly, both in terms of available carriers and actual costs. Not all tools are easily kept up to date in this respect. Usually an update service is purchased or a significant investment in clerical time must be made to keep the information accurate. Selection of a tool to serve a particular organization requires far more detail and attention than has been given here.

NETWORK MANAGEMENT

Once the configuration and disciplines of the subnet are selected, the designer's attention usually turns back to the system's initial objectives. Devices can be selected for the nodes that, in conjunction with the subnet connections, will provide the capabilities and performance specified. Appropriate levels of fault tolerance can be created with redundant links and devices, and the back-up and recovery procedures can be specified. Operational and maintenance requirements can be identified and support staffing plans formulated.

The next important aspect of the design is planning the support necessary for the ongoing evaluation of the network once it is implemented. This may mean including devices to monitor traffic, measure delays, record and analyze the data, and present statistical reports. Such devices not only provide the means of determining whether the original performance objectives are being met, but become the basic tools for a manager to use in adjusting network parameters to improve performance. Increasing effort is being put into automation of these management tasks and some network vendors already offer products called network control centers (**NCCs**).

HIGHER LEVEL DESIGN

Standardization at the higher levels of the OSI model is new enough that the choices available to a communication system designer are not so well defined as within the subnet layers. In fact, the design emphasis shifts entirely from the communication processing to the data processing needs of the application. Where there is higher level support available, it is usually specific to the products of particular vendors, such as in SNA through CICS or in DECnet, and often requires the services of a product specialist. A notable exception to this general rule is the Manufacturing Automation Protocols, whose development is being fostered largely by General Motors (see Chapter 12).

CHAPTER REVIEW

Capsule

Once the problems to be solved by a new system have been identified, goals and specific communication objectives can be established. These include capabilities for resource sharing, connectivity, and simultaneity; performance criteria for response time, availability, reliability, and recovery features; and recognition of constraints imposed by geography, traffic, and growth expectations. Design of the communication subnet begins with ensuring physical compatibility among the devices, transmission medium, and required interfaces. Selection of appropriate link sharing techniques depends on the availability of hardware and software; network modeling and analysis programs are often used to assist in this part of the design process. Network maintenance and management has a large impact at this level as well. Finally, applications software is specified or built on top of the entire underlying design.

Project

Find a real example of a fairly large data communication system. Document the design history and analyze its current performance (this may have to be second-hand or creatively theoretical). Articulate the objectives for expansion or re-design of the network. Design the new network, carefully stating your assumptions and including annotated iterations in your report. Recording the design process steps is a useful learning technique. Prepare a written design recommendation as you would present it to the management group owning the network.

NEW TERMS

adaptive routing   NCC
availability   recovery
fixed routing   reliability
MTBF   response time
MTTR

QUESTIONS

1. Describe a major communications problem currently being experienced with a data processing system (not necessarily computerized) in your school or office. What would be the important organizational goals of any improvements? Translate these into sample system objectives.
2. Talk to a local business that has a computerized system that depends on data communications to support its applications. What backup equipment and procedures are built into the system? What failures have occurred and were the recovery techniques considered adequate?
3. Design a star network for the office system of Figure 10.6. What type of device would be at the center of the star? What patterns of flow and amounts of traffic would need to be supported? What other criteria would be important in selecting an appropriate device? Find a product advertisement for a suitable device.

11 Security and Privacy

CONTEXT

Think about what privacy means to you. Most of us have some data, some statements or opinions or facts about ourselves we would prefer not to reveal to others. Our ability to keep that data from being released is what we call privacy. Historically, the amount of data about individuals and organizations available to the general public was rather limited. Birth records, incorporation papers, and property transactions could be examined by anyone, but only with some expenditure of effort such as going to the data storage locations and retrieving the records. Other than those few public records, we were usually in control of what data were released, and to whom.

In the last fifty years, the situation has changed dramatically. More paperwork has been created to support our personal and business interactions, paper records that are filed away to become a permanent part of our business relationships. These records can be thought of as data beyond our individual control. In fact, legal precedents have established record-keeping organizations as the owners of their records, providing little protection for the subjects of those records. For the most part, we have been willing to give out a certain amount of data to facilitate receipt of goods or services (health insurance, credit cards, business loans, for example). We exchange privacy for convenience.

In the last twenty years, increasing use of computers to store, organize, and retrieve data on demand has raised new concerns. The lack of individual control and the minimal protection against misuses of data have been little

199

recognized except by victims of abuse. The use of data communications to interconnect such computerized storage systems and provide wide accessibility to the data has also increased considerably. Have you thought about what this means?

We live in an information-based society. Organizations and individuals depend more and more on the data available with which to make decisions and conduct business. Computers and communications have allowed more organizations to collect more data about more people than ever before. More decisions are being made on the basis of such records instead of on personal interactions than ever before. In fact, it would be difficult for most businesses to operate effectively now in any other way. Information has become an important means to power in our society. Of course, the information itself is not powerful, but the ability to get and use it can be. Computers and communications have contributed tremendously to making data more accessible and more available, increasing the potential for abuse.

What all this means to development of communications-based information systems depends largely on the organizational environment and the purposes a particular system is designed to serve. **Privacy** is the right of an individual to protection from damage due to inaccurate or inappropriately released data; it is the job of **security** to provide that protection within the information system. In the larger context, legal and social controls would also be needed to complete the protection picture.

SECURITY

There are four capabilities required to provide security in an information system:

- minimize the probability of compromise or intrusion
- minimize the extent of loss or damage
- detect any breaches as soon as possible
- return to a previous state (preferably, one known to be valid).

As an introduction, we focus mostly on the first of these as the primary means of protection.

Physical

Physical security of the on-site hardware components in a data communication system is relatively straightforward. They may be placed in supervised rooms equipped with special fire prevention and extinguishing systems. Environmental protection systems can be installed to maintain appropriate levels of temperature and humidity, provide properly conditioned electrical power, and minimize potential damage from natural disasters such as lightning, windstorm, or flood. Backup equipment can be installed or stored separately so that concurrent damage is unlikely. The extent of this type of protection often depends on management recognition of the tradeoffs between cost of equipment and loss of capability.

Protection from malicious personnel can be accomplished through restricting access, first to the facility or room itself, and then to the individual piece of equipment. Locks may be used that require keys carried by, known to, or inherent to particular authorized personnel, such as magnetic cards, combinations, or voice prints, respectively. Careful screening and limiting total access of individuals is also desirable. Checks and balances, such as dual signatures and access logs are recommended.

The transmission medium is the most difficult hardware component to protect physically. Even on-site media are susceptible to damage from problems with co-located equipment such as electrical power distribution wiring, water or heating systems, and telephone cabling. Physical protection for every inch of wire, cable, or other transmission path is generally not possible, much less feasible from a cost perspective. Even prevention of ineptitude or malice committed by maintenance personnel can be a physical security problem. Separate ducting for data transmission links is a partial solution, but is often not practical or within budget restrictions.

Protection of the transmission process presents as big a problem as the medium, especially when the media are not privately owned, installed, and maintained. Wires can be tapped, radio transmissions intercepted, and radiation leakage detected so that signals are available to unauthorized people. Similar techniques can also be used to inject spurious signals or jam transmission channels. Currently, private optical fiber systems are the only media reasonably safe from such compromise or interference.

Logical

In addition to physical protection of the hardware, it is highly desirable to have logical security built into the software of data communication systems. User authorizations can limit access to hardware, software, or data, depending on the sophistication of the software resources. This is a type of "need-to-know" restriction that is typical in security-conscious organizations. Again, cost of the protection is usually weighed carefully against the benefits expected. The general approach is to make the cost of obtaining unauthorized access far greater than its value to the thief, at a price the protector is willing to pay.

Authorization begins with establishing the *identity* of the user. Most systems handle this through a log-in procedure, with account numbers or names checked for validity against an internal list. The detailed requirements of the log-in procedure itself discourage casual penetrators, at the expense of nuisance for regular users. *Authentication* requires entry of some data supposedly known only to the "real" user. The most common mechanism is the password, and anyone who has used them knows that passwords are generally not very secure because people use easily remembered values or write them down in places accessible to penetrators. More sophisticated approaches can be developed that would construct queries based on a stored user profile, but few systems have been willing to pay either the developmental or operational costs.

Authentication can also be applied to individual communication messages, and is especially appropriate for transaction-processing applications. This technique usually combines the values of certain message data fields into a result that can be appended to the message in much the same way as the transmission checksums discussed for the data link layer in Chapter 5. The destination repeats the combination process on the received data fields and compares the result to the received authentication field. A match provides assurance that the message fields have not been altered.

Procedural Security

Some of the mechanisms for physical protection against unauthorized access are actually security procedures. These include restriction of access, maintenance of logs and escorts when entry is granted to unauthorized personnel, and dual signatures. It is equally important to protect software and data from potential damage. The most familiar physical procedures deal with back-up techniques; the logical ones usually amount to establishing audit trails. Because damage prevention is extremely difficult, procedures tend to be developed that will promote **recovery,** or return to a previous state of the system known to be logically consistent and accurate.

Back-up procedures usually consist of *checkpoints,* that is, copying software and data when they are known to be accurate and have integrity. These copies are set aside in a protected location and maintained as an archive for both historical and recovery purposes. Between copies, an audit trail is maintained so that if a return to a previous copy is required, recent transactions can be examined for validity and applied to re-create a current state for the system.

Sometimes the most difficult security problem is discovering damage so that a timely recovery can be made. Hardware problems are often easier to detect: disk crashes, broken transmission links, failed interfaces, and others usually have recognizable symptoms. Compromised data or altered programs can be nearly impossible to detect. This emphasizes the need for a combination approach to protection which includes access controls, authorizations, and historical records.

Encryption

A different approach to protection is to disguise transmissions so the cost (in dollars or in time) of recovering useful data from them exceeds their potential value. The process of changing data from its natural or *plaintext* form into an unrecognizable or *ciphertext* form is called **encryption.** The reverse process to recover the original data is called **decryption.** Because of a long-

alphabet	ABCDEFGHIJKLMNOPQRSTUVWXYZ
key	PQRSTUVWXYZABCDEFGHIJKLMNO

plaintext	THE FREQUENCY AND PATTERNS HELP
ciphertext	IWT UGTFJTCRN PCS EPIITGCH WTAE

Figure 11.1 A simple substitution cipher

standing military interest in ciphers, a significant body of work exists on coding theory and techniques for ciphering.* Those techniques have been applied to computers for some time; application of the techniques to computer communications is relatively new.

The simplest type of encryption is a *substitution* cipher. Plaintext symbols are replaced one by one with prearranged substitute symbols. This is the way common crossword puzzles called cryptograms are done. Each letter has a particular code substitute to replace it in the encrypted message, as in Figure 11.1. For messages with any length, computer analysis makes it fairly easy to crack simple substitution codes by analyzing the frequency and distribution patterns of the letters. Greater security can be obtained by using a number of substitution alphabets in a prearranged sequence. Since both the sender and receiver must know the entire set of substitutions for every code, maintaining secret key distributions for frequent code changes is a major problem.

Transposition is another simple ciphering approach. It operates on a whole group, or block, of symbols at once by rearranging the position of the individual symbols within the group, as in Figure 11.2. Both the block length and the key must be discovered to crack this type of code.

Neither substitution nor transposition alone is considered adequate for most data communication applications. However, they may be iterated or combined in ways called *product ciphers* that will provide good security

---

* see for example, the special issue on cryptology of *ACM Computing Surveys,* December 1979.

block length: 4   key: 3241

plaintext	SHORT MESSAGES DO NOT SCRAMBLE WELL
blocked	SHOR TMES SAGE SDON OTSC RAMB LEWE LLXX
transposed	OHRS EMST GAES ODNS STCO MABR WEEL XLXL
sent	OHRSEMSTGAESODNSSTCOMABRWEELXLXL

Figure 11.2. A simple transposition cipher

algorithm:	S1 T1 S1
alphabet:	ABCDEFGHIJKLMNOPQRSTUVWXYZ
S1 key:	UVWXYZABCDEFGHIJKLMNOPQRST
T1:	block length = 4 key = 3241
plaintext:	THIS TYPE IS MUCH MORE DIFFICULT
apply S1:	NBCM NSJY CM GOWB GILY XCZZCWOFN
block T1:	NBCM NSJY CMGO WBGI LYXC ZZCW OFNX
apply T1:	CBMNJSYNGMOCGBIWXYCLCZWZNFXO
apply S1:	WVGHDMSHAGIWAVCQRSWFWTQTHZRI

Figure 11.3 A simple product cipher

(Figure 11.3). These more sophisticated transformations require discovery of both the keys and the algorithm.

The Data Encryption Standard (DES) adopted by the National Bureau of Standards is a product cipher that uses 64-bit blocks and 56-bit keys in a complicated scheme of iterated transformation. Extensive analysis was undertaken to demonstrate that the time it would take to use even computers to break the cipher would exceed any data value. More recently, however, short-cut techniques have been developed that indicate longer keys and more iterations might be desirable.

A different approach from DES gaining in popularity uses two different transformation processes, one for encoding and the other for decoding the data. As long as the decrypting technique could not be determined from the encrypting one, the encryption scheme could be made available through a public key library. Only authorized recipients would be able to *decode* messages using their private decryption schemes. This "public key" approach to cryptography (Figure 11.4) eliminates key distribution problems and can be expanded to provide sender authentication as well.

Hardware

Networks incorporating dial-up lines for terminal-to-host connections often use port-protection devices at the host computer. These require that a caller enter a user access code either from the terminal or via the touch-tone pad of the telephone. Some even camouflage the modem carrier signal so that it is not obvious to random callers that the line accesses a computer. Such devices vary in the number of ports or lines protected, the number of user access codes supported, inclusion of call-back capability, and audit trial provisions. For users who can only call from fixed off-site locations, call-back

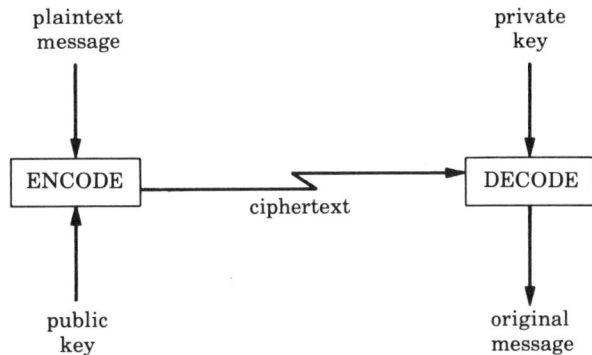

FIGURE 11.4 Public key encryption

is a good protection mechanism. After accepting the user's authorization data, the device breaks the telephone connection and then places a return call to a telephone number listed internally for that user. On answering the return call, the user receives carrier and host connection. Typical port device costs range from about $200 to $1000 per port or line.

Data encryption devices are another useful hardware approach to security. They can be put at the ends of most kinds of communication links because they are usually placed between the communication source or target and the actual transmission device (e.g., between the computer and the modem). This approach removes the software burden of host computation to do the encryption or decryption and also provides protection of protocol headers (including address information) as well as data across the link. Introduction of spurious traffic reduces to a noise problem because improperly coded packets would almost certainly turn into garbage during the decryption process. Such protection also works for terminal devices that are too "dumb" to do their own encryption.

Packet Switching Networks

There are certain inherent aspects of large packet switching networks that tend to counteract their transmission vulnerabilities. The breaking of messages into smaller packets means that most of the packets for a given message would have to be collected to reconstruct the message. If the packets are independently routed through the network across a variety of links, then many listening or tap points would have to be created to glean a particular message from the network. The more taps there are, presumably the higher the probability for detection would be. Every packet header would have to be processed by the penetrator to select the right ones for transmission to a message reconstruction facility. Costs should outweigh potential values in most cases like this. Introduction of spurious packets through penetration taps is much more difficult to prevent. Network management facilities should track and report potential problem areas such as duplicate packets and unusual network flooding or congestion occurrences.

Distribution of resources in a network configuration can actually promote security by partitioning the vulnerability. Data and programs can be placed in locations of most likely use, with only limited remote access allowed. If a site is penetrated, only a portion of the system is compromised. Alternatively, if loss of capability is the more serious concern, copies of hardware, software, or data can be managed so that the maximum degree of fault-tolerance is provided through redundancy. Organizational objectives must be carefully examined in each situation before an appropriate strategy of system security can be developed.

ISSUES

The primary purpose of this chapter has been to raise your awareness of some of the potential security problems and solutions of communication-based information systems. The key concepts are value and cost, both of which tend to be highly subjective evaluations, depending largely on environment or context. It is not information itself that is dangerous, but how people use or abuse it. Until more information systems professionals pay attention to the security concerns within the systems for which they are responsible, it is unlikely that the general public will pay attention. Certainly concerned professionals are needed to advise on the development of reasonable legal guidelines for protection of individual rights. At the same time, reducing the glamour and publicity which is sometimes awarded to youthful penetrators would also be appropriate. News interviews and television take-offs have done little thus far to encourage responsible, ethical computer user behavior. Without professional concern, there is apt to be little societal concern is general.

Another issue which will continue to develop through the 1980s is a consequence of the larger variety of communication services available for both home and business use. As cable systems grow beyond simple distribution of multiple television channels to encompass two-way and data services, it will become easier to focus on individuals as targets for surveillance activities. Billing information, use of particular services, and even detailed patterns of references to particular public data could be collected and analyzed on an individual basis through far simpler "wire-tap" procedures than ever before. Just as personal profiles can sometimes be established by examining individual records of credit card purchases, activities such as home banking and bill paying, access to public databases (such as Dow Jones, for example), or message exchanges through network bulletin boards over a single telephone or cable link can be monitored to provide extraordinary detail about an individual's activities. Societal awareness of the need for legal protection will be crucial to preventing massive abuse of such capabilities. Once again, individuals will have to consider the value to be gained from such services in light of the potential risks.

CHAPTER REVIEW

Capsule

Communication-based information systems and extensive computer networks are leading us to reexamine the roles and vulnerabilities of these systems in society. When we grant an individual the right to protection against misuse of personal data, we create a need for security mechanisms designed to provide that protection. Physical security usually amounts to restricting system access to authorized personnel only. Logical security checks must be used to identify users and verify their authorizations. Computerized information systems must also be protected from intentional or accidental damage to any components; this is usually handled with security procedures such as regular back-up for potential recovery purposes.

None of the security mechanisms which can be developed are totally useful, however, without recognition that it is people who abuse facilities and misuse data. Professional and general public awareness of the vulnerabilities of computerized information systems must increase to create an environment of societal and legal sanctions within which violations of security mechanisms and privacy practices can be punished. Personal and professional guidelines for ethical behavior must be developed through open, public discussion by all types of system builders and users.

Project

Retail credit cards often require telephoning an authorization center to verify sufficient credit for large purchases. Consider the possibility of setting up a system where an intelligent point-of-sale terminal could read the magnetic strip on an inserted card and automatically call for authorization. Discuss what types of protection would be required by law, would be desirable from the retailer's point of view, and might be desired by customers. How could the techniques and equipment covered in this chapter be applied to provide such protection?

NEW TERMS

authorization   privacy
decryption   recovery
encryption   security

QUESTIONS

1. What television shows or series have you seen lately that seem to glorify or sanction breaking into computer systems or networks through communication links?
2. What guidelines have been established for ethical use of computer facilities available to you? What sanctions can be applied to abusers?
3. Find out what a security kernel is. How does it fit into the scheme of physical, logical, and procedural protection discussed in this chapter?
4. What can you as a concerned student of data communication systems contribute to enlarging the scope of professional and public awareness of the need for better system security?

12 Trends in Applications and Technology

CAVEAT EMPTOR

Soothsaying and prediction are always dangerous occupations. In a book, they pose extra peril because details are quickly outdated and miscalculations are so public. Despite the risks, however, even an introductory text would be incomplete without some guidelines on issues and trends in data communications for continuing study. Miscalculated predictions should not dampen curiosity for further exploration.

Out of the broad spectrum of potential application areas, the ones developing most rapidly are offices, general businesses, factories, and telephone companies. In technology, the areas to monitor are fiber optics, distributed systems, and the merging of computing and communications. Overall, we will see the impact of these developments through changes in the communication industry, and changes in the support environment for both information systems and individual workers.

OFFICE SYSTEMS

Context

What is the work of an office that requires communication system support? At first glance, it seems an answer would require knowing to whom the office belongs. Doctors, marketing managers, production supervisors, professors, and corporate presidents might seem to have different requirements. Yet if we look at the individual or underlying activities, the general categories of work that are typical of most offices include paper handling, telephone usage, and scheduling. All these papers, telephones, and schedules are mechanisms for communication of data in and about the office. Let's look at how data communications technology continues to be applied to office systems.

Paper is a very important element of an office's ability to do business. This includes drafting, typing, signing, sending, copying, filing, and so on. We are beginning to learn that we can replace paper with other types of representations. For example, automatic payroll deposit eliminates handling of a paper paycheck, but a record of deposit is necessary to maintain an accurate account balance. Office papers, records, and representations, are generically called **documents.** Since documents contain data, document preparation is a form of data processing. Communication requirements include distribution of documents to recipients, commonly called **electronic mail,** and transfers of documents among pieces of processing equipment, usually called **file transfer.**

Telephone communication requirements are well defined in most office environments to include calling, answering, and taking and leaving messages. Typically, such voice communication has been provided for and managed separately from data communication in the office. The two functions would interact only when significant amounts of data traffic were being handled by modems for telephone transmission. As PBX technology is adapted to serve both voice and data requirements, however, it is likely that voice processing and communication will be handled similarly to data processing and communication. In fact, integration of voice and data will give us enhanced communication mechanisms, such as voice-annotated memoranda or graphs. Documents may even incorporate special symbols to indicate the locations of accompanying voice commentary.

The scheduling activities in an office range from setting up or changing meetings, to establishing production schedules or delivery routes. These have always required inter-personal communication, and attempts to automate the activity and communication have often been frustrated by individual concerns for independence and privacy. People do not always want arbitrary blocks of time commandeered for meetings just because their schedules have not yet allocated that time. Nor do they necessarily want to schedule every detail of their work activities (e.g., thinking, writing, pacing) just to fill up the time. Here the communication problems can be solved rather easily, but the personnel issues cannot.

Hardware

The office-oriented devices we should consider include at least telephones, typewriters, workstations, copiers, printers, and electronic file "cabinets". For communication support, we must add network interfaces to each of these. Physical interconnection is the first concern. RS-232-C will probably continue to serve as a standard until serial speed requirements exceed 19.2 kbps asynchronous and synchronous. 64 kbps will require other standards. Parallel links will follow their own standard, such as the IEEE-488 General-Purpose Interface Bus, or the Centronics-type printer interface.

After physical interconnection, the next concern is network transmission and speed matching among devices with different requirements. Buffering and flow control can be handled by the devices themselves, or be incorporated into the network. When voice and data streams are merged by a common transmission system, the issues become duration and uniformity of delay. Circuit-switching techniques guarantee small and uniform delay for voice traffic, but generally do not offer speeds above 64 kbps for data transfer applications. Packet-switching systems today do not offer any distinction between voice and data packets that could be used to guarantee performance acceptable to voice users. Some PBX systems are beginning to offer common *access* for voice and data traffic, with separate *switching* to accommodate the different needs.

Software and Data

A common office system problem occurs at the data link level. Even if all the devices use the same codes for character representation (e.g., ASCII), no standards have been agreed to for control signals and their interpretation. This is particularly true for word processing equipment, where control characters are commonly used for page and other format purposes. Today's simple solution is to select compatible application and network equipment. In the future, CCITT and other standards will be available, and user pressure will force vendors to conform.

In general, the layered functions we have come to expect in communication software are provided for office system support in a variety of ways. The data link, network, and transport layers are usually part of the network interface, which may be a board inserted in the office equipment or a separately packaged device. Session, presentation, and application layer locations may vary among different types of devices. Some office equipment contains sufficient intelligence to do its own upper layers (e.g., a workstation has its own microprocessor(s), storage, and software); other devices require support from a network host computer or an intelligent interface device. Maintaining compatibility among all the different implementations will be a significant challenge for any office system integrator.

Applications Support

At the application level, data communication support of an integrated office system largely depends on the location and interaction requirements of the various software modules and the special devices. Word processing programs can be either local to an intelligent workstation, placed on a computer host for access by "dumb" typewriter-like devices, or some combination of the two, such as local editing and host storage. This variety of approaches is also typical of other programs. Spelling checks are made by running documents through programs which refer to a *dictionary*. If this is an organizational standard process, the document may have to be sent to a specific node containing the dictionary. Special printing devices and graphics support are usually centralized as well, again requiring document transmission.

Some of the more sophisticated office applications contribute most when they extend beyond the boundaries of a single office. Electronic mail is particularly useful for messages (eliminating "telephone tag", for example) and for distribution of internal documents among offices within an organization. Calendar management programs and automatic schedulers are also most useful when the people or activities to be coordinated are in more than one office.

Although various vendors offer application software for offices, little of it is designed to truly support the collection of different types of equipment and network protocols that are typical of most office installations. Upgrading such systems can involve replacement of existing equipment with specifically compatible devices unless extensive supporting communications expertise is available during the planning and implementation phases.

Depending on the actual work performed in an office, even more complex application-level software may be needed: database management for retrieval of filed data or documents, decision support systems for managers, or graphics for design engineers. These last two encompass capabilities that extend far beyond the typical office information system, and yet the ability to integrate such components with an office system may be important. The extent of the interactions among various devices and users, the willingness to provide intelligent network support for matching or translation of capabilities, and the flexibility of the architectural approach to the system all influence the feasibility of advanced office systems.

Procedures and Personnel

The major goal of an office system is usually to improve productivity. Better data communication will contribute most to improving the flow of information. In some cases, this will require procedural changes in order for office personnel to take advantage of the capabilities an information system represents. Few offices are yet willing to operate in a "paperless" mode, so the first step is to conveniently and reliably reduce the amount of paper handled. The ability, and perhaps more important, the willingness of the staff to adapt to and have confidence in such a different way of doing business will depend largely on accurate analysis of office activities, integration of equipment chosen to support those tasks, and involvement and training of the users. These are certainly not new requirements for a system design, but the communication aspects (paths and flow, and personal and electronic requirements) need increasing attention.

Other Areas of Impact

Much of our focus to this point has been on the clerical or somewhat mechanical activities typical of offices. Communication technology may also have significant impact on an office through **teleconferencing,** the use of television and other media to hold meetings among geographically dispersed people. This is not really a data communication concern, but could have impact on the choice of networking techniques. If a single communications support (hardware or cable) facility is desired for data, voice, and video transmission, then broadband transmission techniques are required. This expands our interest beyond the boundaries of a single office again, but in general, application growth will make the interfacing of internal office networks to larger systems increasingly desirable.

Another area of rising interest is the development of intelligent workstations customized for functions other than word processing, such as for "personal" computing or graphics. The communication requirements of these may be different from the clerical devices (especially in terms of data rates and amounts of traffic), but their interconnection to and through the office network may be very important. Having multiple terminals on your desk for access to word processing, electronic mail, and computing capabilities is undesirable. Office systems available today do not even begin to address all possible issues, much less offer all desirable equipment or support anticipated growth.

BUSINESS SYSTEMS

Context

The two leading trends in general business applications are increasing heterogeneity of computerized equipment and increasing pressure for integration of single-user computers (personal computers, individual workstations, specialized intelligent terminals for graphics, etc.) within the corporate network of resources. Both of these require significant data communication support! As more vendors provide products that conform to accepted standards, and more software is adapted to the micro-mini-mainframe networking environment, we expect that the ability to handle larger and smarter applications will also grow. Thus, it will still be important for knowledgeable, responsible professionals to make known the larger requirements for individual privacy and security that will keep business systems under appropriate control.

Hardware

It is difficult to say whether increased heterogeneity and individual distribution create major impacts on hardware, or whether trends in hardware create the increased motivation for networks of increasingly distributed, heterogeneous resources. In either case, the trend is to isolate more of the communication processing into intelligent network interfaces. Modularity makes it easier to concentrate on development of greater sophistication within the narrower frameworks of either communications or applications. More options are also available for developing communication implementations to offer a range of alternatives in performance costs. For example, early Ethernet interfaces offered only data link and physical layer functions on a single board. Now, interfaces are available with on-board microprocessors that perform increasing amounts of the higher-level communication processing. This frees the attached resources to concentrate on application functions and divides throughput concerns into two areas: application processing and communication processing. Each can be optimized by specialists.

Software

The discussion above should start you thinking that our previous distinctions between hardware and software may not be the important ones in the future. From the perspective of a business with an application to be automated, it is the functional distinctions of what is handled by the application host and what is provided by the network interface that matter, and not which functions are implemented in hardware or software. As usual, the choices for function implementation depend largely on the tradeoffs among cost, flexibility, and performance.

What will continue to be a very general issue for many business systems, however, is the "best" way to first interconnect, and then to integrate, SNA and non-SNA components and applications. No easy solution to this quest is yet apparent. For the most part, today's approach is for non-SNA elements to emulate some component of a standard SNA system, requiring either an extensive software development effort or a hardware investment such as protocol conversion equipment. Neither approach usually provides the best use of the non-SNA resource. Gateway products offer one alternative for access between SNA and other systems, but their effective use often depends on extensive application software development or on data-mapping utilities to mask storage and file format differences between SNA and other hosts.

The future for interconnection with IBM mainframes will be shaped largely by development of IBM and independent vendor products based on "standards" being promulgated by IBM. The various local area network announcements will produce a series of products, each best suited to particular application environments, but eventually there will be one solution encompassing the entire range of requirements. It may not be cost-effective for all, but it will at least offer the potential for complete system integration.

FACTORY SYSTEMS

Context

Certainly the most important trend in factories today is an increasing emphasis on automation and integration of systems for more cost-effective production. General Motors Corporation (GM) has taken a leading role in drawing attention to the communication requirements of factory systems with its fostering of the Manufacturing Automation Protocol (MAP) development. Essentially, MAP is designed to:

- be a tool for factory communications
- provide a standard that will both promote flexible solutions to factory problems and give guidelines for incorporation of multiple vendors and multiple media
- provide OSI compatibility
- evolve into a publicly accepted standard

Ideally, MAP will become the "utility" concept for communications distribution and access, much as there is a North American standard for electric power distribution (110 volts, 60 Hertz, alternating current) and access (the two- or three-pronged plug and receptacle).

Hardware

The kinds of equipment in an integrated factory system range from computerized numerical control machines, through programmable control machines and robots, to host processors supporting inventory control, production scheduling, and material requirements processing. Early networks were strictly vendor-proprietary interconnections of similar equipment types from a single vendor. Figure 12.1 shows a sample Allen-Bradley Data Hiway

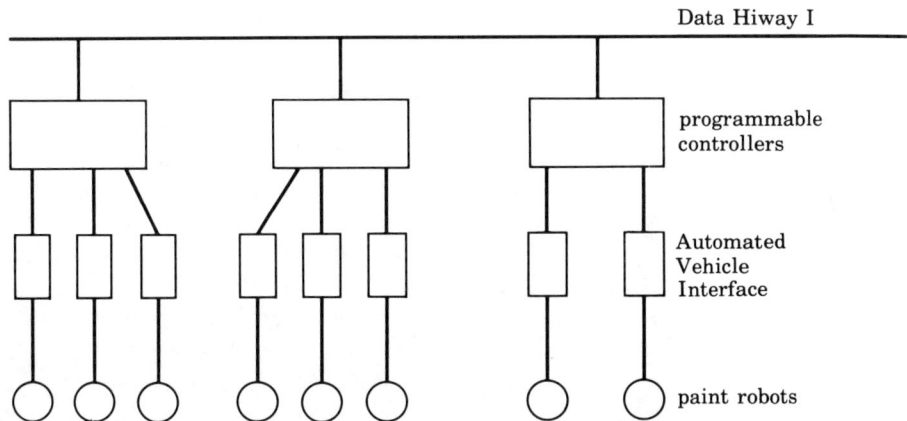

FIGURE 12.1 Early proprietary factory network

OSI layer

ISO CASE	7
(null)	6
ISO SESSION	5
ISO TRANSPORT	4
ISO CONNECTIONLESS	3
IEEE 802.2	2
IEEE 802.4	1

Figure 12.2 Version 2.1 MAP layer specification

I, used to interconnect programmable controllers that guide paint robots in an automobile production line. Connection of an entire factory full of segments of highly specialized equipment from different vendors is a major challenge.

MAP underlays factory application requirements with a communication structure based on the OSI reference model. In fact, MAP's goal is to specify what standardization of function shall be adhered to at each level of the model where standards exist (Figure 12.2). From a hardware perspective, the MAP architecture calls for broadband cable as the fundamental communications medium. Where MAP only provides a backbone network, the interconnected individual subnetworks may use other transmission techniques. The most likely subnetwork candidate is an adaptation of broadband, called carrier-band, that provides a single channel (as baseband would) at a carrier frequency that maintains sufficient signal quality in a factory environment. Some existing vendor-proprietary networks already use carrier-band transmission.

Interestingly enough, selection of broadband as the transmission medium was an early factor in the decision to use token-passing as the sharing discipline for MAP, because no CSMA standard had been agreed to for broadband systems when MAP was being defined in 1982. Then, the more likely reasons for token-passing became the focus of attention: its deterministic performance (except when the token gets lost or during reconfigurations), ease of supporting multiple levels for different priority traffic, and GM's desire to quickly capture the attention and support of the major process control vendors as well as other manufacturers.

Software

One of the most important early aspects of GM's fostering of MAP was the range and scope of vendor commitment and cooperation they obtained. This led to some dramatic public demonstrations of the first implementations of

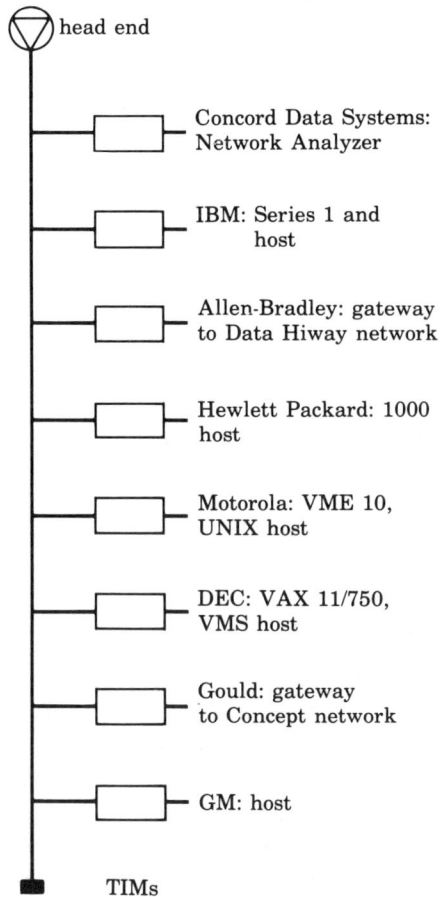

Figure 12.3 NCC '84 demonstration

higher-level software that conformed to ISO standards and was compatible across multiple vendors. The first demonstration was at the National Computer Conference (NCC) in 1984 (Figure 12.3). Equipment from Allen Bradley, Concord Data Systems, IBM, Hewlett Packard, Motorola, DEC, and Gould, coordinated by GM, was interfaced to a broadband cable by Token Interface Modules from Concord Data Systems. Simple message exchanges and file transfers were accomplished between various vendor systems. The major impact of the demonstration was publicity, but the commitment to making it work was clear among all the vendors.

Applications

The next public demonstration occurred in November, 1985, at a conference on factory automation (AUTOFACT '85). More than 20 vendors attended

	OSI level
MAP: network mgmt directory service MMFS subset	user
FTAM (MAP, TOP) ISO CASE kernel (MAP)	7
(null)	6
ISO session kernel	5
ISO transport class 4	4
ISO connectionless	3
IEEE 802.2 link level control class 1	2
IEEE 802.4 (MAP) IEEE 802.3 (TOP)	1

Figure 12.4 AUTOFACT '85 demonstration: software

this conference and the software had grown as in Figure 12.4. In addition, the office protocol effort being fostered by Boeing Computer Services had found an acronym (**TOP:** Technical and Office Protocols) and an alliance with MAP that gave it new visibility as well. A major TOP goal is to be identical with MAP at least at levels 3 through 7 to provide for the eventual interconnection of office and manufacturing systems. The MAP and TOP efforts have now become largely the responsibilities of their user group organizations, coordinated by a MAP/TOP steering committee, and all operating under the auspices of the Society for Manufacturing Engineering (SME). Boeing and GM continue to play very active roles at all levels of standards and implementation development.

Many challenges remain in factory systems. There are still some underlying communication problems to be solved, such as making sure all broadband modem implementations work together, and developing adequate testing and verification procedures and facilities. Definition of presentation layer protocols will develop as they are needed or are produced by other standards groups. Meanwhile, increasing attention will be paid to operational issues (e.g., timer settings, network management mechanisms) and applications development (e.g., how to design manufacturing applications to capitalize on MAP features, what and how to integrate between manufacturing and business systems). There are also questions on the use of fiber optics as a transmission medium.

TELEPHONE SYSTEMS

Context

The most significant trend in telephone systems is certainly the gradual change from analog transmission facilities to entirely digital signal handling. As we saw with private branch exchanges, switching techniques have been digital for some time. With the advent of inexpensive codecs to convert analog signals into digital format, it is reasonable to extend digital signaling beyond private networks into general public telephone systems. In fact, when telephone networks can transfer digital signals from one end to the other without needing to convert them into analog, any type of digital traffic such as voice, data, alarms, and video can be sent, subject only to the speed constraints of the interfaces and the level of subscriber service. This potential is being explored formally as **ISDN,** the Integrated Services Digital Network concept. CCITT has been working on definitions and standards in support of ISDN since 1980.

The basic concept and structure of ISDN are shown in Figure 12.5. A so-called digital pipe provides subscribers with access to telecommunications transport facilities through a standard network interface. In the United States, where regulation requires separation of transport (basic) from information (enhanced) services, the pipe will actually provide "transparent" data transportation. Subscribers will be responsible for aggregating their traffic, and will be able to interact with intelligent network controllers to

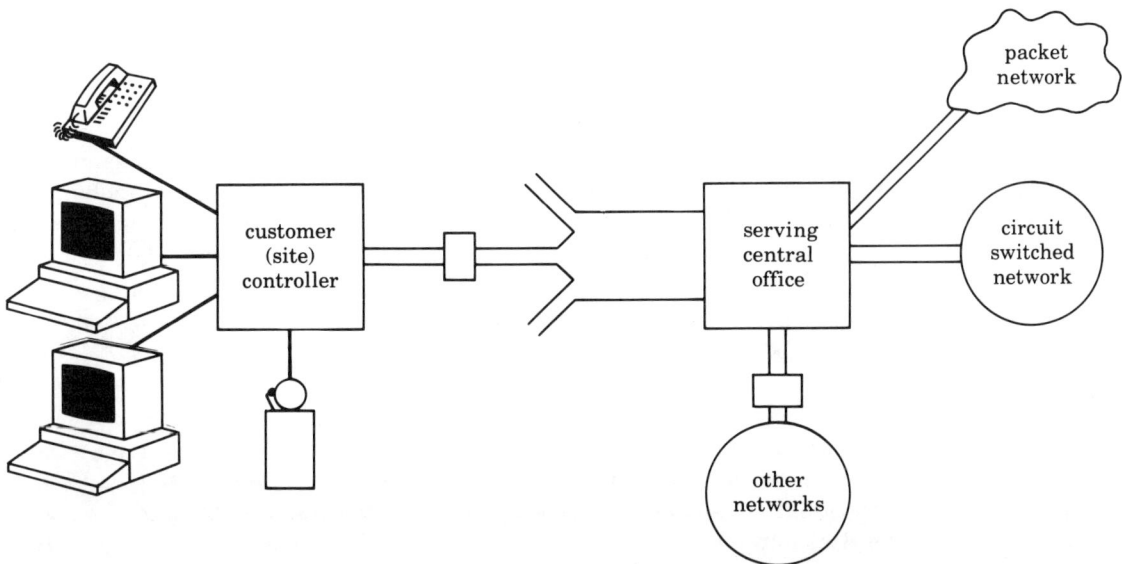

FIGURE 12.5 Local access to multi-bandwidth ISDN transport

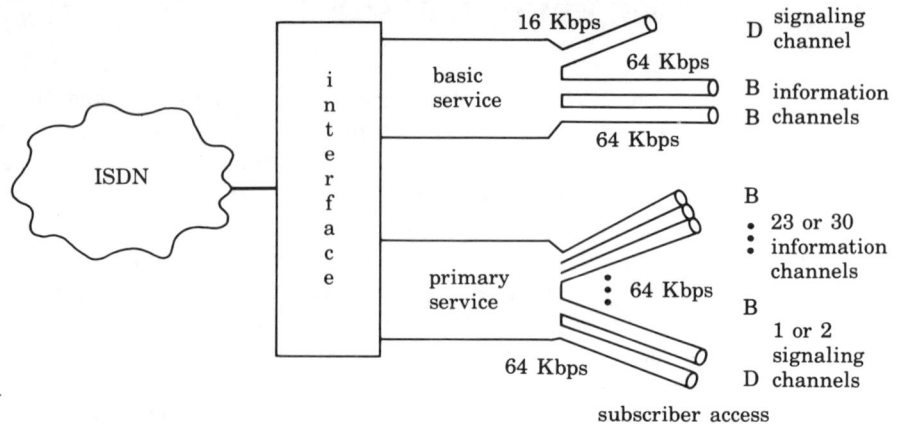

FIGURE 12.6 ISDN access alternatives

specify the various characteristics and options needed for transport. The ideal result, of course, is for both subscribers and network operators to experience optimal efficiency and performance.

Outside the U.S., where regulation is not at all the same, the ISDN concept has expanded toward an enormous, completely integrated information system. The differences in national requirements for boundaries between transport and processing services has made agreement on the approaches and details of ISDN even slower than for some other international standards efforts. Significant commitments will be required from many participants to achieve a level of standardization that will allow compatibility among pieces both within the U.S. and internationally.

The second major issue of compatibility is definition of the two ISDN access rates. The basic rate offers subscribers 144 Kbps of total bandwidth, subdivided as shown in Figure 12.6. The primary rate offers wideband access. In the U.S., T1 will evolve to provide 23 B channels and one D channel within the 1.544 Mbps total bandwidth capacity. Europe prefers to evolve their 2.048 Mbps standard into 30 B channels and two D channels. Most likely, CCITT will be forced to adopt both as standards, even though the two will be incompatible.

Hardware

U.S. telephone companies are hard at work upgrading their transmission systems and switching centers to handle digital signals all the way out to individual subscribers. However, without standards defined to the lowest level of detail, there is much concern over ultimate compatibility of even these pieces. Figure 12.7 shows the reference points established to minimize wasted effort among ISDN proponents. The interface points (S, T, and U)

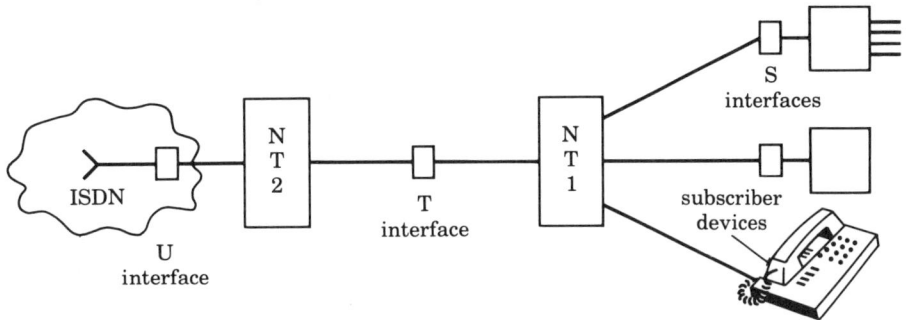

FIGURE 12.7 Reference points for interface definition

should be thought of as plugs and receptacles, although it is unlikely they will be implemented independently. The two processing points will probably end up as PBX interface cards to terminate the subscriber connection pairs (NT1), and network channel-terminating equipment (NT2).

Software

One area of ISDN progress is in the definition of standards for the Common Channel Signalling (CCS) system portion. This is a separate channel specifically set up to provide call control signaling. It will be shared by all types of telecommunication services, instead of having control information transferred on each channel along with the user traffic. CCS will handle call set-up for telephone and circuit-switched data calls, exchange of management and maintenance information among switching and specialized centers in the telephone system, and any other types of control traffic. The definition of common channel signaling for ISDN is called Signaling System Number 7 (**SS7**), and its layered structure is shown in Figure 12.8. Its major purpose is to provide reliable exchange of control and management information in support of ISDN services.

The layers of SS7 are related to the OSI reference model: levels 1 and 2 of SS7 correspond directly to OSI levels 1 and 2, SS7 levels 3 and 4 together are equivalent to OSI level 3. The remaining SS7 components do not match OSI; they are simply modules convenient in partitioning the functions of SS7's level 4.

Levels 1, 2, and 3 of SS7 are collectively known as the Message Transfer Part (MTP) because they provide connectionless data transport for the control traffic. Level 1, the physical layer, is responsible for the physical signaling interface with the transmission network, as would be expected from the OSI reference model. Level 2 performs data link control. It handles the framing of traffic (Figure 12.9) and controls one physical communication link. Error control is accomplished with data frame sequencing, acknowledg-

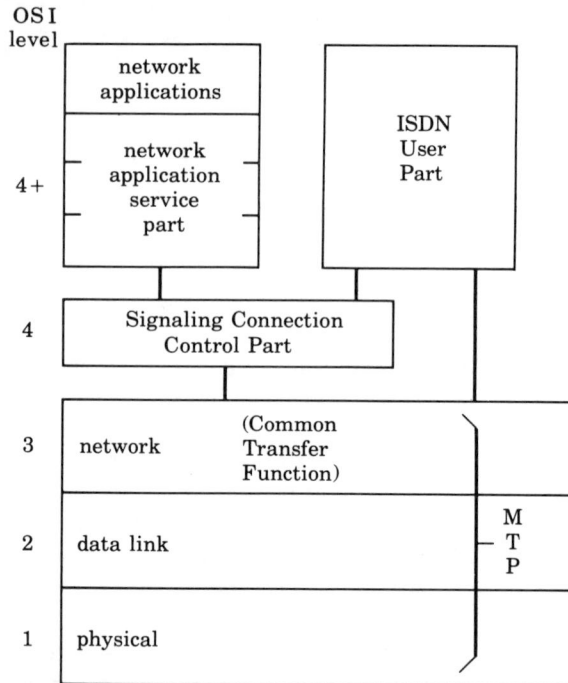

FIGURE 12.8 Layered architecture of signaling system number 7

ments, retransmissions triggered by negative acknowledgments, and a timer for the excessive delay of acknowledgment caused by a link failure condition. Level 3, the network layer, is called the Common Transfer Function (CTF). It is responsible for routing traffic toward its specified destination and for managing the flow of traffic through the signaling network, including redirecting traffic around network failures or congestion, exchanging information about the status of network components, and providing facilities for testing in support of fault isolation. The upper-level components of SS7 support various applications, such as coordination of pairs of hosts that cooperate in providing network user services.

TECHNOLOGY

It is difficult to predict future developments in communication technology. If we knew which inventions or improvements were going to have significant impact on future information systems, we would certainly have a good chance to invest wisely. Even without a crystal ball, however, there are some definite trends that can be expected to continue.

flag	BSN	B I B	FSN	F I B	LI	✕	SIO	signaling information field	...

| 8 | 7 | 1 | 7 | 1 | 6 | 2 | 8 | 8n, n ≥ 2 |

←	...	check bits	flag

| 16 | 8 |

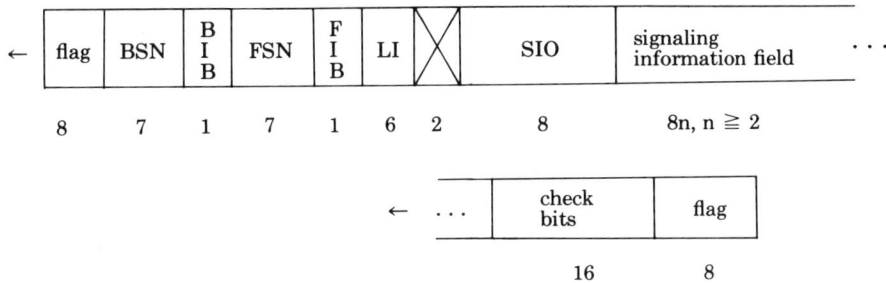

BSN   backward sequence number
BIB   backward indicator bit
FSN   forward sequence number
FIB   forward indicator bit
LI   length indicator
SIO   service information octet

Figure 12.9 Frame format of message signal units in SS7

Fiber Optics

Increasing use of fiber optics for telephone systems communication links will broaden the base of components and expertise to the point where more information systems will take advantage of their inherent speed, bandwidth, and security. Transatlantic cable systems are expected to have repeaters as far apart as 100 kilometers by 1988, instead of the one to ten kilometers common today. Predictions have even been made that by 1990, optical fiber will be within two miles of more than ten percent of home loop subscribers.

The first widespread use of fiber in computer networks is already being seen as point-to-point links for interconnection of individual nodes. This was common for PBX components even in the early to middle 1980s, and soon spread to host-to-host computer and host-to-peripheral connections with the advent of the 100-Mbps Fiber Data Distributed Interface (**FDDI**) standardization by ANSI. As transmission speeds over fiber continue to increase, and transmitter/receiver technology catches up, we can expect to see a renewal of discussions about implementation tradeoffs between parallel and high-speed serial links.

Distributed System Applications

The trend to distribution of computer system resources to provide better response, availability, fault-tolerance, and security will certainly continue. With enough experience, we will begin to understand enough about partitioning application software to take advantage of the aggregate capability of an entire collection of resources. As more standardization is achieved among higher level network protocols, we can also expect to see development of tools to assist designers in the development of distributed applications. Integration of microprocessors into more different kinds of devices will press further development of local area networks in terms of coordination strategies based on applications rather than interconnections. Performance will continue to be an issue as demands stretch beyond the limitations of existing equipment and techniques. For example, increased use of intelligent graphics workstations to present the results of sophisticated data manipulation by super-computers began pushing LANs for effective individual throughput rates better than 2 Mbps even in the early 1980s.

"Compunications"

One of the largest influences on information system design is the merge taking place between computing and communication technologies, sometimes called **"compunications"**. It is nearly impossible to communicate over any distance today without having computers involved in the process. Similarly, effective computer systems depend on communication techniques far more sophisticated than simple direct-wired connections. Designers in each area must become increasingly knowledgeable in both areas in order to develop new systems with enhanced capabilities.

INDUSTRY

Here again, it is difficult to predict which products and companies will remain viable. While smaller companies may be able to continue offering just specific devices or software products, larger ones will probably look to provide, or fit into, some overall system architectural plan. Acceptance of standard network approaches across large segments of the computer industry will foster greater compatibility, or at least clearer choices, among selected hardware and software components. On the other hand, companies and organizations with unusual requirements for technical innovation or new application development will still have to blaze their own trails.

One of the biggest growth areas in the data communications industry will be for new services. Organizations that have developed private communication systems for their own internal use are discovering that such communication capabilities can be the key to their own expanded futures. For example, a large retail company with its own credit operations and an extensive computer and communication system could certainly consider expansion to provide home shopping and home banking, as well as network access and various financial services for businesses. The larger its network of internal facilities, the easier it should be for a company to offer services to organizations other than its own. This means a whole new set of vendors could participate in the arena of new service development.

ENVIRONMENT

What will all of these developments look like to us at home and in business? There is some concern that the improvements in technology will encourage more and more isolation, allowing people to hide behind their communication devices instead of participating directly with other people. Some will fall into such a trap, as has happened with various pervasive technological changes in the past (widespread use of television to distract children, for example). Any technology seems to provide avenues for misuse or abuse, but only *people* can choose the usage paths to be traveled. As individuals knowledgeable about information and communication systems, we will be responsible for paying attention to, and increasing general awareness of, the implications of various applications of our expanding technology.

Certainly with the divestiture of AT&T and the increasing competition for current and future services, an obvious change will be more choices among vendors and services. We will have to learn to "shop" for communications similarly to the way we choose a car or television set today. Two-way communication across CATV cable systems, for example, will need careful scrutiny from both subscribers and community interests to ensure useful, non-intrusive services. Home banking, shopping, and videotext experiments have shown the potential for other types of service. Increasing interest in home computers for personal business, homework, and recreation may fuel growing demands for convenient and inexpensive data communications from the home.

We can already see many of the anticipated changes beginning to take place in our offices: microprocessors make commonplace devices such as telephones and typewriters more intelligent, local area office networks offer increasing levels of interconnection, and more functions are integrated into fewer devices. It is easy to imagine a single device on every desk that will combine interpersonal communication capabilities (video/telephone), computing access (personal workstation or terminal), and word processing (keyboard and printer), with access to extensive data storage (electronic file cabinet as well as large databases). As input alternatives to the keyboard improve, our new device may look more and more like a large television set with various accessories.

IN CLOSING

While progress toward the future is inevitable, we must remember that *we* are still in charge of how that future will look. If we take the responsibility seriously and are willing to shape "the future" in a way that improves the quality of life for all, development of data communication technology may contribute much to our general ability to live with and enjoy each other.

CHAPTER REVIEW

Capsule

Data communication has contributed much to our ability to implement improvements in the communication activities typical of most offices, businesses, and factories. Newly intelligent hardware, more capable software, and broader applications offer great potential for services that we can now only imagine. The challenges are intriguing, the promises exciting, and the responsibilities awesome, for both information and communication system professionals.

NEW TERMS

CASE	ISDN
documents	SS7
electronic mail	teleconferencing
FDDI	TOP
file transfer	

QUESTIONS

1. Letter-quality printers produce print that looks as though it came directly from a typewriter. They tend to be much slower and more expensive than utility printers. What differences between these two apply to the communication requirements of letter-quality printers vs. intelligent copy machines?

2. If workstations have local intelligence and storage, what benefits could be gained from applications and data resident on a network host computer?

3. In some office with which you are familiar, find out what the reaction would be to replacing a telephone receptionist with a voice message system. What are the desired characteristics of such a system?

4. Find out the current state of the standards for message exchange and document exchange. Why are these important, and how do they fit into TOP?

5. In addition to OSI CASE, there is a concept of SASE. Find out what these mean. Has any progress been made in standards for SASE?

6. Research the experience of McDonald's Corporation in being a test installation for ISDN services. What other tests are in progress?

7. Compare this year's top fifty companies involved in data communications with those from five years ago (see *Data Communications* magazine). Discuss the significance you see in the major changes.

References

GENERAL REFERENCES, USEFUL THROUGHOUT THE COURSE

Data Communications, (magazine) McGraw-Hill, New York (monthly)

Telecommunications Products + Technology, (magazine) PennWell Publishing, Littleton, Mass. (monthly)

"Proceedings, Ninth Data Communications Symposium" Computer Communication Review 15, no. 4 (September 1985).

Computer Communication Review, (magazine) ACM SIGCOMM, New York (quarterly)

Telecommunications, Horizon House-Microwave, Dedham, Mass. (monthly)

SUGGESTIONS FOR ADDITIONAL READING

Chapter 1. A System Approach

Adams, David R., Gerald E. Wagner, and Terrence J. Boyer. *Computer Information Systems: An Introduction.* Cincinnati: South-Western Publishing, 1983.

Adams, David R., Michael J. Powers, and V. Arthur Owles. *Computer Information Systems Development: Design and Implementation.* Cincinnati: South-Western Publishing, 1985.

Chapter 2. Basic Concepts

Transmission Systems for Communication. 5th ed. Bell Telephone Laboratories, 1982.

McNamara, John E., *Technical Aspects of Data Communication*. 2d ed. Bedford, Mass.: Digital Equipment Corp., 1982.

Stallings, William. *Data and Computer Communications*. New York: Macmillan, 1985.

Chapter 3. Hardware

Chou, Wushow, ed. *Computer Communications, Volume I: Principles*. Englewood Cliffs, N.J.: Prentice-Hall, 1983.

Pooch, Udo W., William H. Greene, and Gary G. Moss. *Telecommunications and Networking*. Boston: Little, Brown, 1983.

Chapter 4. Software

Green, Jr., Paul E., ed. *Computer Network Architectures and Protocols*. New York, Plenum Press: 1982.

Green, P. E. "An Introduction to Network Architectures and Protocols." *IBM Systems Journal* 18, no. 2 (1979): 202-22.

IBM Corp. *Systems Network Architecture, Concepts and Products*. 1981.

Proceedings of the IEEE, Special Issue on Open Systems Interconnection 71, no. 12 (December 1983): 1331-1448.

Chapter 5. Protocols and Interfaces

Chow, Wushow, ed. *Computer Communications, Volume II: Systems and Applications*. Englewood Cliffs, N.J.: Prentice-Hall, 1985.

Davies, D. W., D. L. A. Barber, W. L. Price, and C. M. Solomonides. *Computer Networks and Their Protocols*. New York: John Wiley & Sons, 1979.

Martin, James. *Computer Networks and Distributed Processing*. Englewood Cliffs, N.J.: Prentice-Hall, 1981.

Schick T., and R. F. Brockish. "The Document Interchange Architecture: A Member of a Family of Architectures in the SNA Environment." *IBM Systems Journal* 21, no. 2 (1982): 220-44.

Chapter 6. Communication Environments

Gagliardi, Robert M. *Satellite Communications*. Belmont, Calif.: Lifetime Learning Publications, 1984.

Tanenbaum, Andrew S. *Computer Networks*. Englewood Cliffs, N.J.: Prentice-Hall, 1981.

Chapter 7. Local Area Networks

Bellamy, John. *Digital Telephony*. New York: John Wiley and Sons, 1982.

Fine, Michael, and Fouad A. Tobagi, "Demand Assignment Multiple Access Schemes in Broadcast Bus Local Area Networks." *IEEE Transactions on Computers* C-33, no. 5 (December 1984): 1130-58.

Stallings, William. *Local Networks, An Introduction*. New York: Macmillan, 1984.

Thurber, Kenneth J., and Harvey A. Freeman. *Tutorial: Local Computer Networks*. 2d Ed. New York: IEEE Computer Society Press, 1981.

Chapter 8. Distributed Processing

Cohler, Geoffrey L. "A Star is Born." *Digital Review*. (April 1985): 34-38 [VAX Clusters]

Gray, J. P., and T. B. McNeill. "SNA multiple-system networking." *IBM Systems Journal* 18, no. 2 (1979): 263-97.

Kaplan, Ray. "Cluster Support in VAX/VMS." *Digital Review* (April 1985): 41-45.

Lorin, Harold. *Aspects of Distributed Computer Systems*. New York: John Wiley & Sons, 1980.

Needham, R. M., and A. J. Herbert. *The Cambridge Distributed Computing System*. London: Addison-Wesley, 1982.

Stankovic, John A. "A Perspective on Distributed Computer Systems." *IEEE Transactions on Computers* C-33, no. 12 (December 1984): 1102-14.

Thurber, Kenneth J., ed. *Tutorial: A Pragmatic View of Distributed Processing Systems*. IEEE 1980.

Chapter 9. Network Management

Westcott, Jil, John Burruss, and Vivienne Begg. "Automated Network Management. In "*Proceedings, IEEE INFOCOM 85,* 26-28, March 1985: 43-51.

Chapter 10. Design Techniques and Issues

Ahuja, Vijay. *Design and Analysis of Computer Communication Networks*. New York: McGraw-Hill, 1982.

Davies, Donald W. and Derek L. A. Barber. *Communication Networks for Computers*. New York: John Wiley & Sons, 1973.

Stuck, B. W., and E. Arthurs. *A Computer and Communications Network Performance Analysis Primer*. Englewood Cliffs, N.J.: Prentice-Hall, 1985.

Chapter 11. Security and Privacy

ACM Computing Surveys, Special Issue: Cryptology 11, no. 4 (December 1979): 283-356.

Chaum, David. "Security without Identification: Transaction Systems to Make Big Brother Obsolete." *Communications of the ACM* 28, no. 10 (October 1985): 1030-44.

Davies, D. W., and W. L. Price. *Security for Computer Networks*. New York: John Wiley & Sons, 1984.

Hsiao, David K., Douglas S. Kerr, and Stuart E. Madnick. *Computer Security*. New York: Academic Press, 1979.

Voydock, Victor L., and Stephen T. Kent. "Security Mechanisms in High-Level Network Protocols." *Computing Surveys* 15, no. 2 (June 1983): 135-71.

Chapter 12.   Trends in Applications and Technology

ANSI T1X1.1 Working Group. *American National Standard Specification of Signalling System No. 7.* 1984+.

Goodenough, Frank. "Telecommunication Integrated Circuits." *Electronic Design* (January 10, 1985): 199-218.

Nussbaum, Eric, and Walter E. Noller. "Integrated Network Architectures--Alternatives and ISDN." *IEEE Communications Magazine* 24, no. 3 (March 1986): 8+ [Several other articles of interest also appear in this issue].

Personick, Stewart D. *Optical Fiber Transmission Systems.* New York: Plenum Press, 1981.

Glossary

access control Restriction of access to specified areas, equipment, or programs to authorized users only.

ack Positive Acknowledgement—A control signal indicating that a message or data item was received with no apparent error.

adaptive routing A method for path selection through a network that dynamically updates the information on which routing decisions are made.

alarm A visual or audible indication that an event of interest has occurred in the network.

Aloha A multiple-access channel sharing technique developed at the University of Hawaii that allows a station or node to transmit whenever it has traffic.

AM Amplitude Modulation—Information to be transmitted is superimposed on a carrier signal by varying the signal amplitude.

amplitude The volume, intensity, or loudness of a signal. In a sine wave representation of a signal, it is the distance from the X axis.

analog A continuously varying signal where the value at any instant is chosen from an infinite number of possible values within the defined range.

application layer The highest level of communication function prescribed by the Reference Model for Open System Interconnection.

ARPANET The first large experimental packet-switching network in the United States, originally funded by the Advanced Research Projects Agency.

ASCII American Standard Code for Information Interchange—A binary digital coding scheme for representation of letters, digits, punctuation, and control characters.

asynchronous Occurring at an arbitrary time relative to other devices or events (compare with synchronous).

audit trail A set of records giving enough detail so that a sequence of events can be reconstructed.

authentication Verifying a user's identity or a message's source.

authorization Permission to use some resource.

availability Capability and readiness to perform on demand.

B channel Designation for a channel that can carry subscriber traffic in an Integrated Services Digital Network.

bandwidth A portion of the frequency spectrum, as the 200 Hertz band between 5100 and 5300 Hertz; now used more generally to mean the carrying capacity of a transmission medium or the capacity requirements of a signal.

baseband Single-channel transmission at the basic signaling frequency natural to a particular transmission medium (compare with broadband).

basic rate A proposal for subscriber access to an Integrated Services Digital Network, consisting of two information channels of 64 kilobits-per-second capacity and one signaling and control channel of 16 kilobits-per-second capacity.

baud rate The number of discrete signaling elements transmitted per second (compare with bit rate).

bit rate The number of binary digits transmitted per second.

bit error rate The number of binary digits per second that are received in error if compared to the bits transmitted.

bit-stuffing A technique for inserting zero bits into the transmission of a long sequence of one bits to prevent loss of clocking information.

BOC Bell Operating Company—Any local telephone company once owned by AT&T, made independent of AT&T by the 1984 Divestiture Decree. These were allowed to consolidate into seven regional holding companies according to an economical and geographical distribution scheme.

boot To initialize all hardware characteristics, operating parameters, and software modules.

bps bits per second—A measure of transmission speed or rate of data transfer.

bridge A mechanism for joining two previously independent networks of the same type.

broadband A transmission technique with the capacity divided into multiple, independent channels (compare with baseband).

BSC Binary Synchronous Control—A character-oriented IBM coding scheme for information and control signals across a communication link.

BTAM Basic Telecommunications Access Method—An early consolidation of communication control functions by IBM.

bus A high-speed, shared multiple-access interconnection mechanism.

carrier-band Single-channel transmission using only one carrier frequency on a broadband medium.

CASE Common Application Service Elements—An application layer standard being developed by the International Standards Organization for functions common to a variety of applications.

CATV Community Antenna Television—A common application of multi-channel transmission over coaxial cable to distribute television channels to a community of subscribers.

CCITT Consultative Committee for International Telephony and Telegraphy—An international group heavily involved with data communications and telecommunications standards.

Carterfone A legal decision based on a suit brought by Carterfone that first allowed equipment manufactured by other than Bell Telephone companies to be connected to Bell Telephone transmission networks.

central office The local telephone switching center to which individual subscriber loop connections are made.

centralized Located in or controlled from a single point.

checkpointing A technique that uses periodic snapshots of the state of a system to provide for returning to a known recent state after detection of failure or security breach.

CICS Customer Information Control System—One of IBM's application subsystem program products.

ciphertext The coded version of a message.

circuit A complete connecting loop. In the case of an electric circuit, there must be both a path over which the current can flow and a ground path.

circuit analysis Techniques for establishing that the physical interconnection between two devices is working properly.

coaxial cable A transmission medium consisting primarily of a central conductor and an outer ground sheath.

collision Interference of two signals transmitted simultaneously in the same shared medium.

common carrier A company with legal permission to offer transmission and basic communication services for sale to public subscribers.

common channel signaling Sending control signals on a separate channel from the data signals being controlled instead of inserting control bits among the data bits on a single channel. Often, a single control channel is shared by several independent data channels.

communication access method A consolidation of common communication function available to various users.

communications subnet (1) A small network connected with other small networks by some backbone. (2) A portion of a network that has an independent identity. (3) The aggregate functions of the three lowest layers of the OSI reference model.

compunications A word coined to emphasize the increasing technological dependence and similarities between computing and communications.

concentration Combining intermittent transmissions of multiple users into one channel offering less capacity than the simultaneous aggregate requirements of all potential users.

conditioned line A transmission line and associated equipment to counteract common signal impairments or distortions, such as the frequency dependencies of attenuation and phase distortion.

congestion Having more traffic than capacity; usually occuring when all buffers are full.

connectivity The extent to which an individual member of a network has access directly to the other members.

Consent Decree A 1956 settlement of the U.S. Department of Justice attempts to break up the AT&T monopoly of telephone services—It provided for AT&T retention of the manufacturing capabilities of Western Electric Company, but forced licensing agreements making the technology available to other companies. AT&T was also prohibited from engaging in businesses outside the provision of regulated common-carrier transmission and telephone services.

contention Multiple users competing simultaneously for the same limited resource.

CRC Cyclic Redundancy Check—Bits added to the end of a message for detecting transmission errors. In this case, polynomial arithmetic is used to compute the additional bits from the data bits themselves and from a special, agreed-upon generator polynomial.

critical resource A resource whose failure prevents normal operation from occurring.

cross-subsidization Charging more than necessary for one service in order to make up for losses in providing another service.

CSMA Carrier-Sense Multiple Access—A technique for sharing a common transmission medium among multiple users, where each must listen before transmitting to be sure no other transmission is already in progress.

CSMA/CD Carrier-Sense Multiple Access with Collision Detection—A variation of CSMA. Each user must continue to listen while transmitting to ensure that no other transmission interferes.

CTF Common Transfer Function—Level 3 of Signaling System Number 7, a common channel signaling standard for Integrated Services Digital Network.

D channel Channel for common signaling in Integrated Services Digital Network.

data A major component of an information system. Usually distinguished from information as the unsorted, unclassified, unorganized, unstructured, and uninterpreted basic elements out of which information is created.

data flow A tracing of the paths followed through a system by data.

data link layer Layer 2 of the Reference Model for Open Systems Interconnection.

datagram A transmission service in which each message is independently handled by the network with no guarantee of delivery or sequence.

DCA   Document Content Architecture—A standard proposed by IBM to define the format, structure, and interpretation of documents to be transferred among computer systems.

DCE   Data Circuit (–terminating) Equipment—(1) The modem side of a terminal-to modem-connection. (2) The network side of a host-to-public data network connection.

DDBMS   Distributed Data Base Management System.

DDCMP   DEC (Digital Equipment Corporation) Digital Control and Monitoring Protocol—A character-oriented link protocol developed by DEC in support of its Digital Network Architecture.

DDD   Direct Distance Dialing—Long-distance telephone service from AT&T.

DDS   Dataphone Digital Service—Digital telephone service from AT&T.

deadlock   No activity can proceed because all participants are waiting for one of the others to do something.

decentralization   The opposite of centralized. Having multiple points of (or locations for) resources and control.

DECnet   A networking philosophy and a set of products from Digital Equipment Corporation.

decryption   The process of decoding ciphertext back into plaintext.

DES   Data Encryption Standard—Promulgated by the U.S. National Bureau of Standards, a technique for protective encoding and decoding of digital messages.

destination   The target of a communication or message.

deterministic routing   A method for selecting a path for traffic through a network where the choice of destination drives the decision at each point, regardless of changing conditions in the network.

device driver   Software specifically designed for management and control of a particular device (type), to be shared by various users while isolating them from the details of device operation.

DIA   Document Interchange Architecture—A standard developed by IBM for the communication of documents among computer systems.

diagnosis   The process of determining the source of a problem or failure in a system.

digital   Representation from a finite set of discrete values, where changes in value are perceived as occurring instantaneously.

distributed control   Data and the responsibility for decision-making are present at, and shared by, multiple entities in the system.

distributed data   Data elements required for processing are located at, and managed by, multiple entities in the system.

distributed function   Dividing the processing requirements of a system among multiple processing elements.

distributed processing   Multiple, independent processing systems cooperating to share significant responsibility for the total processing requirements.

distributed system   A system of multiple elements, often geographically distant, that share portions of the total responsibility for accomplishing the jobs for which the system was designed.

divestiture   A process by a business organization of relinquishing control and support of some portion (or sub-organization) of its activities. The primary use in this text is in reference to an agreement between AT&T and the U.S. Department of Justice that the Bell Operating Companies would become completely independent of AT&T beginning on 1 January, 1984.

DNA   Digital Network Architecture—A philosophy and structure for communications and network product development by Digital Equipment Corporation.

DSR   Data Set Ready—A circuit defined in the RS-232-C standard for device interconnection.

DTE   Data Terminal Equipment—The attached host side of an interconnection with a public data network.

DTR   Data Terminal Ready—A circuit defined in the RS-232-C standard for device interconnection, usually indicating that a terminal device is operating in such a way as to be capable of exchanging control or data signals.

dump A simple output report, typically showing the contents of a series of processor memory locations at the time of request, that is used for diagnostic or debugging purposes.

EBCDIC Extended Binary-Coded Decimal Interchange Code—An IBM standard coding scheme for binary representation of character (text, numeric, punctuation, and control) information.

echo checking An error-detection technique that checks a returning echo against the original information transmitted.

electronic mail A computerized store-and-forward system for electronic delivery of text messages.

encryption The process of transforming text so that the meaning of the original is no longer obvious, but can be recovered through a suitable reverse transformation (called decryption).

Ethernet A local area network definition put forth by Xerox, Intel, and Digital Equipment Corp. that specifies the physical and data link layers, including media, connectors, signaling, and access control mechanisms. The term is sometimes used generically to refer to coaxial cable networks using Carrier-Sense Multiple-Access with Collision Detection, CSMA/CD.

explicit permission A technique for sharing a common transmission medium that requires acquisition of some symbol of permission in order to transmit.

fault detection The process of discovering that a problem or error exists in a system.

fault isolation The process of identifying the cause of a problem or error in a system.

fault tolerance A characteristic of a system that allows it to continue operating effectively even though certain errors occur or some devices fail.

FCS Frame Check Sequence—Information added to a transmitted data stream that allows the receiver to detect errors that might have occurred during transmission.

FDDI Fiber Distributed Data Interface—A standards effort directed at the use of fiber optics to interconnect distributed elements of a computer system or network.

FDM Frequency Division Multiplexing—A technique for sharing a common transmission medium by dividing the frequency range carried by the medium into multiple channels so that modulation of a carrier frequency within one channel does not interfere with signals in any other channel.

FDX Full Duplex—A method of transmission that carries signals in opposite directions simultaneously.

FEP Front-End Processor—A computer attached to a general-purpose processing host, used to offload some special activities that tend to slow down the performance of the host.

file transfer Transmission of a computerized file from one processing device to another, usually from one computer system to another.

fixed routing A store-and-forward network delivery technique, where the next leg of a path to any destination is always the same for each destination at any point in the network.

flag A special pattern of bits that is agreed to by sender and receiver as having a particular meaning, especially to indicate the beginning or end of a message unit.

flow The ability of traffic in a network to move across a link or set of links.

flow control A mechanism to stop and start traffic according to the availability of resources required to support that traffic.

FM Frequency Modulation—A technique for slightly modifying the basic carrier frequency of a signal in a way that superimposes additional information that can be recovered by a receiver.

forward channel A channel that carries signals from a main transmitter to its destination receivers, as in a cable television system. In data networks, this usually applies to a channel carrying data from the head-end retransmission facility to the attached listening stations.

frame A unit of transmission at the data link level that distinguishes between packaging information and the data being carried.

frequency The number of cycles per second in a periodic signal.

FTP File Transfer Protocol—a set of rules for exchanging files among computer systems.

full-duplex A method of transmitting signals in both directions simultaneously.

gateway A communication system providing connection between two computers or networks that use different protocols or are geographically distant.

go-back-N A negative acknowledgement with retransmission scheme for handling errors. If an error is detected by a receiver, the transmitter is notified and requested to retransmit everything following the last correctly received transmission.

half-duplex A transmission mode that can send signals in only one direction at a time. In practice, this means that first one side talks while the other listens, then the other side talks while the first listens.

HDLC Higher-level Data Link Control—Standard international rules for exchanging data over a single communications link. It is recommended by CCITT for the data link layer supporting X.25 attachment to a public data network.

HDX Half-Duplex—a transmission mode that can send signals in only one direction at a time.

head end The location and equipment of a central retransmission facility. It allows multiple devices to hear all signals transmitted on a shared, uni-directional, multiple-access medium such as broadband coaxial cable.

header The initial packaging information added to the front of some unit of data to be transmitted, usually containing addressing and control information.

Hertz The unit of frequency, number of cycles per second, in a periodic signal.

hub-go-ahead A polling scheme for sharing access to a common communication medium. A central authority, or hub, initiates the poll by giving permission to send to the first device in a sequence. If that device has traffic, it transmits, and the hub gives permission to the next in sequence. If a device has no traffic to send, the permission is passed directly to the next device in sequence without going back to the hub in between. Only when traffic is sent does control return to the hub.

hybrid service Service offered to the public that is enhanced beyond basic transmission capabilities. Often value-added carriers lease bulk transmission capacity from a regulated communications company and provide more than just transmission for resale. Value-added services may include character set or protocol conversion, packet assembly and disassembly, error detection and correction, as well as data processing services.

IEEE Institute for Electrical and Electronics Engineers.

IEEE-488 A parallel interface standard also known as a GPIB, general-purpose interface bus, used for interconnection of devices at speeds higher than can be provided over serial links.

IEEE 802 A set of subcommittees engaged in defining communication standards for local area networking. Areas of interest include bus and ring systems, baseband and broadband transmission, contention and token-passing multiple-access sharing disciplines.

IMP Interface Message Processor—Originally a communication node providing front-end host access to the ARPANET, and now referring more generally to an access node for any networks using ARPA-like protocols.

interface A well-defined boundary across which communication flows. This may be a logical separation of functions (as between layers in the Reference Model for Open Systems Interconnection), or a physical package of functions providing access to something (as a network interface unit containing the sharing discipline functions and physical connections to a local area network transmission cable).

IP Internet Protocol—A scheme first proposed in association with the ARPANET for addressing, control, and packaging suitable for communication among interconnected networks.

ISDN Integrated Services Digital Network—An international standard being developed for digital networks that will be able to accommodate voice, data, video, and various other types of traffic.

ISO International Standards Organization—A group responsible for identifying areas for standardization and for developing recommendations for the definition of such standards.

isochronous A transmission method with intervals between non-adjacent characters restricted to even multiples of a character.

IXC Inter-Exchange Carrier—A company licensed to provide public communication service across the boundaries of a LATA (local access and transport area).

kHz kiloHertz—1000 cycles per second; a measure of the frequency of a periodic signal.

kbps kilobits per second—1000 bits per second; a measure of transmission speed or data transfer rate.

LAN Local Area Network—Usually smaller than a few miles in extent, owned by a single organization, offering high-speed data communication at very low error rates.

LAPB Link Access Protocol, Balanced—An international standard for the data link level in support of recommendation X.25 from CCITT for host access to public data networks. It is effectively equivalent to HDLC, higher-level data link control.

LATA Local Access and Transport Area—A geographical area within which a licensed local operating company may provide telephone service, according to the January 1, 1984, AT&T divestiture arrangements. For telephone service crossing a LATA boundary, access must be provided to the facilities of an interexchange carrier (IXC).

layers Groups of functions arranged in a hierarchical format so that the services provided by a layer through the functions within that layer are built strictly on top of the functions offered by the layer below—often a convenient way to modularize hardware and software for ease in understanding, building, and modifying.

leased services Public telephone facilities dedicated to the use of the leasing customer. Often higher quality transmission capability is available at higher cost.

levels The distinct functional responsibilities assigned to the layers in an hierarchical system.

life cycle The total time period during which costs are attributed to a system—beginning with the initial problem statements, feasibility analysis, and design, and running through the entire development, installation, useful operation, and decline periods, up to replacement by a successor system.

line A single communications circuit between two points, typically made up of some number of twisted-pair copper wires.

line driver The transmitter equipment required to put digital signals onto a single communication link, especially for twisted-pair copper wire connections.

link The general term for a single communications circuit, including point-to-point and multipoint connections over various transmission media (wire, coaxial cable, microwave, optical fiber, light wave, etc.)

local area A restricted geographical area within which a single organization wants a single data communication network.

local loop The complete local communication circuit between a telephone system central (service) office and an individual subscriber.

logging The recording of certain events or activities for historical, auditing, or back-up purposes.

logical As distinct from physical, something which gives the appearance of its physical counterpart (e.g., a logical connection may require a series of actual physical connections between pairs of intervening communication nodes).

loopback A testing technique that returns signals to the originator from specifically pre-defined points instead of being forwarded to a destination.

MAP Manufacturing Automation Protocol—Initiated by General Motors Corp., it is an effort to standardize the communication functions required for integrated factory system.

master/slave A control and sharing discipline. One of the participants is in charge (the master) and delegates permission for various activities to the others (the slaves).

Mbps Megabits Per Second—One million bits per second, used to describe both the transmission rate and the carrying capacity of communication links.

medium The physical entity or mechanism that carries signals from one point to another, encompassing things as diverse as a copper wire carrying electronic signals and light signals broadcast through space.

MHz MegaHertz—One million cycles per second. A measure of the frequency of a periodic signal.

microwave A portion of the electromagnetic radiation spectrum used for private or restricted (as opposed to entertainment broadcast) radio communication, especially for earth-to-satellite and line-of-sight terrestrial links.

modem MOdulator/DEModulator—A device that transforms signals into analog representations at frequencies that can be carried by the intended transmission medium.

modem eliminator A device used in place of a pair of modems over short distances to connect the necessary circuits.

modulate To modify the basic transmission characteristics of a "carrier" signal so that the information to be sent is superimposed and carried along with the "carrier."

MTBF Mean Time Between Failures—An average value for how long a piece of equipment can be expected to operate properly.

MTP Message Transfer Part—A subset of the communication functions defined for Signaling System Number 7, an international standard technique for common channel signaling.

MTTR Mean Time To Repair—An average value for how long it can be expected to take to repair a failed or faulty device.

multiplexer A device that combines several independent signals into a form that can be transmitted across a communication link and then separated (or de-multiplexed) into its original components.

multipoint A communication link to which three or more devices are attached. Typically, some sharing discipline is needed to resolve or prevent simultaneous transmissions that would interfere with each other.

nak Negative Acknowledge—A report that an error was detected in a transmission or package of data.

NCCF Network Communications Control Facility—In IBM's Systems Network Architecture (also used to stand for network configuration and control facility), a network management component usually responsible for coordinating the control, observation, and diagnosis of a network.

NCC Network Control Center—A logical or physical entity containing the major responsibility for control, observation, and diagnosis of a network.

NCP Network Control Program—(1) A network management component of DECnet. (2) An IBM software product containing sophisticated front-end communication responsibilities in support of Systems Network Architecture.

network An interconnected set of computers and components that offer services and resources to a set of users.

network architecture The organization, plan, and philosophy for communication services to interconnect computer or other component systems. SNA is IBM's Systems Network Architecture and DNA is Digital Equipment Corp.'s Digital Network Architecture.

network control The ability to define and modify physical and operational characteristics, start and stop, test, and otherwise manage the devices in a network.

network diagnosis The ability to look for and detect problems or failures in a network, as well as to determine their cause or isolate them to a particular component.

network layer A set of communication functions grouped together at a certain level of a network architecture, especially the third layer of the reference model for Open Systems Interconnection advocated by the International Standards Organization.

network management All functions necessary to ensure the coordinated, useful, proper behavior of a network, especially one containing computer resources.

network observation Collecting and displaying information about the devices and operations of a network, usually for identifying problems, potential problems, or actual error conditions.

network planning The activities, including assessment of network performance, projection of user requirements, and evaluation of a network's ability to serve its users, leading to a determination of whether additional resources or a network is needed.

network startup The activities involved in powering up, checking out, and making network resources available to their users.

NICE Network Information and Control Exchange—A network management protocol defined for Digital Equipment Corp.'s Digital Network Architecture.

NLDM Network Logical Data Manager—A component of the network management capabilities in IBM's Systems Network Architecture responsible for recognizing sessions rather than just physical devices in the network.

node An independent entity cooperating with similar systems connected together to form a network.

noise Signal or signal elements received at a destination that were not intentionally transmitted as part of (or in support of) the information being communicated.

non-blocking Having adequate access and resource capabilities so that a request for service is never denied.

NPDA Network Problem Determination Application—A network management component of IBM's Systems Network Architecture that allows network operators or managers to automate some of the management tasks (such as observation, testing, and fault isolation).

optical fiber A strand of glass, plastic, or other material capable of conducting light from a source to a destination with minimal signal lost to the surrounding medium.

OSI reference model A definition and organization of communication functions required for Open Systems Interconnection; that is, for the connection of computerized systems from various manufacturers, regardless of their internal hardware and software design and implementation details.

packet An independent unit of transmission carrying all the address and control information required to get it from the source to the destination location in the network.

packet switching A network technique that makes switching decisions independently for each packet, based solely on its source and destination, rather than on any relationship it may have to other packets traveling between that source and destination.

PAD Packet Assembly/Disassembly (or the machine accomplishing those functions)—The division of data into chunks packaged into independent units called packets, and the specification of addressing and control information to get the packet delivered to its intended destination.

parallel Multiple transmission paths between the same source and destination that carry portions of a data signal simultaneously, as in a character-width connection where the eight character bits are put one on each wire and transmitted all at the same time instead of one after another on a single transmit wire in a serial link.

parity The even or odd characteristic of a counter value, as in how many one bits are contained in a binary character representation. It is often used to add redundant bits to transmitted data for the purpose of error detection.

partitioned Separated into disjointed, non-overlapping, non-duplicating segments that compose the whole.

path A sequence of steps or links, through whatever intermediate points intervene, to arrive at a destination from a source (or origination point).

PBX Private Branch Exchange (also known as PABX for Private Automated Branch Exchange)—A privately owned set of switching equipment providing primarily telephone communication service to a set of subscribers within the owning organization, and offering interconnection with the public telephone networks.

PCM Pulse-Coded Modulation—A technique for transmitting digital signals, often used with sampling techniques applied to analog signals to allow digital representation and transmission of analog data.

PDN Public Data Network—A data network offering communications services for sale to the general public on a subscription basis similar to public telephone networks. Offered services may include basic transmission or value-added, enhanced service (such as protocol conversion), access to data processing or database resources.

peer cooperation A control and sharing discipline where no participant has authority over any others, using one of various strategies such as voting to ensure all participants make the same (or at least compatible) decisions about actions and events in the network that affect more than one participant.

phase The characteristic of a periodic signal that describes the instantaneous position relative to the beginning of a cycle.

physical Real or actual, as opposed to logical, which gives the appearance of something real.

physical layer The first (bottom or lowest) level in a layered approach or model of communication functions, such as the reference model for Open Systems Interconnection or IBM's Systems Network Architecture.

plaintext The unmodified, undisguised, original version of data whose security is of concern.

PLP Packet Level Protocol—The third layer of communication function as specified by the CCITT in Recommendation X.25, built over a data link level called LAPB (for link access protocol, balanced, equivalent to HDLC, higher-level data link control).

PM Phase Modulation—A transmission technique which superimposes information on a "carrier signal" by changing its phase so that the original information can be reconstructed by the receiver.

point-to-point Direct linkage between two systems not shared by any other signal source.

polling A technique for sharing multiple-access transmission media where a single, central authority controls all permission to transmit; typically each subservient participant is invited to transmit (polled) periodically according to a scheme or list held by the central authority.

POP Point Of Presence—A point within a LATA (local access and transport area) where a connection can be made for access to telephone service from an interexchange carrier (IXC) to get across the LATA boundary.

port The physical interconnection point and equipment for a single communication link.

POTS Plain Old Telephone Service—An affectionate term commonly used in the Bell telephone system community for simple voice communication service with no enhancements for either voice or data capabilities.

presentation layer Usually the sixth level up in a layered communication system model or architecture. It collects together some commonly useful functions that support a variety of applications, such as encryption, file compression, display screen formats, etc.

primary rate The bulk communication access interface being specified as part of the ISDN (Integrated Service Digital Network) standard. In the U.S. it consists of 23 "B-channels" to carry traffic at 64 kbps and 1 "D-channel" at 64 kbps for control; in Europe, it consists of 30 B-channels and 2 D-channels.

product cipher An encryption or encoding

technique built from two simpler mechanisms to disguise and protect sensitive information.

protocol A set of rules defining communication mechanisms.

public key An encryption/decryption technique using separate keys for encoding and decoding information to be protected where neither key can be figured out from the other.

recovery The process of returning to a known consistent operating state after a failure or breach of security.

reliability The characteristic of a system that means it will consistently operate properly, producing repeatable results.

reservation In a multiple-access system, the ability to request resources that will then be dedicated to that user for some period of time.

resource sharing Providing multiple users with access to system capabilities and facilities, typically across a network, regardless of whether users and resources are co-located.

reverse channel In a multiple-channel (typically broadband cable-based) system, a channel that carries traffic toward the head-end or central retransmission facility.

ring A network configuration in which every member of the network has a predecessor and successor for network transmissions.

roll-call A polling scheme in which a central authority maintains a list of devices participating in the network, and offers permission to transmit to each in turn according to the central list.

routing The mechanism by which network traffic makes its way from a source to a destination location.

RS-232-C A standard definition for the physical level interconnection of computer (and peripheral) devices, including definition of the electrical, mechanical, and procedural connection requirements, which handles asynchronous data traffic at speeds up to 19.2 kbps.

RS-449 A standard definition for the physical level interconnection of computer and peripheral devices, including definition of the electrical, mechanical, and procedural connection require-ments, which handles asynchronous data traffic at speeds up to 19.2 kbps and synchronous data traffic at speeds up to 64 kbps.

satellite A vehicle carrying transponders to receive and retransmit microwave communications over long geographic distances.

SDLC Synchronous Data Link Control—A data link level protocol defined and used in IBM's Systems Network Architecture.

security The characteristic of a system that ensures no damage to, or loss of, any component.

selective retransmission A negative acknowledgement error correction scheme that involves retransmission only of the piece(s) reported to be missing or in error.

serial A type of transmission that puts only one signal on the link at a time. This usually means one bit at a time on a single circuit connecting the two devices, so that multiple bit transmissions mean a series of bits, transmitted one after another.

session A unit of interaction between two parties, with a well-defined beginning and termination.

session layer Usually the fifth level up in a layered network architecture such as the reference model for Open Systems Interconnection. It is the main level of user interaction with the communications system, especially for building distributed applications on the basis of inter-task communication.

signals The physical forms of data being transmitted and received, or the basic mechanism of exchange underlying communications.

simplex One-way communication that always occurs in a fixed direction.

simultaneity Occurring at the same time, or appearing so.

slot A regularly repeating, fixed unit of time—usually imposed on a transmission medium or traffic stream.

slotted Aloha A multiple-access sharing scheme that imposes slightly more discipline on when a user can transmit than is required in the original Aloha contention scheme.

SME Society for Manufacturing Engineers—The group that assumed responsibility for definition and development of the Manufacturing Automation Protocols originally proposed by the General Motors Corp.

SNA Systems Network Architecture—A philosophy, structure, and product set from IBM for networking computer resources.

source The originator of signals, transmissions, and communications.

space division A physical method of sharing communication capabilities.

splitting/recombination A technique for dividing and reconstructing messages that are larger than the unit of transmission in a particular network environment.

SSCP System Services Control Point—A controlling entity in a network adhering to IBM's Systems Network Architecture through which network resources are allocated and managed.

SS7 Signaling System Number 7—An international specification of the architecture and protocols for common channel signaling in support of the Integrated Services Digital Network standards and development.

star A network configuration with a single central switching facility and all other devices connected directly to that hub.

STATDM STATistical Time-Division Multiplexing—a sharing technique for multiple access to a physical transmission capability that allocates transmission time dynamically according to the demands of active users.

static routing A technique for determining the path to be followed by network traffic in which the information and algorithms used to make decisions are fixed at the time of network generation.

STDM Synchronous Time-Division Multiplexing—A sharing technique for multiple access to a physical transmission capability that has a fixed allocation of capacity to each of the users, regardless of whether they are active or not.

stochastic routing A technique for determining the path to be followed by network traffic in which the results of individual decisions vary according to the conditions in the network at decision time.

stop-and-wait An error detection technique that waits after each individual transmission for positive or negative acknowledgement from the receiver. If the response is positive, the next transmission is begun. If the response is negative, the previous transmission is repeated.

store-and-forward An asynchronous network transmission that does not require active participation of the destination receiver to allow transmission to take place; that is, if the destination is not active, the transmissions can be stored at some intermediate location.

subchannel An independent logical or physical portion of a communication channel that is subdivided in such a way as to support multiple users.

substitution cipher An encryption technique that disguises messages by replacing the original characters one by one with some other characters.

sub-voice grade Transmission capability for signals that do not require the quality or speed of a voice channel.

switched service Transmission capability that dedicates a path through the network for the duration of a "conversation" (data or voice), where access to the network facilities is provided on demand (up to capacity) to a community of users called subscribers.

synchronous A method of communication requiring the source and destination to be in step during an entire transmission, agreeing precisely to the time definitions of bits and that the time between successive bits or characters in a single transmission stream is completely deterministic rather than arbitrary.

TAF Terminal Access Facility—A component of the network management capabilities of IBM's Systems Network Architecture that allows a network manager or application to take advantage of the display tools in other IBM software.

TARA Threshold Analysis and Remote Access—A component of the network management capabilities of IBM's Systems Network Architecture that allows observation of the network beyond the local hierarchy.

tariff A filing by a communications carrier with the FCC describing services and prices offered to the public.

TCAM Telecommunications Access Method—An IBM software component providing enhanced capabilities in focusing application access to communications through a single, common resource and control mechanism.

TCP Transmission Control Protocol—A transport level standard originally developed to provide reliable, end-to-end communication for ARPAnet applications.

TDM Time-Division Multiplexing—A sharing discipline for multiple access to a single, high-capacity transmission medium that creates independent subchannels of smaller capacity out of the total by dedicating the assignment of successive transmission time intervals to different devices.

TDMA Time-Division Multiple Access—The application of time-division multiplexing techniques to broadcast transmission media.

teleconferencing Interconnection of geographically dispersed conference participants by means of various telecommunications capabilities, ideally including voice, data, and video connection.

Telenet A U.S. public data network owned by GTE.

timesharing A technique for sharing computer resources among multiple users by giving each in turn a short period of access, and cycling through the active group quickly enough that each has the appearance of a dedicated resource.

token The mechanism symbolizing permission to act (usually transmit permission) in the distributed polling technique for sharing multiple access to a common transmission medium.

TOP Technical and Office Protocols—A standard definition for communications in support of office and technical information systems, originally developed by Boeing Computer Services.

topology The arrangement, structure, and interconnection pattern of elements in a network.

total connectivity An arrangement of network elements where each has a direct physical link (no intermediaries) to every other.

trailer The bits appended to the end of a message or information to be transmitted. Typically this includes redundant information for error detection and flag bits to signify the end of all the related information belonging to a single transmission.

transceiver The physical transmitting and receiving device providing access to a communication medium. It is most often used in connection with Ethernet coaxial cable networks.

transmission The process of putting signals on or into a communication medium.

transparency The characteristic of being invisible to a user.

transport layer The fourth level up in an hierarchically structured network architecture such as the reference model for Open Systems Interconnection.

transposition cipher An encryption technique that disguises the content of an original message by rearranging the characters according to a fixed pattern.

tree A branching network topology with a single root or central hub, and no cycles or interconnections that form a ring.

trunk (1) A connecting link between subscriber switching equipment and a telephone company central office. (2) A link between telephone offices. (3) A general term for the high-capacity link interconnecting switching equipment.

twisted copper wire pair, or twisted-pair copper wire A pair of conducting copper wires twisted together in such a way as to minimize the interference that can be generated in one by signals in the other. In multi-pair cables, the twist length of adjacent pairs is varied to minimize interference from one pair to another, as well.

VAN Value-Added Network—A network offering services enhanced beyond simple transmission from one location to another, including such things as character set conversion, protocol conversion, and actual data processing services.

virtual Giving the appearance of existing, but not necessarily implying the dedication of real physical resources.

virtual circuit Application of network resources with the appearance of a dedicated physical interconnection.

voice-grade A quality of transmission service suitable for voice traffic. For digital service, this means a 64 kbps transmission capability.

VTAM Virtual Telecommunications Access Method—The component of IBM's Systems Network Architecture responsible for providing coordinated, central control over and access to the communications facilities.

WATS Wide Area Telephone Service. A bulk-rate long-distance service offering from AT&T. Charges are monthly by the line rather than by the call.

wideband A transmission service offering higher capacity than required to support a single voice conversation.

word processing A computerized application for the creation, modification, and production of text documents (character-oriented as opposed to graphics).

X.21 An international recommendation by the CCITT for the standard physical level interconnection of communicating devices.

X.25 An international recommendation by the CCITT for standard attachment to public data networks. It includes specification of three levels (physical, data link, and packet) in analogy to the layered network architecture of the reference model for Open Systems Interconnection.

X.75 An international recommendation by the CCITT for the standard interconnection of public data networks to one another.

Index

WE VALUE YOUR OPINION—PLEASE SHARE IT WITH US

Merrill Publishing and our authors are most interested in your reactions to this textbook. Did it serve you well in the course? If it did, what aspects of the text were most helpful? If not, what didn't you like about it? Your comments will help us to write and develop better textbooks. We value your opinions and thank you for your help.

Text Title _____ Edition _____

Author(s) _____

Your Name (optional) _____

Address _____

City _____ State _____ Zip _____

School _____

Course Title _____

Instructor's Name _____

Your Major _____

Your Class Rank _____ Freshman _____ Sophomore _____Junior _____ Senior

_____ Graduate Student

Were you required to take this course? _____ Required _____Elective

Length of Course? _____ Quarter _____ Semester

1. Overall, how does this text compare to other texts you've used?

_____ Superior _____Better Than Most _____ Average _____Poor

2. Please rate the text in the following areas:

	Superior	Better Than Most	Average	Poor
Author's Writing Style	_____	_____	_____	_____
Readability	_____	_____	_____	_____
Organization	_____	_____	_____	_____
Accuracy	_____	_____	_____	_____
Layout and Design	_____	_____	_____	_____
Illustrations/Photos/Tables	_____	_____	_____	_____
Examples	_____	_____	_____	_____
Problems/Exercises	_____	_____	_____	_____
Topic Selection	_____	_____	_____	_____
Currentness of Coverage	_____	_____	_____	_____
Explanation of Difficult Concepts	_____	_____	_____	_____
Match-up with Course Coverage	_____	_____	_____	_____
Applications to Real Life	_____	_____	_____	_____

3. Circle those chapters you especially liked:
   1   2   3   4   5   6   7   8   9   10   11   12   13   14   15   16   17   18   19   20
   What was your favorite chapter? _____
   Comments:

4. Circle those chapters you liked least:
   1   2   3   4   5   6   7   8   9   10   11   12   13   14   15   16   17   18   19   20
   What was your least favorite chapter? _____
   Comments:

5. List any chapters your instructor did not assign. _____

6. What topics did your instructor discuss that were not covered in the text?_____

   _____

7. Were you required to buy this book? _____ Yes _____ No

   Did you buy this book new or used? _____ New _____ Used

   If used, how much did you pay? _____

   Do you plan to keep or sell this book? _____ Keep _____ Sell

   If you plan to sell the book, how much do you expect to receive? _____

   Should the instructor continue to assign this book? _____ Yes _____ No

8. Please list any other learning materials you purchased to help you in this course (e.g., study guide, lab manual).

   _____

9. What did you like most about this text? _____

   _____

10. What did you like least about this text? _____

   _____

11. General comments:

   May we quote you in our advertising? _____ Yes _____ No

   Please mail to: Boyd Lane
                     College Division, Research Department
                     Box 508
                     1300 Alum Creek Drive
                     Columbus, Ohio 43216

   Thank you!